License to Steal

The Gambling Studies Series

JEFF BURBANK

License to Steal

*Nevada's Gaming Control System
in the Megaresort Age*

3 1336 05322 0704

University of Nevada Press ▲▲ Reno & Las Vegas

The Gambling Studies Series

Series Editor: William R. Eadington

University of Nevada Press, Reno,

Nevada 89557

Copyright © 2000 by University of

Nevada Press

All rights reserved

Manufactured in the United States

of America

The paper used in this book meets the

requirements of American National

Standard for Information Sciences—

Permanence of Paper for Printed Library

Materials, ANSI Z39.48-1984. Binding

materials were selected for strength and

durability.

Library of Congress Cataloging-in-

Publication Data

Burbank, Jeff, 1945–

License to steal : Nevada's Gaming

Control Board and Commission in the

megaresort era / by Jeff Burbank.

p. cm. — (The gambling studies series)

Includes bibliographical references and

index.

ISBN 0-87417-339-6 (hard : alk. paper)

1. Nevada. State Gaming Control

Board.   2. Nevada Gaming Commis-

sion.   3. Gambling—Nevada—Las

Vegas.   4. Gambling—Nevada—Clark

County.   I. Title.   II. Series.

HV6721.L3 B87 2000

363.4'2'09793135—dc21   99-050648

FIRST PRINTING

09 08 07 06 05 04 03 02 01 00

5 4 3 2 1

To my wife, Andrea

Contents

Illustrations

Preface

Before I arrived in Las Vegas in 1987, my experience as a journalist in San Francisco, Washington, D.C., and Los Angeles was mainly writing news stories about the typical goings-on in overbuilt suburban areas—development issues, redevelopment issues, schools, and traffic congestion. But Las Vegas was a much more invigorating place for a news reporter with the desire to cover the strange and unusual. Compared to where I had been, the town was wholly different—slot machines in supermarkets, gas stations, and laundries; limousine services offering rides to legal rural brothels; and a local government and populace that were absolutely pro-development. Not long after joining the staff of the daily *Las Vegas Sun* in October of that year, I was writing stories on things such as Nevada's state brothel lobby, wealthy but unsuccessful Japanese casino owners, on-the-job illegal drug use by casino workers, call girls (with beepers) who serviced casino customers, and a mayor of Las Vegas who, as a slot machine sales manager, sold machines to casino operators after voting in favor of their requests for more machines. The *Sun*'s newsroom itself was completely unlike any other newsroom I had been in. Each week during pro football season, for instance, a reporter or an editor would go to the managing editor, the city editor, the copy editors, and the reporters to collect their picks for the week and then drop the picks off at the sports book of a local casino. Once, a *Sun* reporter, after winning money in a media poker tournament at the Binion's Horseshoe casino, announced he was going to a pawnshop so that he and his wife (a frequent video poker machine player) could "finally" get their wedding rings out of hock.

One thing I learned quickly about Las Vegas is how self-conscious and defensive residents of this desert valley can be about the area's peculiarities and how sensitive some are about the opinions of out-of-towners. Since the city is necessarily dependent on the gaming industry and the whims of tourism, its casino, hotel, and convention officials spend tens of millions each year promoting its good side throughout the country. This "up with Las Vegas" mentality frequently carries over to the town's print and broadcast news coverage of people and events. The Las Vegas news media often appear to play it safe, with a homeboy, wide-eyed, public relations approach to news stories, particularly about the casinos and entertainment offerings on the Las Vegas Strip.

I observed the town's sensitivity almost right away at the *Sun*. As the paper's new business reporter, I was instructed to cover things unrelated to the city's ubiquitous gaming industry. What I had heard was that more than a year before I was hired, the *Sun*'s gaming reporter wrote a story that apparently offended a local casino figure. The reporter left the paper soon afterward, and *Sun* publisher Hank Greenspun, tired of hassling with his casino friends and foes, abruptly instructed his managing editor not to replace the position. To take any future heat from the industry off the *Sun*, so to speak, the task of writing gaming stories for the publication fell to the Las Vegas bureau of United Press International, then headquartered inside the *Sun*'s newsroom. But after writing stories on nongaming topics for a couple of months, I decided to try to slip in a few gaming articles. I gradually wrote more gaming-related stories with no apparent objection from management. Greenspun didn't seem to care or notice. Yet, even though my stories got into print, my editors at times raised objections when the articles appeared, in their minds, to make the town look bad. A story I did on trick rolls by prostitutes (who drugged the drinks and then robbed the wallets of their customers) in hotel-casinos angered one editor who threatened to punish me if I wrote on the subject again. One of the higher-ups at the paper also objected to a story I did on legal brothels in Nye County (about 65 miles west of Las Vegas), a potentially embarrassing subject matter that he thought was better left uncovered. "Why did you have to write on that again?" he asked. And a casino owner once objected to one of my stories so much that he pulled all his advertisements (temporarily) from the *Sun*. But, finally, the *Sun*'s managing editor quietly acquiesced and allowed me to report on gaming full-time—the best beat in town.

Most of the chapters in this book are based on stories I covered while at the *Sun* and, later, its crosstown rival, the *Review-Journal*. The period, from the late 1980s to the mid-1990s, was a pivotal time for the gaming industry, for which Las Vegas is as central as Detroit is to cars, Silicon Valley is to high-tech, and Winston-Salem, North Carolina, is to tobacco.

In 1988, Congress passed the Indian Gaming Act, which permitted American Indian tribes to sign agreements with states to operate forms of gambling that are legal in the state. That started the rush toward legalization. Legislatures in South Dakota, Iowa, and other states soon began permitting, in selected cities, most types of casino gaming available in Las Vegas and all over Nevada. By the early 1990s, about two dozen states allowed casino gaming in one form or another on riverboats or on land. In Las Vegas a record number of new visitors and the availability of junk bond financing ushered in the age of the so-called megaresort: massive hotel-casinos with new, multi-million-dollar attractions and shopping opportunities in addition to gaming. The first of the megaresorts was the $640 million, 3,400-room Mirage hotel-casino in

1989; followed by the $290 million, 4,000-room Excalibur in 1990; and then the Luxor, Treasure Island, and MGM Grand (the latter built with a record 5,005 rooms at a then-record cost of $1 billion) in 1993. For a while at least, family vacationers, not just serious adult gamblers, drew the attention of casino marketing executives on the Strip. One by one, private, family-owned casinos, such as Palace Station and Binion's Horseshoe, went public and sold shares on the stock market to raise money for renovations, expansions, acquisitions, and new casinos. Gaming companies based in Las Vegas successfully entered the new out-of-state gaming jurisdictions.

The rise of the megaresort era upped the stakes for survival in the Las Vegas gaming scene. The influence of the old, individual, risk-taking, quirky, and in some cases downright strange casino operator was declining. The rules and judgments of Wall Street, a presence in Las Vegas since the late 1960s, had virtually taken over the casinos on the Strip and elsewhere in town by the early 1990s. And the stakes grew ever higher. From July 1, 1996, to June 30, 1997, the Nevada State Gaming Control Board reported that Nevada's gaming industry employed more than 188,000 people, grossed $7.6 billion—about two-thirds of it in the Las Vegas area—and paid $445 million in taxes, equal to 33 percent of the state's operating funds.

This book focuses on major licensing and policy issues considered by Nevada's gaming regulatory bodies—the Nevada State Gaming Control Board and the Nevada Gaming Commission—during that absorbing period in time. I chose the subjects for the first seven chapters from among the most controversial and unusual issues considered by the board and the commission in those years. For some reason, this particular era—a few years before and the early years after the first wave of modern megaresorts in Las Vegas—produced some of the strangest situations ever considered by state gaming regulators. Some former Nevada gaming officials I talked to for this project told me that regulatory matters in Las Vegas in the late 1990s were tame by comparison.

Most of the situations covered in these chapters prompted the board and the commission to stiffen enforcement of existing rules and to make crucial, if at times late, changes in state gaming statutes that either prevented the problems from happening again or provided a precedent to guide regulators in the future. It holds true, however, that almost any applicant for a nonrestricted license (tables games and/or 16 or more gaming machines) or a restricted license (15 gaming machines or less) in Nevada can raise an unexplored issue or a new policy dilemma for the board and the commission.

The chapters describe how the board and the commission dealt with such often subjective issues as how to decide who is "suitable" to receive a gaming license, how to regulate new computerized gaming machines, how to punish violators of casino accounting regulations, how to make sense of and pass judgment on complicated financial deals involving casinos, how to investigate license applicants from foreign countries, and even how to deal with a rare case of corruption within the gaming board itself.

While the book essentially examines case studies of the ways the board and the commission approached these challenges, I treated each chapter as I would an individual news feature story, that is, by including significant elements—such as criminal investigations, lawsuits, and adverse publicity—to give the reader a fuller picture of each case.

The introduction is meant to serve as an overview of the history of legalized gambling in Nevada from the mid-19th century up to nearly the end of the 20th century. While surveying books and other materials for this history, I noticed that little had been written about Las Vegas and Clark County in the years leading up to the legalization of casino gambling in Nevada in 1931 and the decade or so that followed. The results of my research into this period—based on the minutes of meetings by city and county commissioners from the 1920s to the 1940s—provide new insight into this period and for that reason are included at length in the introduction. A series of brief profiles of current and former members of the board and the commission are outlined in chapter 8. In the introduction and in each chapter, I've interspersed my own reporting and recollections with other sources of information—including books, news articles, and people whom I interviewed for this book—that are cited numerically in the endnotes to each chapter.

I want to acknowledge the following people for their time, aid, and insight during the research and writing of this book: Dennis Amerine, Jimmy Bryson, Carole Case, Joseph Cronin, Gerald Cunningham, Steve DuCharme, William R. Eadington, Marilyn Epling, Ron Farrell, Char Faulkner, Gary Harris, Paul Hejmanowski, Ronald Hungridge, Charlotte Matanane, Lisa Miller-Roche, Shannon Nadeau, Owen Nitz, John O'Reilly, Robert Peccole, Gregory Peters, Paul Pusateri, Thomas Roche, David Roger, Michael Rumbolz, Scott Scherer, Frank Schreck, David Thompson, William Urga, Sue Wagner, and Ellen Whittemore. I also want to thank Marsh Starks and the photo staff of the *Las Vegas Sun* for providing most of the photos used in the book. Kudos as well to Michael Green, a professor of Las Vegas history at the Community College of Southern Nevada, for providing valuable suggestions and assistance in editing the manuscript. I also want to acknowledge those I do not mention here who spoke off the record but who nonetheless contributed to this volume. I further want to kindly thank Trudy McMurrin of the University of Nevada Press for her help and continued enthusiasm for this project. And, of course, I thank my wife, Andrea, a paragon of patience.

Introduction

An Overview of Gambling in Nevada
1861 to 1999

Gambling, whether prohibited or regulated, has played a major role in Nevada throughout its more than 135 years of history. The unprecedented expansion of legalized casino gambling into nearly half the United States in the 1990s came after state and Indian tribal governments sought to duplicate Nevada's economic success. The state governments used Nevada's approach as a guide for taxing, licensing, and controlling legalized gambling. But Nevada carries an association with gambling like no other state.

A former territory of Spain and Mexico, Nevada—which means "snow clad" in Spanish—was first seen on maps in the 16th century. The state, mostly within the Great Basin, an ancient former sea, now covers 110,540 square miles, including the most remote land in the continental United States.[1] The U.S. government owns about 86.5 percent of the state, most of which is national forest land, military land, and Indian country.[2]

Throughout its history as a state, Nevada has taken full advantage of the states' rights provision in the U.S. Constitution. Nevada used these rights to engage in what Gilman M. Ostrander, author of *Nevada: The Great Rotten Borough, 1859–1964,* called "legal mischiefs"[3]—liberal divorce and marriage laws, legal bordellos, easy incorporation, and legal gambling. Thus, it has been Nevada's legacy to enact laws that accommodate the human impulse for quick riches, marriage, divorce, or sex. The legacy got its start in the mid-19th century with the lure of riches, and the rest followed.

Before the 1850s, Nevada's primarily barren western landscape provided little to the early pioneers beyond fur trapping or a gateway to California. But in 1858 the discovery of the huge Comstock lode beneath Virginia City in northern Nevada started the "silver rush" that attracted thousands of prospectors and adventurers, absorbed by the idea of making a fortune. A similar desire, accompanied by boredom and a need for entertainment after work, would prompt silver miners, gold miners, and others—who had arrived in northern Nevada from 39 foreign countries and every American state—to haunt Virginia City's bordellos and its 42 saloons.[4] Nevada's population surged to more than 16,000 in 1861 from just 6,857 in 1860.[5]

1

But as Nevada established this rowdy identity, its politicians moved rapidly to abolish gambling. In 1861, Congress designated Nevada a territory, and in October of that year, the territorial legislature, in its first session, adopted the common law of England,[6] designated Carson City as the state's capital, and made operating "games of chance" a felony—punishable by two years in prison, a $500 fine, or both—and wagering a misdemeanor. Legislators agreed to award district attorneys $100 per conviction for gambling offenses.[7] Nevada's first territorial governor, a native New Yorker named James Nye, was staunchly antigambling. In a speech before territorial legislators, Nye declared that of "all the seductive vices extant, I regard that of gambling as the worst. It holds out allurements hard to be resisted. It captivates and ensnares the young, blunts all the moral sensibilities and ends in utter ruin."[8] But lawmakers would soon realize that gambling was difficult to control out of existence in Nevada. Gambling convictions were rare. Legislation did not stop underground operators from running games of chance to entice the freewheeling hordes of silver miners. In 1863, the beginning of a second mining boom, Virginia City was a compilation of taverns, Victorian mansions, tent neighborhoods, boardinghouses, a grand opera house, and the four-story International Hotel. The city also boasted of a lifestyle that featured gambling—specifically the card game faro—operating 24 hours a day for the convenience of miners from all shifts.[9]

While the Civil War was being fought back east, Nevada's lucrative mining industry was valuable to the Union side. The territorial legislature had pledged support to President Lincoln in 1863, when the take from the Comstock was $12.4 million a year, more than double the $6 million in 1862, although the output merely equaled expenses.[10] In March 1864, Lincoln, seeking another loyal state to vote for the 13th Amendment abolishing slavery, signed the Nevada Enabling Act, allowing the territory to seek statehood. A constitutional convention convened in Carson City, on July 4, 1864, and drafted a constitution that included a tax on the net proceeds of mines. After voters approved the document, Nevada was proclaimed a state on October 31, 1864, in time for it to vote for Lincoln's reelection and for its two newly elected senators and congressman to scurry to Washington to vote for the 13th Amendment. But in its maiden gathering that year, the Nevada state legislature, seeing how much the territory's gambling law had been ignored, reduced the punishment for operating games of chance to a misdemeanor. Gambling was now even easier to offer. Public posturing against it, however, continued. Governor Henry Blasdel, a fervent opponent of gambling, vetoed a bill in 1865 that would have permitted it as a legal, licensed activity.[11] But in 1869, the legislature overrode his second veto of the bill, and gambling became lawful in Nevada. It was Nevada's first effort at controlling and licensing gambling. The state charged operators licensing fees of $250 to $500 per quarter and prohibited gambling in the front rooms and first floors of buildings.[12]

In the last decades of the 19th century, as mining in the state declined, gambling remained legal in Nevada, with the legislature prescribing new policies aimed at control. The state set penalties for offering gambling without a license, excluded minors from gambling businesses, and made county sheriffs responsible for enforcement.[13] Proceeds from gambling license fees were distributed to the counties and cities. In 1879 a new state law made it a misdemeanor to permit cheating in licensed gambling halls.[14] The state even allowed operators to offer gambling on first floors.

But soon after the turn of the century, the state experienced a mood swing. Many of Nevada's top politicians banded together with Progressive reformers and antialcohol organizations united in opposition against gambling on moral grounds. The national prohibition movement caught steam, and in 1909 the state legislature agreed to ban gambling and make it a felony again in Nevada. What followed was a repeat of the 1861 experience—games of chance continued in backrooms. Many Nevadans, in keeping with the western libertarian tradition, seemed ambivalent about gambling, legal or illegal.[15] Bribery of law enforcement officials by gambling operators was common, as was organized crime involvement in gambling activities.[16] In its next session in 1911, the legislature moved to permit poker games, only to make all gambling illegal again in 1913 and then legalize nonbanking poker games (where players alternated the deal) in 1915. While operators sought and received city and county licenses for poker games, most players enjoyed the added appeal of illegal, but tolerated, casino gambling in backroom speakeasies throughout Nevada. In 1915, the legislature permitted slot machines and social games awarding drinks, cigars, or other prizes worth no more than $2.[17]

With the outbreak of World War I, Nevada's copper mining, livestock, and agriculture industries flourished with the increased need for goods.[18] In the 1920s, copper and other mining accounted for most of the state's economy, thanks to demand from American industries.[19] By 1929, the state's economic future looked bright and was unaffected, at least at first, by the October 1929 stock market crash on Wall Street. In the next couple of years, the state received a settlement of almost $600 million from the federal government for money loaned by Nevada during the Civil War.[20] The U.S. government also decided to build a $3.5 million munitions storage depot in southwestern Nevada and in April 1931 to begin the $125 million Hoover Dam project on the Colorado River south of Las Vegas. Governor Fred Balzar told legislators in 1931 that the state was on "solid financial standing" thanks in part to the federal spending.[21] But Balzar painted an all-too-rosy picture of the state. As the rest of the country suffered from the Depression, Nevada's top industries, mining and agriculture, were in deep decline. Agriculture, which attracted a gross income of $22.1 million in 1928, fell to just $6.4 million in 1932.[22] Gross income from mining in 1932 was only a seventh of what it was in 1928.[23]

In 1931, the new legislature believed that the time was right to legalize gambling again, because of the lack of success of its prohibition to contain it, and that legal gambling might add to the state's attractions and enhance its economy. Legislators lifted the 20-year-old ban in March 1931, permitting most casino-type games. Assemblyman Phil Tobin of Humbolt County in northern Nevada is credited as the sponsor of the legalization bill, but several other legislators were said to have thought about introducing it.[24] There was also an indication that Clark County officials were in favor of it early on. On January 24, 1931, the *Reno Evening Gazette* wrote that "no one will admit having been approached to offer such a bill, but all of the legislators profess a lively interest in one. None of the Clark County delegation has an idea in mind of introducing a gambling bill, although the latest agitation started in that county."[25] State lawmakers at the time also thought that liberalizing divorce laws would attract visitors and business to the state. In May 1931, legislators reduced the length of residency for divorce from three months to only six weeks.[26]

The new gambling law mandated that Nevada's county governments were responsible for granting licenses with five-member boards, including the three county commissioners, the sheriff, and the district attorney. Individual cities were also given the authority to grant licenses for gambling within city borders. One-quarter of the fees paid by gambling licensees to the counties went to the state, and the counties got the other 75 percent. Incorporated cities got one-quarter of the fees from the licenses they granted, with one-half going to the county and a quarter to the state. For the city of Las Vegas and for Clark County, legalized gambling would be a godsend. So too would be the repeal of laws banning another vice—the sale and consumption of alcoholic beverages—two years later. Las Vegas enjoyed its first gaming boom during the 1931–1936 construction of Hoover Dam. Still, while gaming in the 1930s laid the foundation for the casino industry in later years, gaming did not produce a large amount of revenue during the decade.[27]

"Gaming" in Las Vegas and Clark County from the 1920s to 1940s

While "gambling" was the more popular term used outside Nevada, the word "gaming" was coined in the state since at least the 1920s in the context of regulation. In the city of Las Vegas during the 1920s, when only poker-related games were permitted by law, licenses for "gaming" were routinely approved

by the Las Vegas Board of City Commissioners after applications had been reviewed favorably by the city's police and fire commissioner. At a meeting held
January 4, 1924, for instance, city commissioners approved a "gaming license"
for A. T. McCarter for two poker games at the Exchange Pool Hall, after "the
same having heretofore approved by Police and Fire Commissioner [C. R.]
Shield."[28] The commissioners also granted gaming licenses to three partners
in the Las Vegas Bar for seven poker games and a license to the owner of the
Big Four Club for three of the games. The city fathers, however, ordered an application by E. H. Edwards for a license for two games at the Arizona Club to
be "held up for investigation" (Edwards received a license at the following
meeting).[29]

In the years before casino gambling was legalized in 1931, Las Vegas, which
was founded as a townsite in 1905 and incorporated in 1911, had a hard time
meeting the expenses of government and used gaming and other license
fees to supplement its thin treasury. License fees accounted for $10,293.60, or
28 percent of the city's total revenue of $36,393.60, at the end of 1923.[30] Most of
the city's money came from property taxes, including a tax on the net income
of local mines: $15,292, or 48 percent. In 1924, the city charged 5 cents on each
$100 worth of taxable property to pay for city employee salaries, plus 12 cents
for its street fund, 3.5 cents for interest on sewer bonds, 1.5 cents toward re-
deeming sewer bonds, 7 cents for interest on highway bonds, 8 cents devoted
to paying the principal on the highway bonds, and 1.5 cents for city lighting.
Expenditures during 1923, including administration, police and fire, and bond
payments, added up to $44,923, nearly $9,000 more than the city took in. Auditors estimated that Las Vegas needed to collect $5,000 more in taxes in 1924
to meet expenses by the end of the year. The city responded by raising property taxes. Revenues from gaming fees soon became less significant. Gaming
and other licensing fees, as well as court fines, served as a little extra revenue,
with most of it going to police and emergency services. But the city's fiscal
woes continued throughout the 1920s. In 1925, city commissioners voted to
seek an "emergency loan" from First State Bank to help with expenses. In January 1928, the city, still making payments on the emergency loan, managed to
raise only $1,450 from gaming fees.[31] The city charged poker room operators
fees of $75 for one gaming table, $150 for two tables, and $250 for three.

In January 1931, gaming fees, other permit fees, and court fines totaled
$3,063 in Las Vegas, and the city sent $1,434.25 of it to the general fund, $1,500
to police and fire, $70 to the cemetery fund, and $59.50 to water, sewer, and
lighting.[32] But the city still had needs it could not afford to meet. An official of
the state highway department urged city commissioners to seek federal funds
to pave Fremont Street and other downtown roads. The city's 1932 budget
showed Las Vegas's income amounted to $169,329.05 during 1930. The largest

source of city revenue came from bond proceeds ($55,928.90)—loans that
had to be paid back. Licensing fees still accounted for a smaller proportion of
city revenue than in 1924: $23,055.50, or 13.6 percent. The city also collected
$11,568.05 in court fines and miscellaneous fees. Las Vegas officials realized
the city was in an emergency situation and desperately needed extra income
to operate. While auditors estimated that Las Vegas would collect more than
$56,000 in taxes in 1930, city officials said more than $68,000 in tax revenue was
required to meet its obligations for 1931. Revenue-raising options remained increasing property taxes or offering yet more bonds for sale. The property tax
rate for the city's employee salary fund was already 15.6 cents per $100 as-
sessed valuation, triple what it was in 1924. With little choice, city commissioners voted to raise property taxes by 14 percent—from a rate of $1.16 per
$100 in 1931 to $1.35 in 1932. The total worth of all property in Las Vegas, valued at $2.5 million in 1924, was estimated to top $5 million at the end of 1931,
but the city still needed the hefty tax increase.

When the prohibition on casino gambling was lifted in 1931, Las Vegas responded immediately. Obviously, gaming activity meant increased city revenue from license fees as well as new income opportunities for local businesses. On March 20, 1931, the commissioners and Mayor J. F. Hesse passed
what they described as "an emergency ordinance deeming that an emergency
exists for the collection of fees hereunder for the benefit of the City."[33] The new
law would "prohibit gaming and operation of slot machines without first obtaining a license therefore regulating the same." The ordinance gave the city
the right to set the number of licenses issued and prescribed penalties for violators. Commissioners wanted the law so bad they gave it a first and second
reading the same day. The first city gaming licenses were awarded the following month, on April 7, 1931. According to the minutes of the meeting, the
commissioners took the license applications from Ethel W. Genther, C. J.
Mackey, J. R. Boyer, and Jack Butler off the agenda, saying their forms were in-
complete.[34] The minutes show that the first license was granted to the Boulder
Club, located at 118 Fremont Street, and other licenses (in order) were approved for the Las Vegas Club at 21 and 23 Fremont, A. T. McCarter's Exchange Club at 123 First Street, and the Northern Club at 15 Fremont. Four local residents then asked the commissioners to consider granting additional
licenses, and eight others admonished the city to create a district zoned for
gaming and to set a limit on new licenses. In response, city commissioners
passed, with Mayor Hesse opposed, an ordinance limiting licenses to those
held in the previous quarter, meaning that no new licenses would be granted
"until a zone is established for the operation of gambling houses and a policy
is adopted by the Board [of Commissioners] governing the issuance of new
licenses."[35]

Two days later, on April 9, 1931, the city took up the second proposed gaming ordinance. Disappointing some members of the audience who wanted more licenses, city commissioners agreed on a policy limiting gaming licenses to those approved in the previous quarter and at the April 7 meeting. The law also contained a curious provision: "This Resolution shall not be construed to prevent the consideration of an application for and the granting of a license to a person of the Ethiopian Race for the conduct of a game or games in a place cattering [sic] exclusively to persons of the same race only." [36] Las Vegas would remain a segregated city for another three decades.

The city had entered the modern era of casino gaming, but tough times remained. On April 13, 1931, city commissioners, citing a "pressing need for the extension of the present sewer system," moved to place before voters a $150,000 bond measure to pay for one. City officials also discussed the refusal by Clark County to allow Las Vegas to increase the property tax rate to $1.32. The county revised the figure down to $1.12 per $100 assessed valuation, requiring Las Vegas to rewrite its budget with lower forecasted revenues. The city adjusted its tax rates down across the board. But the city's rewritten budget for 1932 contained an even more significant change: The $25,000 in projected expenses for the police department and municipal court—which was to have been paid by a property tax rate of 6 cents, plus $11,000 in "receipts other than taxes" in the old 1932 budget—was to be covered in full by nontax revenue.[37] City officials, in a bind, were banking on the new gaming law to provide additional license fees to help solve the city's financial predicament in the year ahead.

In the rush to formulate city policy on gaming, changes occurred behind the scenes. At the April 17, 1931, meeting, Las Vegas commissioners granted gaming licenses to four people already licensed for poker tables. They then voted to rescind the gaming law they had passed in March. A new ordinance was approved, limiting licenses for each "gaming house" to one per 1,500 persons in Las Vegas, or only six total licenses. The law stated that such a limitation "will not contravene public interest and will not require an excessive amount of police protection for a city of the size of Las Vegas, Nevada, having in mind the funds provided for police protection under the city's 1931 and 1932 Budgets . . . and the state of the city funds applicable to police protection."[38] However, the revised law did not limit licenses for slot machines, and those who held a valid gaming license could apply for additional slot machines at any time during each quarter for a fee. After adopting the revised law, the city denied gaming house applications from 14 people, citing the six-license limit. But they okayed 12 other applications for slots only, including five machines to the Boulder Club, six to the Las Vegas Club, six to the Boulder Drug Company, two to A. T. McCarter, and two to Ethel Genther. The slot machine license had made its debut in Las Vegas. For drugstores, coffee shops, barbershops, and other small businesses seeking additional profits from slot machines in Las Vegas, it was off to the races in the months that followed.

On April 22, 1931, the city passed another emergency ordinance, this time to establish separate and distinct residential, industrial, and commercial districts within the city. City Attorney F. A. Stevens then reported that in his opinion, the city commission was within its power to pass the March gaming law and to limit the number of gaming licenses. Commissioners then approved slot licenses for the State Cafe (three machines), R. C. Andred (two machines), the Deluxe Barbershop (one machine), and J. T. Watters (23 machines). Gaming license and other fees in April brought the city $3,727.50, more than 50 percent of the city's revenue of $6,368 from all other sources for the month. The city turned over $3,557 of it to the police and fire fund.[39]

The first legal challenge to Las Vegas's new gaming law came in May 1931, when the city was sued in the state supreme court in Carson City by Roy Grimes, who along with his partners was denied a gaming license to operate a proposed casino, the Lorenzi Resort. Commissioners voted to send City Attorney Stevens to the state capital to argue their case against granting the license.[40] But later that month, the city gave in and granted Grimes and his partners six slot machine licenses.[41]

Meanwhile, the city continued to feel financial pressure. Voters, by 956 to 737, defeated its bond measure for the proposed sewer system. Then, on May 19, 1931, city commissioners voted to reprimand Clark County Sheriff Joe Keate, whom the city claimed had withheld 6 percent of the $5,104.20 in gaming license fees for businesses within the Las Vegas city limits from April to May.[42] The city passed a resolution, demanding that Keate, whose office collected all the gaming fees in the county and issued the paper gaming licenses, return the balance of the funds to Las Vegas. The next day it was business as usual. The city granted three licenses for a total of six slot machines. Sheriff Keate reported he had given the city the rest of the $5,104.20 in back gaming fees, and city commissioners duly sent $1,500 of the total to city police and fire services, $3,602.74 to the general fund, and $1.46 to the Library Checking Fund.[43] On May 29, 1931, the city rejected pleas from Grimes and others to issue still more gaming licenses.

The financial situation for Las Vegas improved rapidly in the weeks to come in 1931. As gaming-related controversies subsided, the city issued new gaming and slot licenses and swiftly spent the fee money. On July 6, 1931, the city voted to lease a street sweeper and called for bids so that the city could buy two cars for the police department, a dump truck for the street department, and a year's supply of tires and tire tubes for all city-owned vehicles.[44] The city also hired a new police chief; passed an ordinance governing street curbs, gutters, and driveways; and enacted a law regulating traffic on public streets. On the gaming front, the city expanded its gaming house limit to seven and granted or renewed a total of 19 gaming house and slot licenses, allowing 68 slots, 8 table games, and 11 gaming "devices." Slot licenses were awarded to four drugstores and six restaurants. The Vegas Sweet Shop alone was approved for 17 slots, more than any other licensee on the list. J. R. Boyer, a previously unsuccessful applicant, was granted the city's seventh gaming house license.

Clark County's own fiscal troubles, both just before and after 1931, were similar to those of Las Vegas. The Clark County Board of Commissioners also levied property taxes to pay for expenses in the 1920s, including interest on bonds for each of the county's 10 public schools (the state provided additional funds for schools). The county's property tax rate in 1929 on county land outside of Las Vegas was $1.70 per $100 assessed valuation.[45] Special taxes were charged on gasoline, mining revenue, "near beer" stands, livestock, and sheep. The county's budget for 1929 estimated receipts totaling $788,964. Of that, $330,000, from bond proceeds, was the single highest source of revenue, and property tax revenue was next with $236,125. Expenditures for the year included paying off a $5,000 emergency loan. Revenues from gaming and other licenses amounted to only $8,900, and only $10,670 was collected from fines and fees.

On March 5, 1929, despite pleas from local residents and Nevada's state health officer to appoint and compensate a county health nurse, county commissioners put the matter off until the new budget could be drawn up in 1930. County commissioners even ordered the county clerk to send a letter to the legislature, expressing their opposition to a state bill that would direct counties to pay residents a bounty for each jackrabbit they trap, saying that "it appeared to the Board that the bill mentioned would not result favorably for this County."[46] On March 7, 1929, county commissioners passed a resolution to urge the legislature—which was set to adjourn in only a few days—to immediately grant the county authority to create bonded indebtedness. The county, they reasoned, would suffer a great deal to wait any longer since the legislature would not meet again for two years. "[S]uch delay would mean a great loss to the community and an expense upon the county government which could not be borne at this time."[47] The county also asked for state assistance to pay for a highway to Las Vegas from the planned Hoover Dam. The state later agreed and created the Clark County State Highway Fund. By 1930, Clark County's budget was expected to drop from $893,116.68—inflated by $357,510.54 in bond proceeds—to $298,218, with its property tax rate raised to $1.74. On August 5, 1930, the county commissioners had to transfer $7,000 from the general fund to the county's depleted Indigent Fund.

After the legislature voted to bring back casino gambling in 1931, Clark County drafted its gaming ordinance, creating a licensing board made up of the county's commissioners, district attorney, and sheriff, who served as chairman. The new board fixed and imposed license fees and passed judgment on issuing and revoking licenses on gambling games. The county's law stated that the board "in the exercise of their judgment and discretion may refuse to grant or renew the license provided for in these regulations."[48] The law also gave the licensing board the authority to revoke a license if it appeared that the licensee "is not a proper person, firm, association or corporation to carry on or conduct the slot machine, device and/or games for which the license was granted, or that such slot machine or device and/or game is not being properly or fairly conducted."

The county's law also declared that no one in Clark County was permitted to conduct "any game of faro, monte, roulette, keno, fan-tan, twenty-one, stud poker, draw poker" or any banking game without first obtaining a license. Nonrefundable fees for gaming licenses were set at $50 a month for each table game in the county, payable to the sheriff for each quarter (three months) in advance. Slot licenses were $10 a month per machine. Licenses were valid only for the quarter and had to be renewed by paying the same fees. The quarters would expire on March 21, June 21, September 21, and December 21. Applications had to be submitted at least 30 days before the county could consider granting a license. License holders were permitted to request additional slot machines throughout the quarter. Card games played for money, such as stud and draw poker, bridge, whist, solo, and pangingue, were to be licensed separately from the casino games at $25 a month.

The county set up its new License Board on March 21, 1931. Sheriff Keate was appointed chairman. Other members were County Commissioners E. G. McGriff, A. L. Jones, and E. F. Davidson and District Attorney Harley E. Harmon. In addition to gaming, the board would issue or revoke licenses for pool halls, dancing halls, bowling alleys, theaters, and "soft-drink establishments." Applications for gaming licenses swarmed in, both inside and outside Las Vegas. On April 1, 1931, the License Board approved 25 gaming licenses. First on the list was the Meadows Casino, owned by Louis D. Cornero, for two crap tables, two roulette tables, two 21 tables, one English Hazard, one faro table, a Big Six wheel, two poker tables, and five slot machines. Also licensed for casino table games were the Northern Club, the Las Vegas Club, the Boulder Club, the Exchange Club, the Rainbow Club, and the Red Rooster Night Club. The other 18 licensees were for slots only. The Texaco Cafe, for instance, was approved for two nickel machines; J. Warren Woodward's Auto Camp for one quarter, one dime, and one nickel machine; and the Park Home Cafe for one nickel machine. The tally was 38 casino games, 19 poker games, and 61 slot machines, or $2,985 in gaming license fees for the month. That meant the county's first take from gaming fees would be $11,940 for the quarter, with some to go to the city of Las Vegas, where many of the table games and slots were based.

County auditors initially estimated that revenue from gaming license fees during all of 1931 would amount to $11,600, up from $5,100 in 1930. The good news was that with the legalization of gaming, fees collected in the county would be more than four times that. But the new funds were slow in coming. With gaming now in place, Clark County nonetheless remained unable to meet general expenses, mainly because of the costs of providing hospital, pension, and other benefits to the poor. On April 6, 1931, county commissioners voted to raise the property tax rate for 1931 to $1.81, up from $1.74 in 1930. On April 29, 1931, they passed a resolution, stating that tax revenues estimated for June 1931 "will not be sufficient to pay general county expenses and expenses which will necessarily be incurred in the relief of indigent persons."[49] The resolution asked the state finance board for permission to borrow $20,000 from a bank to establish an emergency fund for "indigent persons," to be paid off with higher property taxes. Meanwhile, on May 5, 1931, the county License Board approved 10 casino games and two poker tables to six new applicants (amounting to $2,200 in fees for the quarter) and put off the application of a seventh "until the applicant could be further investigated." One of the approved applicants was Oscar E. Klawitter, who had requested a roulette table, a blackjack table, and a crap game for the Pair-O-Dice Casino, three miles southwest of Las Vegas, on what was then called the Los Angeles Highway, near the area known years later as the Las Vegas Strip. On May 20, 1931, a letter from E. J. Seaborn, the secretary of the state finance board, was entered into the record, authorizing the county to seek the emergency loan. Seaborn wrote that the loan was appropriate because "a great necessity or emergency has arisen in Clark County." The county obtained the $20,000 from First State Bank in October 1931.

On July 7, 1931, the county commission revoked its first gaming license. With Prohibition still in effect, liquor sales were illegal across the country. Federal agents had raided and pressed charges against the Red Rooster Night Club, just outside Las Vegas, for which the county had approved one blackjack table and three slot machines on April 1. The county commissioners voted to reject the Red Rooster's request for another license, even though a new owner had applied for it. Commissioners also delayed a licensing bid by the Midway Amusement Company, "pending investigation of the applicant," and postponed action on applicant L. A. Ethridge for a month, since Ethridge did not file within the required 30 days before a license could be granted.

The expansion of local businesses following the legalization of gaming continued in the Las Vegas valley. But 1933 would bring a new major change—the legalization of alcoholic drinks, which had perhaps even a larger impact on Nevada at the time than the addition of legalized gaming. Casino gambling, drinking, and other forms of legal entertainment had merged for the first time in decades in Nevada. Prostitution was also legal and licensed in the city of Las Vegas, with brothels situated on the Block 16 section of downtown on First Street between Ogden and Stewart Avenues.[50]

In January 1933, Clark County approved gaming licenses for two gaming clubs and granted dance hall licenses to the Blue Heaven, the Sunset Dance Pavilion, and the infamous Red Rooster.[51] On April 5, 1933, following the national repeal of Prohibition, the county passed a liquor ordinance that set licensing and fee requirements and created the Liquor Board, with the same members as the License Board. The ordinance specified that beer and other liquor sold in the county contain no more than 3.2 percent alcohol by weight. Licenses would be issued for the sale of liquor by retailers and wholesalers. An immediate crush of first-time liquor license applicants followed, all of them wanting to sell beer only. Just a day later, on April 6, the new Liquor Board granted beer licenses to 35 businesses, including the Boulder Inn, Pair-O-Dice, and Railroad Pass casinos; the Blue Heaven and Red Rooster dance halls; and various small bars and restaurants. Six other applications were held for further investigation. During the same meeting, the board members changed hats and, as the License Board, approved licenses to 21 businesses to dispense soft drinks, holding over eight others. Most of the soft-drink applicants were service stations, an indication of the increased auto traffic to Las Vegas. The Midway Amusement Company received licenses to sell soft drinks and to run a crap game, a dance hall, and concert saloon. In just one day, a brand-new, legal lifestyle had taken hold in the Las Vegas area.

After the first wave of liquor licenses had passed, the county decided to rewrite its relatively brief liquor ordinance on November 21, 1933. The new ordinance said that to serve liquor in the county, bars and saloons had to pay a fee of $1,000 per quarter and restaurants $500 a quarter, although businesses in towns with fewer than 1,000 people had to pay between $200 and $300. Other businesses serving beer or other liquor with 4 percent alcohol or less had to cough up only $50 a year. To be eligible for a liquor license, applicants had to be residents of the county for at least six months. The law further prohibited owners of liquor-serving bars, nightclubs, and social clubs from allowing women to "loiter in and around" their businesses, unless the women were employed there. Also, female dancers in bars and clubs serving liquor had to obtain permits from the sheriff before they could work, and such businesses could not "employ more than 10 female persons as dancers or entertainers." The law further prohibited "any gambling devices games or devices within a room where a bar is maintained and liquor is sold or served." However, gambling games could be conducted "within the same building" where liquor was sold or served.[52]

The county's Liquor Board would eventually take over the gaming license oversight of the License Board. In fact, throughout the middle and late 1930s, meeting records show that the county commissioners spent a high proportion of their time simply acting as the Liquor Board, sifting through piles of liquor license applications and hearing about the problems of licensees and violations of the liquor law. On November 5, 1935, the fusion of gaming, liquor, and dancing girls got one establishment, the Meadows Casino, into hot water. The Meadows was located outside downtown Las Vegas next to Boulder Highway and was built in 1931 to target locals and workers from the Hoover Dam project. District Attorney Roger T. Foley told the commission that the owners of the Meadows, Dave Stearns and Larry Potter, had permitted "a dance commonly known as the Fan Dance in an indecent manner."[53] Foley had sent a letter to the Meadows, ordering that "if it was their desire to continue said Fan Dance, that it must be done in the legal manner." Foley said, however, that his letter was ignored, and the dance continued in the "indecent" manner. The License Board accepted an offer from another owner, Sam Stearns, to take over as operator of the casino. By 1937, the Liquor Board was granting both gaming and liquor licenses, which the board continued to do routinely into the 1940s.

In 1938, after a new mayor was elected in Los Angeles, bent on eliminating illegal gambling from the city, a corrupt Los Angeles police captain named Guy McAfee—who, while a commander of vice enforcement operated illegal gambling there for years—decided to come to Las Vegas.[54] McAfee bought the Pair-O-Dice casino, about a mile south of the city limits on Highway 91, which he is credited for nicknaming the "Strip," after the Sunset Strip in Los Angeles.[55] In 1940, hotel man Thomas Hull bought land on Highway 91 and a year later opened the El Rancho Vegas, regarded as the first Las Vegas resort on the new "Strip." The El Rancho featured hotel services, horseback riding, a travel agency, a swimming pool, and a casino.[56]

World War II would bring the biggest boom period yet to Las Vegas. While gaming revenues in area casinos rose by 50 percent from 1931 to 1941, revenues increased 56 percent from 1941 to 1943.[57] Entertainment offerings in casinos blossomed. In 1941, a casino in Elko in northeastern Nevada hired a well-known orchestra to attract visitors, and casinos in Reno and Las Vegas soon began hiring name entertainers.[58]

The next hotel-casino to appear on the fledgling Strip, the Last Frontier—built at the site of the Pair-O-Dice casino—opened in 1942. County officials in the early to mid-1940s still devoted most of their time granting or denying local liquor licenses, according to minutes of commission meetings. But with the influx of American servicemen, curious about casinos they saw in the Las Vegas area, attention shifted back to gaming. Out-of-staters attracted by casino gambling poured into Las Vegas throughout the 1940s. In January 1944, the county's new licensing agency, the Liquor and Licensing Board, started the year off with 215 gaming applications, mostly from the owners of bars, cafes, liquor stores, markets, and other small businesses requesting slot machines.[59] The largest casinos, all in the city of Las Vegas, were the Pioneer Club, which requested 45 slot machines and 22 casino games; the Frontier Club, 41 slots and 17 games; the Boulder Club, 37 slots and 18 games; and the Las Vegas Club, 29 slots and 12 games. The Last Frontier, in the county's jurisdiction, applied for 34 slots and 10 games. Each of the 215 applications were approved, except for one—a request by Mack H. Shell for a 21 table at the Four Star Ranch, although the minutes do not indicate why. The Liquor and Licensing Board then approved 30 additional gaming applications over the next four months.

In 1945, the legislature amended the state's 1931 gambling law to require gaming operators to apply for state gaming licenses from the Nevada Tax Commission, thus removing primary licensing authority from the cities and counties.[60] The intent was not so much to control gaming as to collect taxes on it. The state imposed a 1 percent tax on gross gambling receipts of licensees (a tax that would increase to 2 percent in 1947) collected by the Tax Commission.[61] Gambling operators, however, would now have to use proper accounting procedures to ensure that the state received the tax money they owed. The Tax Commission, which served as overseer of state tax laws, had seven members appointed by the governor, who served as chairman. Each commission member represented a different classification of state business: mining, cattle, industry, land, banking, utilities, and general business. In 1945, Governor E. P. Carville selected Robbins Cahill, a former school board trustee and state legislator, to serve as the new executive secretary of the Tax Commission. Cahill hired a small staff of investigators, who began to peer into the backgrounds of gaming license applicants and monitor gambling operators for compliance with the new state gaming tax.

Clark County saw another deluge of gaming applications in 1945, again mostly for slot machines in small businesses. The county Liquor and Licensing Board had to hold meetings on Friday and Saturday, January 5 and 6, 1945, to consider and approve 207 gaming licenses. Some applicants were awarded more than one license. One applicant, listed as R. Roschl, was licensed to operate slot machines in 27 taverns, cafes, grocery stores, and other locations. Lee Hughes obtained 19 of the 207 licenses, all for slots in small businesses. Wilbur Clark, who would later operate the Desert Inn hotel, was licensed to run the Hotel El Rancho casino, on Highway 91, on January 6.

In 1946, the flood of new gaming licenses continued. On August 5, 1946, County Sheriff Glen Jones, chairman of the Liquor and Licensing Board, presented the application of the Nevada Project, Inc., also known as the Flamingo Hotel, "for a retail liquor and gaming license."[62] Representing the Flamingo and its infamous operator, East Coast mobster Benjamin "Bugsy" Siegel, was Las Vegas attorney Louis Wiener, Jr. The board, however, took no action and held it over for further investigation. Jones introduced the application again at the board's meeting on August 14. The Flamingo's application, the only item on the agenda, was granted, but the minutes recorded no discussion about it. What would become the most famous Las Vegas casino was licensed.

Siegel, a key associate of mob figures Lucky Luciano and Meyer Lansky, bought the Flamingo from original owner William Wilkerson in 1945. Since the early 1940s, Siegel had controlled the race wires that transmitted results of out-of-state horse races to legal bookmakers in Las Vegas. He charged huge fees for the service and used the profits to buy into the unfinished Flamingo project and purchase interests in the Golden Nugget and the Frontier Club casinos in downtown Las Vegas. Because the state's gaming statutes did not direct the Tax Commission to investigate the background or character of applicants, Siegel's group obtained local and state gaming licenses despite his infamy as a member of an organized crime syndicate, his past involvement with illegal gambling ships off the coast of Los Angeles and other illegal casinos in Southern California, and his arrest for murder in the early 1940s. It was Siegel who laid the foundation in Las Vegas for the eventual infiltration of the casino business by interests tied directly to mob bosses Meyer Lansky and Frank Costello in New York, Joseph Stacher in New Jersey, Moe Dalitz from Cleveland, and other crime syndicate chieftains from Florida, Detroit, Brooklyn, Louisiana, Florida, and Kansas City.[63] Siegel's other past associates included top hoodlums Al Capone, Vito Genovese, and Abner "Longie" Zwillman.[64]

In Las Vegas, local and state officials both tolerated and rationalized the licensing of Siegel and others with criminal records. The prevailing attitude was that people with criminal or otherwise bad backgrounds were acceptable if they behaved themselves while in Las Vegas.[65] Arrests for illegal gambling in other states could be excused since gaming was legal in Nevada. And, as it happened, members or associates of organized crime were the most experienced in managing casinos. Thus, with the knowledge of state officials, some of the most prominent early casino operators and partners in Las Vegas in the 1940s and 1950s had criminal records, including arrests for illegal gambling. Others had once been arrested for much more serious crimes, such as murder, kidnapping, and burglary. Mobsters and mob associates would soon come to own most of the early casinos in Las Vegas.[66]

Ironically, since casino gaming was illegal everywhere else, hoodlums and criminals were among the most professional casino gambling operators. Jerome Skolnick, author of the 1978 book *House of Cards—the Legalization and Control of Casino Gambling,* wrote that it "would have been the end of the industry" had Nevada failed to license mobsters, who laid the foundation for the industry before the Nevada State Gaming Control Board was formed in 1955.[67] Illegal gamblers from Texas, California, Ohio, and Kentucky converged on Las Vegas to join the fray in the 1940s.[68]

In January 1947, the county approved a record 352 gaming licenses. But important changes were on the way. After Siegel was shot and killed in Beverly Hills, California, in June 1947, the wave of bad publicity encouraged state officials to consider toughening state gaming laws. Nevada Attorney General Alan Bible said in a landmark opinion that the Tax Commission, empowered to make rules and regulations on gaming, could refuse to grant licenses to certain persons if deemed in the public interest.[69] In 1949, the legislature adopted the state's first regulations on gaming license applicants. Applicants for new gaming licenses now had to meet the approval of the Tax Commission, which was given the authority to set rules and regulations on gaming and, for the first time, empowered to look into and pass judgment on the backgrounds of applicants. The state also required casino employees to be fingerprinted.

The Rise of Modern Gaming Regulation in Nevada

In the months before his 1947 death in a gangland execution, Ben Siegel had a bad reputation in Las Vegas, and most locals steered away from the Flamingo. He had racked up cost overruns while building the casino, which lost money after it opened in December 1946. Siegel also defied his mobbed-up backers, who believed he was stealing construction money. But his gangster partners were ready to move right in. Literally minutes after Siegel was slain, apparently on orders from Luciano and Lansky, underworld members Moe Sedway, Morris Rosen, and Gus Greenbaum entered the hotel's lobby to announce they were taking over. Mob involvement in Las Vegas had begun to hit stride. A week after Siegel's murder, Rosen, Sedway, and Siegel's brother Solly, a Los Angeles doctor, snatched up the dead man's interests in the Golden Nugget and Frontier Club. A man named Connie Hurley took over the late Siegel's race wire business.[70]

When he was alive, Siegel had decided who would and would not have access to the results from the race wire and then demanded a share of the profits from each of the race books. Resentful race bookies had complained to the district attorney in Las Vegas, but nothing was done by either Las Vegas or

Nevada authorities for more than a year after Siegel's death. From 1947 to 1948, disreputable race book operators fostered a dangerous environment in Las Vegas. A pair known as the Stearns brothers, who operated a downtown betting parlor called the Santa Anita Club, slipped a hidden microphone into the competing Frontier Club next door so that when race results were announced there they could also be heard in the Santa Anita.[71] The Frontier Club complained about the theft of its race reports to the Federal Communications Commission and the U.S. attorney's office. Clark County District Attorney Robert E. Jones sent a letter to the Nevada Tax Commission, warning of a possible outbreak of gang warfare.[72] With the heat on, in October 1948 Governor Vail Pittman ordered hearings on the race wires, out of which the legislature passed the Race Wire Service Law. The law authorized the Tax Commission to set rates for race wire services and prevented wire operators from refusing service to a gaming licensee. Under the law race wire owners could not raise the prices they charged race books as of March 1948 without the approval of the Tax Commission. State officials figured that would be enough to take care of the problems that began with Siegel years earlier. However, the race wire already operating in Las Vegas, dominated by Continental Press out of Phoenix, Arizona, was allowed to function without any additional state oversight.

Meanwhile, media reports about the notorious Las Vegas gaming scene, including Siegel's death, mob influence, and the race wire controversy, attracted the attention of Washington. In 1950, the Special Committee to Investigate Organized Crime in Interstate Commerce, chaired by the ambitious U.S. senator Estes Kefauver (D-Tenn.), held hearings throughout the country to gather information about mob activities, and Las Vegas was one of its main targets. The Kefauver Committee came to Las Vegas on November 15, 1950, to interrogate, in executive session, a list of state and local politicians, businessmen, and casino operators, including some with reputed mob ties. The hearings revealed the weaknesses in Nevada's approach to controlling its gaming industry, one being the state's acceptance of gaming regulators themselves having financial·interests in the industry they regulated. Under the state's political climate and mentality of the time, state officials still thought nothing of permitting people with illegal gaming convictions outside Nevada to hold gaming licenses since, they reasoned, gaming was legal in the state. Convictions for far worse crimes also remained forgivable in Nevada. The 1949 state gaming control law included a "grandfather" clause, conveniently exempting past licensees—including those with extensive criminal records and other blots on their backgrounds—from the scrutiny that might prevent new applicants from being licensed.[73]

Nevada's gaming policies came under examination by the Kefauver Committee during the closed hearings. What emerged was that state officials tolerated apparent conflicts of interest involving the growing gaming industry. The list of witnesses called before the Kefauver body in Las Vegas included William J. Moore, a member of the Tax Commission, and Nevada's lieutenant governor, Clifford A. Jones, both of whom owned considerable investments in Las Vegas casinos and thought nothing of it. Moore, originally from Dallas, Texas, was the architect of the Last Frontier hotel-casino before it opened in 1942. The money to back construction of the Last Frontier came from R. E. Griffith, owner of a 200-screen movie theater chain based in Dallas.[74] Tax Commissioner Moore testified that he owned about 8 percent of the company operating the casino, which included 10 other partners who received shares of the net proceeds. Moore himself also received a salary of $10,000 and 5 percent of the net receipts. In 1949, he said he earned between $75,000 and $84,000 from the operation. Moore reported that the Last Frontier grossed $4 million in 1949, $2 million of it from gaming. Despite that, the hotel-casino reported to state and federal tax authorities a net profit of only $135,000.

Moore had been on the Tax Commission since 1947, representing business interests for the state. Kefauver Committee members and committee counsel Rudolph Halley grilled him about his casino income and the state's oversight of race wire services. Under questioning, Moore said the Last Frontier was paying only $200 a month to the Continental Press wire service for race results. When a senator told him the Kefauver Committee had learned one customer paid Continental $6,000 a week, or $24,000 a month, for the same service, Moore replied that it "doesn't surprise me."[75] He then denied that the much lower fee charged his casino was the result of a side deal or blackmail. Moore, in a way typical of some Nevadans of the time, also did not sound particularly interested in ridding the race wire business of unsavory characters who held state gaming licenses.

SENATOR TOBEY: Are most of these gamblers and bookmakers crooked?
MR. MOORE: No.
SENATOR TOBEY: Are most of them members of high integrity?
MR. MOORE: Well, it depends on how you describe "high integrity."
SENATOR TOBEY: You know what integrity is as well as I do: character.
MR. MOORE: I would say that it is probably like any other profession. There are some—
SENATOR TOBEY: No more in this business than there are in any commercial line?
MR. MOORE: Yes, I would say a few more shady characters.
SENATOR TOBEY: What hope do you ever see of getting rid of them?
MR. MOORE: That I have never thought of.

SENATOR TOBEY: Would that be a desirable thing, in your judgment?

MR. MOORE: Some individuals, maybe, yes.

SENATOR TOBEY: For the common good, I mean.

MR. MOORE: Yes.[76]

Moore later testified that the Tax Commission had refused to license "several hundred" people and had revoked 75 to 100 licenses since obtaining full licensing authority in 1949. Applicants were rejected on the basis of their background and character, he said. However, he revealed some contradictions to the Kefauver Committee. Moore acknowledged that the Tax Commission had recently denied a license to a St. Louis man, James Carroll, a major figure in the horse racing business who had no criminal record, simply because of Carroll's "national prominence in the race book business." He admitted, however, that the Tax Commission had licensed Sanford Adler for the Cal-Neva Club in Lake Tahoe, despite Adler's arrest record, and two other men, William Graham and James McKay, who had been convicted of altering government bonds stolen from a New York bank. When asked how he could reconcile that, Moore replied that a "granddaddy clause" exempted previous licensees and that other government agencies overseeing licenses for attorneys, engineers, and other professions had done the same thing.

"Are you going to throw out a man with a three-and-a-half million dollar investment?" Moore asked, referring to Adler. "In other words, the sheriff gave him a license. He had been operating in the state several years. You can't correct overnight a situation that existed prior to your enactment of a new law. . . . Just because you get the privilege of controlling the thing, is that any reason why you should put the man out of business, if he is operating in the State of Nevada?"[77]

"Yes, I think it is," replied Senator Tobey, "but you and I might differ on that. I think if you have a man that is crooked and shown to be crooked, and a lawbreaker, I wouldn't give him any privilege at all."

Later, Moore was asked about a man, referred to only as Wertheimer from Detroit, whom the Tax Commission granted a license, even though the man had convictions for illegal gambling.

MR. HALLEY: Haven't you ever heard of Wertheimer's gambling activities in a state where it is not legal?

MR. MOORE: Sure, but, as far as that is concerned, the man gambles. That is no sign that he shouldn't have a license in a state where it is legal.

MR. HALLEY: It makes no difference to you whether he gambles in a state where it is not legal?

MR. MOORE: No. How is he going to learn the business?

MR. HALLEY: In other words, you take a position that, because gambling
is legal in the state of Nevada, that anybody who has been convicted for
gambling in other states is not to be considered in any way disqualified;
is that right?

MR. MOORE: That is right.

MR. HALLEY: Is that a basic policy of the commission?

MR. MOORE: Yes.

MR. HALLEY: With regard to people who have been convicted for anything else, that doesn't disqualify them so long as they were in business
here in 1948, is that right?

MR. MOORE: That is right.[78]

Next to testify was Lieutenant Governor Jones, a Las Vegas attorney who
owned percentage share interests in gaming proceeds at the Thunderbird Hotel, the Golden Nugget, and the Pioneer Club casinos. Jones told the committee over the past year he had received $12,000 in cash from his 1 percent share
in the Golden Nugget and $14,000 from his 5 percent of the Pioneer's net
profits. Jones said he owned 11 percent of the stock in the Thunderbird's operating and ownership companies but received no income or return from them
since the casino opened in 1948. Jones's main partner in the Thunderbird was
Marion Hicks, an association Jones would one day live to regret. In his testimony before the committee, Jones echoed Moore's opinions about the propriety of the 1949 state law that allowed former criminals and mobsters to retain
gaming licenses.

CHAIRMAN KEFAUVER: But you blanketed in a lot of racketeers who
were already doing business?

MR. JONES: Yes; in other words, it is kind of like a grandfather clause.
They were here in business, and in operation, some of them, and had a
lot of money invested. In other words, you can't legislate them out of
business . . .

MR. HALLEY: So what you are really talking about is the Tax Commission at its discretion has decided to allow these who had previous—
well, first, that had been here prior to 1949, to continue to operate?

MR. JONES: That is right.

MR. HALLEY: Whether or not they are qualified?

MR. JONES: That is right. In other words, they have kind of taken the attitude that if they had been here and had been operating and had conducted themselves properly, that they were qualified by that.

MR. HALLEY: Since you are Lieutenant Governor of the state, I am going
to presume to ask an over-all policy question, which you may or may
not see fit to answer.

MR. JONES: All right.

MR. HALLEY: It is definitely a statement of opinion. Wouldn't you say prior to 1949 a great many undesirable characters, with bad police records, were engaged in gambling operations in the State of Nevada, such as Graham and McKay, Wertheimer, Bugsy Siegel? I could name a great many more, of course.

MR. JONES: Well, of course.

MR. HALLEY: Moe Sedway?

MR. JONES: Some of those I could very definitely concur with you on. Some of them are people who have been in the state long before I was here, so I wouldn't presume to pass judgment upon their qualifications to conduct their business.

MR. HALLEY: Well, there had been a lot of people—

MR. JONES: There were some people that you might say had police records and reputations of gambling in other places. But this seems to hold true, that people who came here when the state started to grow, to gamble in the gambling business, they weren't particularly Sunday school teachers or preachers or anything like that from out of the state. They were gamblers. In other words, they came here to gamble.

MR. HALLEY: We have one more question. As a matter of over-all state policy, do you believe it is good policy to allow people whose previous records have been bad, to continue in the gambling business in this state for the simple reason and sole reason that they were in business prior to 1949?

MR. JONES: I would say that I believe as long as they conduct themselves properly that I think there is probably no harm comes to it.[79]

The Kefauver Committee's inquiry was seen by many in the state as an intrusion into the state's legal activities. Nevada Tax Commission Executive Secretary Cahill maintained that the hearings were held to promote Kefauver's own future candidacy for president "by being against sin and for motherhood."[80] But Nevada officials felt the pressure to tighten controls on gaming. A bill was introduced in the U.S. House Ways and Means Committee to levy a 10 percent tax on gross gambling profits that could have effectively closed Nevada's casinos. But Nevada's powerful senior senator, Pat McCarran, who did not think much of casino gaming, pulled strings and used his seniority in committees to help defeat the bill before it reached the House floor.[81]

Nevada's state lawmakers responded by imposing rigid licensing requirements on gaming applicants, ones that would be eased in the years to come to provide gaming authorities more flexibility in considering the backgrounds of applicants. In 1953, the legislature enacted a law deeming all applicants unsuitable for a gaming license if they were convicted of larceny, narcotics, firearm violations, or any other felony crime or if they were under the age of 21 or not a U.S. citizen.[82]

In the early to mid-1950s, a slew of major casinos opened on and off the Strip, starting with the $4.5 million Desert Inn in 1950, the $5.5 million Sahara in 1952, and then the Sands, Showboat, Royal Nevada, Riviera, Moulin Rouge, Dunes, Stardust, Martinique, Tropicana, Continental, Trade Winds, Vegas Plaza, Casa Blanca, San Souci, and Horizons.[83] The Desert Inn's casino was organized in a way considered typical for the time: 1 manager, 2 assistant managers, 85 dealers, 19 pit bosses and box men, 7 change girls, and 3 slot machine supervisors.[84] By the mid-1950s, there were 10 Strip resorts, 35 hotels, and 250 motels in Las Vegas. Tourists spent $164 million in Las Vegas in 1955.[85]

During this boom period, construction money for casinos was difficult to obtain, as banking institutions, even in Las Vegas, declined to give loans to casino projects because of the industry's reputation as being mob influenced.[86] Reputed hoodlums stepped in with clandestine investments in the new Las Vegas casinos. In the case of the Horseshoe casino in downtown Las Vegas, a former Dallas street hood ran the show, with the state's blessing. In 1951, the Tax Commission licensed Lester "Benny" Binion to operate the Horseshoe, at 128 East Fremont Street, even though he was under indictment by a grand jury in Dallas for operating a multi-million-dollar illegal gambling racket.[87] Nevada governor Charles Russell, a member of the Tax Commission, defended the licensing, saying that Binion signed an affidavit and offered "proof that he is not engaged in gambling in any state where gambling is illegal."[88] Binion, who also held interests in the Las Vegas Club and the Westerner Club in Las Vegas, was a violent former numbers runner in Dallas whose record included two arrests for murder. He fled to Las Vegas with a suitcase full of cash in 1946 to escape the Internal Revenue Service (IRS), which eventually caught up to him. Binion was convicted of tax evasion in 1953 and served five years in a federal prison.[89]

Another infamous gangster-backed casino was the Sands Hotel, opened in 1952. The main investor in the Sands, lurking behind a "front man" with a clean background who was set up to apply for the license, was Joseph "Doc" Stacher, an associate of Lansky, Siegel, and New Jersey Mafia leaders Willie Morretti and Gerardo Catena. Stacher's record included 10 arrests for larceny, battery, robbery, and other charges in the 1920s, all of which were dismissed. Stacher also held interests in the Fremont casino and the Horseshoe.[90] Other mobbed-up hidden investors in the Sands included Lansky, former Capone associate Joe Fusco, Minneapolis hoodlum Isadore Blumenfeld, and one-time Capone attorney "Longie" Zwillman.

This time, the Tax Commission considered Stacher's background unacceptable, and commissioners denied licenses to two Sands investors who submitted applications, Jake Freedman and Mack Kufferman, several months before the Sands opened. Commissioners viewed Kufferman as an associate and a mere front for Stacher and felt Freedman did not deserve a license because he knew Kufferman. But the commission soon turned around and approved Freedman after he said he had bought out Kufferman's investment for $789,000. Freedman's license, however, was held up for a few weeks by the Clark County Commission after County Commissioner Harley E. Harmon complained about constantly receiving new reports of lists of investors in casinos the county did not know of when granting a license. The county, however, soon relented and agreed to license Freedman. Not long afterward, the states' rights rationale was used again in Nevada, to its detriment. The Tax Commission decided to stop requiring gaming license applicants to submit detailed financial background information on their holdings, reasoning that the facts might subject important gaming industry figures to audits and penalties by the IRS.[91]

The list of organized and convicted criminals with interests, licensed or not, in Las Vegas casinos in the 1950s went on and on. In 1954, those still involved with the Flamingo casino featured Minneapolis mob member and alleged contract murderer Israel "Ice Pick Willie" Alderman and former Siegel enforcer and convicted kidnapper Davie Berman.[92] Alderman also had invested in the Riviera from 1954 to 1959. But a turning point in Nevada gaming control history occurred in the mid-1950s, when an exposé in the *Las Vegas Sun* revealed that Jake Lansky, brother of Meyer Lansky, was involved with the casino revenue counting room at the Thunderbird hotel and casino. The results of a state investigation would bring needed reform to Nevada's gaming control system.

Meyer Lansky was then considered the most infamous member of organized crime in the United States. His many mob associates included Siegel, Luciano, Costello, and Dutch Schultz. He was a contract killer in the early 1930s with Siegel in the Bug and Meyer Mob.[93] In the mid-1950s, it was Jake Lansky's financial interest in the Thunderbird that prompted the Tax Commission to order a show-cause hearing against the nine partners in the Thunderbird Hotel Company, who would have to argue before the commission why their license should not be revoked. Marion B. Hicks held the controlling interest in the Thunderbird, which included a copartnership in the casino operation (the Thunderbird Hotel Company) and a hotel corporation named Bonanza Hotel, Inc. Another licensee in the Thunderbird operation targeted by the state was Clifford Jones, who held a smaller share than Hicks's. Jones, while the lieutenant governor of Nevada in the 1940s, was the first state politician to receive a Nevada gaming license.

The Thunderbird case showed the public how hidden money from the underworld helped finance Las Vegas casino projects. In hearings on March 30 and April 25, 1955, the Tax Commission reported that Hicks had obtained a $160,000 loan in 1947 from Frank Saldo, an associate and close friend of Jake Lansky. The loan went toward construction expenses for the Thunderbird. Saldo, said to be a close friend of Hicks, was identified as the conduit through which the Lanskys operated the Thunderbird. Meyer Lansky was identified as an adviser for syndicate figures who built the Desert Inn, Tropicana, Stardust, Riviera, and Fremont in the 1950s (his advisory role also extended to the creation of Caesars Palace, which opened in 1966).[94]

The issues raised in the Thunderbird investigation, the fear the federal government might make another move to control gaming in Nevada, and the desire to obtain its rightful share of state taxes prompted the state legislature in 1955 to approve Governor Russell's request to create a gambling control agency within the Tax Commission. Commission Executive Secretary Cahill would chair the new Nevada State Gaming Control Board. The state hired an ex-FBI agent to head a team of investigators for the new agency. The law also made casino gambling a privileged business, allowing the board to revoke licenses without having to prove cause. In April 1955 the new gaming board suspended the Thunderbird's license and made the owners remove Jones as an investor as a condition to receiving a new one. A year later the board issued a list of new regulations regarding qualifications for licensees and rules pertaining to accounting procedures, stockholders, revoking licenses, and the reporting of interest transfers and loans. As for tax revenue, the state made out. From the late 1950s to the early 1960s, about 20 percent of winnings from Nevada casinos went to the state's general fund from taxation.[95]

Still other trouble, however, was headed for Las Vegas. The city would attract more embarrassing national attention in 1957, this time all the way from New York City. There, on May 2, 1957, top hoodlum and Meyer Lansky buddy Frank Costello was shot outside his apartment complex at Central Park West. Costello survived, but police found in his pocket a piece of paper listing $651,284 in gross casino receipts from the Tropicana Hotel on the Strip as of April 27, 1957, the first month the hotel opened. The note also listed payments of $30,000 to "L." and $9,000 to "H."[96] Nevada gaming officials determined later that the note had been written by a Tropicana cashier who previously worked at a New Orleans club owned by Costello, mobster Phil Kastel, and mob leaders Meyer Lansky and Carlos Marcello. Also, at about the same time, Jimmy Hoffa, the mob-connected chief of the Teamsters truck driver's union, started convincing trustees of the Teamster Central States, Southeast, and Southwest Areas Pension Fund to filter millions in loans to Las Vegas casinos, including $4 million to the Dunes Hotel in 1958 and $4 million to the Fremont in 1961. By 1962, 22 percent of the pension fund's loans were in Nevada businesses.[97] In 1964, Hoffa was convicted of obtaining money under false pretenses for diverting $1 million in pension money to himself and other defendants.[98]

The state's government struggled, slowly, to keep up. In 1957, supporters of maintaining strong controls over gaming were aided by the defeat of Senate Bill 92 in the legislature. The bill would have permitted people whose licenses were suspended by the board to file their case in state court and to use testimony and cross-examination of witnesses to overturn the Gaming Control Board's ruling. The defeated proposal also would have removed the board's authority to order a casino closed. Top casino operators had gone on record against the bill. On March 4, 1957, owners of seven major Las Vegas casinos— Gus Greenbaum, Jake Freedman, Beldon Katleman, Al Parvin, T. W. Richardson, Milton Prell, and Major Riddle—wrote a telegram to Governor Russell opposing any bill that would restrict the Gaming Control Board's right to suspend or revoke the license of a casino operator for a cheating offense.[99]

In another victory for gaming control that year, the state supreme court, while ruling that the Thunderbird's license must be reinstated, added that the Tax Commission retained the right to investigate licensees and revoke the licenses of unlawful casino operators and to make decisions on gaming-related policies.

In the late 1950s, reformers thought more had to be done to assure the public that gaming in Nevada was free of corrupt influences. News stories were appearing in the national media of mob involvement in Nevada casinos. In 1959, receipts from Nevada's gaming industry accounted for 21.9 percent of all state tax revenue.[100] Nevada could not afford to be passive about regulating gaming. Newly elected governor Grant Sawyer made gaming reform his top priority when he took office in January 1959. The state legislature that year adopted the Gaming Control Act, containing major regulatory changes recommended by Sawyer. The board, the law stated, was to require that gaming businesses be "operated in a manner suitable to protect the public health, safety, morals, good order and general welfare of the inhabitants of the state, to foster the stability and success of the gaming industry and to preserve the competitive economy and policies of free competition of the State of Nevada."[101] The governor's revised system included a paid, part-time, five-member Nevada Gaming Commission and a full-time, paid, three-member Nevada State Gaming Control Board. The Gaming Control Board was made a separate agency from the Tax Commission, which Sawyer said would strengthen gaming control. The board, given more independence than it had under the Tax Commission, would serve as the state's full-time regulatory agency for gaming. It would collect taxes from the gaming industry, enforce gaming laws, perform investigations, and make recommendations on gaming license applicants and gaming policies to the commission, which would make the final decisions. The governor would appoint each member of the board and commission to four-year terms. The gaming statutes required the board to include at least one member with five years of experience in public or business administration; one who had been a certified public accountant for five years or more or who was an expert in finance, auditing, gaming, or economics; and a third member who had a law enforcement background.[102]

"In my inaugural address to the Legislature [in January 1959]," Sawyer said in his 1993 oral history *Hang Tough!* "I said that it was the policy of my administration that we would not tolerate any organized crime influence in Nevada, and I invited the FBI to tell us if they knew of any mob presence in the state. I wasn't so dumb that I didn't realize that some of the licensees came out of organized criminal backgrounds. There wasn't really anything I could do about those who were already here and licensed before I was elected except watch them carefully; but when a new applicant for a gaming license came along, one of our first [inquiries] would be to the FBI to see if they had a rap on that person (they would always provide us with a copy if they did), and during my eight years as governor I don't believe we licensed anybody who later turned out to have ties with organized crime. Ultimately, all the people who were suspected died off or left the state, so there's virtually no organized criminal activity in gaming in Nevada now." [103]

Sawyer remained a proponent of strict controls on gaming throughout his political career. In 1960, he endorsed the Gaming Control Board's adoption of the so-called Black Book, a list of individuals by law ordered to stay out of all gambling establishments in Nevada for life. Casino licensees who permitted Black Book members in their establishments risked fines and the loss of their licenses. Later renamed the List of Excluded Persons, the roster was directed at keeping known hoodlums or those whom state officials dubbed as "unsavory people" out of the state's casinos. State officials wrote that allowing notorious mobsters in Nevada casinos "tends to discredit not only the gaming industry but our entire state as well." The first list, selected by Gaming Control Board chairman and former FBI agent R. J. Abbaticchio, Jr., contained the names of 11 people, all reputed mobsters, most with ties to syndicates in Chicago, Kansas City, or Los Angeles: John Battaglia, Marshal Caifano, Carl and Nicholas Civella, Michael Coppola, Louis Dragna, Robert Garcia, Sam Giancana, Motel Grzebienacy, Murray Humphreys, and Joseph Sica.[104] The list, of course, was not complete, but it was a start. The legislature formally approved the List of Excluded Persons in 1967 as part of amendments to the Nevada Gaming Control Act.

But the state still had problems with hoodlums, some of whom enjoyed influential political connections in Las Vegas. Three men placed in the Black

Book by the Gaming Commission in 1965—Rudy Kolod, Israel "Ice Pick Willie" Alderman, and Felix Alderisio—were promptly removed the same year.[105] All three had been convicted of extortion in connection with threatening the life of a Denver lawyer. Governor Sawyer had strongly urged they be named to the list as a way to show Nevada's determination to keep undesirables out of the gaming industry. Kolod, the only one of the three with a gaming license, had about $1 million invested in the Desert Inn and Stardust casinos. One of his fellow investors was former Cleveland mobster Moe Dalitz, who had moved to Las Vegas. Dalitz, who headed a group of investors in the Desert Inn, Stardust, and Royal Nevada that included Kolod, used his considerable political clout to pressure and convince state gaming authorities to take Kolod and Alderman off the list. Alderisio, said to be a paid associate of Chicago mobster and Black Book member Sam Giancana, also was removed later in the year. Still fuming, Kolod made a $200,000 contribution to the 1966 campaign of Paul Laxalt, Sawyer's Republican opponent for governor. Laxalt defeated Sawyer, and no additional people were placed in the Black Book while Laxalt was in office. By 1994, 45 people had been placed on the List of Excluded Persons (counting Kolod, Alderman, and Alderisio), 18 of whom were removed only after their deaths.[106] Since it was instituted, Nevada has won court challenges on the constitutionality of the list. A U.S. court of appeals struck down a suit by Marshal Caifano in 1962, ruling in favor of Nevada's case that entering a casino is a privilege the state could enforce and not a basic right under the 14th Amendment's due process provision. Critics, meanwhile, have complained over the years that the effectiveness of the Black Book is limited and that it has been used simply to impress on the public that the state is doing something about keeping mobsters, gambling cheaters, and other potentially dangerous people out of the gaming industry.

In the early 1960s, the new Kennedy administration made Nevada feel threatened once again with possible federal intervention in the operation of casinos and heavy taxation of gaming proceeds. Attorney General Robert Kennedy saw Las Vegas as a hotbed of organized crime and was determined to eliminate the mob involvement there. In 1961, Sawyer succeeded in persuading President Kennedy to call off a raid by a federal strike force on Nevada casinos, planned by the attorney general.[107] Nonetheless, Robert Kennedy later assigned 86 investigators from the U.S. Justice Department to Nevada as part of "Operation Big Squeeze" to probe organized crime activities in casinos and to investigate the race wires and reports of skimming of casino revenue to avoid taxation.[108] In 1963, the FBI began gathering evidence (illegally obtained and thus inadmissible in court) of skimming from conversations intercepted by wiretaps placed in the offices and homes of Las Vegas casino executives. The Justice Department concluded in 1966 that operators of the Fremont,

Sands, Flamingo, Horseshoe, Desert Inn, and Stardust had skimmed large amounts of money from the casinos.[109] After learning that FBI Director J. Edgar Hoover had wiretaps of conversations regarding skimming and films of henchmen delivering skimmed cash, Governor Laxalt went to Washington and convinced Hoover that the state could curb skimming on its own with stricter auditing controls. As a result, Hoover did not send the evidence to Congress.[110] The only convictions on the evidence came in 1973, when the owner of the Flamingo admitted that Meyer Lansky shared in casino proceeds from 1960 to 1967.[111]

But Nevada officials remained defiant. In 1966, the Nevada Gaming Commission issued a report claiming that casino money was not being filtered to organized crime contacts and chiding the federal government's enforcement tactics in the state. (Nevada, however, would learn a decade later that mobsters indeed were still siphoning millions from Las Vegas casinos.)

With Nevada's gaming industry still under attack from federal authorities over alleged organized crime investments in Las Vegas casinos in the late 1960s, the state saw a chance for an out. In March 1967, the billionaire Howard Hughes, who long enjoyed vacationing in Las Vegas, bought the Desert Inn hotel—where the eccentric Hughes had been staying in a ninth-floor penthouse since November 1966—from Moe Dalitz, formerly of the Mayfield Road Gang in Cleveland, for $13.2 million.[112] Over the next several months, Hughes, using some of the more than $546.5 million he got from selling 6.5 million shares of stock in Trans World Airlines, then bought up the Sands, Castaways, and New Frontier casinos on the Strip. Nevada gaming authorities welcomed Hughes. By the time he bought the Frontier casino (formerly the Last Frontier) for $14 million in September 1967, two of the hotel's six partners, Maurice Friedman and T. Warner Richardson, had been indicted and convicted in the infamous Friar's Club card cheating case in Beverly Hills, California.[113] The case received nationwide news coverage, often making mention that Friedman and Richardson were part owners of a Las Vegas casino. Furthermore, Clark County Sheriff Ralph Lamb announced he was investigating the possibility that Detroit-based mob figures held hidden interests in the Frontier. These embarrassments led the Gaming Control Board and the Gaming Commission to hold a rare telephone conference meeting in late 1967 to grant Hughes a license to own the Frontier.[114]

While Hughes's purchase appeared to be good news on the surface, most of Dalitz's crew at the Desert Inn stayed on. Mob figure Johnny Rosselli, who lived at the Desert Inn in the early 1960s, told mobster-turned-government-informant Jimmy "the Weasel" Fratianno that the skimming by organized crime continued at the resort after Hughes bought it.[115]

In 1968, Hughes added the Silver Slipper and the Stardust to his Strip casino collection. Hughes now controlled about a quarter of the gaming business in Las Vegas and more than a third of the gross receipts by casinos along the Strip. More significant, Hughes, with his suitable background, had acquired casinos thought by many to have included investors with ties to organized crime syndicates. Hughes's purchases, having removed some of the taint of mob involvement—at least in the public's mind—in the casino business, encouraged more legitimate corporate interests to consider investing in Las Vegas casinos. That attraction increased in 1969, when the legislature passed the Corporate Gaming Act, a law allowing public corporations to own casinos without each shareholder having to apply for a gaming license. Legislation in 1977 required holders of 10 percent or more of a company investing in a casino to apply for a license and gave the Gaming Commission the right to demand those with as little as 5 percent to submit an application.

By the mid-1970s, Nevada was the fastest growing state in the country and saw revenues from tourism and gaming reach $1 billion.[116] Major public companies, including Hilton Hotels and Metro-Goldwyn-Mayer, entered the gaming scene. Experts were saying that Hughes, who did little to improve his Las Vegas casinos, did not do much for the town except promote investment into the industry by making it look more respectable.[117] Despite the potential for profits in the casino industry, which averaged a return of 15 to 20 percent in Nevada, Hughes's gaming operations performed poorly. The return on his casinos was only 6.15 percent in 1968 and 1.63 percent in 1969, and together they posted a loss of $10 million in 1970.[118]

In 1972, the Gaming Commission denied a request by the Hughes organization to restructure its corporation. In March 1973, Governor Mike O'Callaghan flew to London with the chairman of the Gaming Control Board to see whether Hughes was actually alive and coherent. The governor met with Hughes, and after he determined that Hughes was more or less normal, the state approved his corporate restructuring.[119]

After Hughes's death in 1976, Las Vegas ended a brief, relative lull in gaming control problems and entered a period of crisis. During the 1970s, the legislature authorized the Gaming Control Board and the Gaming Commission to regulate employee unions and license limited partnerships. But by far the most significant gaming control issue of the period came with the discovery of hidden ownership and skimming by organized crime members in three Las Vegas hotels: the Fremont in downtown Las Vegas and the Stardust and the Tropicana on the Strip.

The Fremont and the Stardust were operated in the mid-1970s by Argent Corporation, headed by Allen Glick, a real estate man from the San Diego area whose company obtained a gaming license to buy the ailing Hacienda Hotel in 1972.[120] The 33-year-old Glick later made a deal to buy the Stardust and the Fremont for $62.7 million, which he borrowed from the Teamsters Central States Pension Fund, the same one that made loans to mob-controlled Las Vegas casinos in the 1950s and 1960s. Glick got his loan in only nine days with the help of Allen Dorfman, a shady Teamsters official who oversaw the pension fund after Hoffa was put in prison. Teamster loans to Las Vegas casinos amounted to $240 million by 1977, or one-fourth of the fund's holdings.[121]

Gaming Control Board and Gaming Commission members approved the Glick-Teamster transaction after expressing doubts about it but finding that no laws had been broken. Glick and his Argent company would later obtain a total of $146 million in loans from the pension fund to buy Nevada casinos and make investments outside the state. But in 1975, the Gaming Control Board ruled that one of Glick's top executives, Frank "Lefty" Rosenthal, had to apply for a gaming license as a key employee—casino employees with a certain amount of authority who made $40,000 or more per year. Rosenthal's salary was $250,000 a year, and the board believed he held considerable sway over Argent's casino operations. The board learned that Rosenthal, an expert sports handicapper and former illegal bookmaker, was a longtime associate of violent Chicago mob henchman Anthony "Tony the Ant" Spilotro. Rosenthal was convicted of illegal bookmaking in 1959. In the early 1960s, Rosenthal did not contest a charge of bribing a New York college basketball player to fix a game and was fined $6,000.[122] Rosenthal also had been named as an organized crime associate in a report by the Chicago Crime Commission in 1969, the year the Gaming Commission licensed him to hold a 2.84 percent interest in the Circus Circus hotel-casino in Las Vegas.[123] In 1976, the board recommended denying him a key employee license, and the commission turned Rosenthal down. He sued the agencies in both federal and state court, maintaining that Nevada's gaming laws were vague and thus violated his due process rights. In December 1976, District Court Judge Joseph Pavlikowski in Las Vegas ruled in Rosenthal's favor, saying that Nevada's gaming laws were an unconstitutional violation of due process rights contained in the 14th Amendment. It came out later that Pavlikowski had a potential conflict of interest: He had performed Rosenthal's wedding ceremony in Las Vegas, and the judge's own daughter's 1974 wedding took place at the Stardust, which paid for $2,800 of the expenses incurred for it.[124] Still, the case put Nevada's entire gaming control operation into question. The judge's decision was later reversed by the Nevada Supreme Court, which ruled that gaming was a privileged business and that an applicant for a gaming license did not have an actual property interest protected by due process. The U.S. Supreme Court refused to hear Rosenthal's appeal. Nevada's gaming system won another big legal victory. Rosenthal returned to the Stardust to serve as entertainment director, which the state at first did not consider a key employee position. However, in 1978 the Gaming Commission determined it was and forced him out of the job.

Meanwhile, Nevada Gaming Control Board agents had uncovered a major skimming operation at the Stardust back in 1976 while Glick and Rosenthal worked there. Gaming Control Board agent Dennis Gomes led a team of agents in two raids at the Stardust and learned that the casino had altered the "hard count" scale that measured coins from slot machines. The scale undercounted the coins, and the conspirators converted the rest into currency to complete the skim. The state estimated that from $7 million to $15 million had been siphoned at the Stardust and the Tropicana from 1974 to 1976.[125] The skimmed cash was distributed to organized crime family members in Kansas City, Chicago, and Milwaukee. Still other money was skimmed at Argent Corporation's Fremont casino.

Another large skimming scheme was disclosed in the late 1970s at the Tropicana, involving most of the same crime syndicate members involved in the Argent skim. Federal prosecutors in Kansas City alleged that Nicholas Civella, Carl Civella, and fellow Kansas City mobster Carl DeLuna each held secret investments in the Tropicana. They employed casino executives Joseph Agosto and Carl Wesley Thomas to help them skim money from the casino and keep it quiet. The skimmed cash was distributed to DeLuna and Charles Moretina in Kansas City, Joseph Aiuppa in Chicago, and others in Milwaukee. The Civellas (both entered into the original Black Book in 1960), DeLuna, Agosto, Caruso, and Thomas were indicted in 1979 and convicted of felony crimes in October 1983.[126] In a related case in October 1983, Agosto and former Minnesota businessman Deil Gustafson were convicted and sentenced to prison in connection with their floating $4 million worth of checks at the Tropicana.[127]

In December 1983, a federal grand jury in Kansas City indicted 15 people in the Argent skimming case. The 15 defendants included Nicholas Civella, Carl Civella, DeLuna, Agosto, and Thomas, once a respected Las Vegas casino operator, on charges of skimming and hidden interests at Argent casinos. Nicholas Civella had already died in the spring of 1983, and Agosto died days after he, DeLuna, Carl Civella, Thomas, and two others were convicted in the Tropicana case.

FBI authorities maintained that Rosenthal managed the skimming of Stardust casino receipts in the 1970s, but neither he nor Glick was indicted. The Gaming Commission placed DeLuna and Agosto into the Black Book in 1979. The commission that year also revoked Glick's license. Rosenthal was placed into the Black Book in November 1988. Spilotro, entered into the book in 1978, was killed in a gangland slaying outside Chicago in 1986.

The Gaming Control Board further learned that Detroit mobsters had secretly received cash skimmed by James Tamer, an entertainment executive at the Aladdin Hotel, in the mid-1970s.[128] In 1979, Tamer and three Detroit gangsters were convicted in federal court of illegal ownership and conspiracy in the Aladdin skimming case. The commission added Tamer to the Black Book in 1988.

The issue of mob influence in Las Vegas casinos had waned by the 1980s. So too would the prevalence of the private and independent casino owner. More and more public companies used federally regulated stock and debt offerings to raise funds to buy, expand, refurbish, or build casinos. Corporate executives from the out-of-state public companies started replacing people who had backgrounds only in Las Vegas casinos. Public companies, fearful of the opinions of federal regulators, shareholders, and stock analysts, would not allow people with questionable backgrounds to run their casinos. In the 1980s, the Gaming Control Board focused on related issues, such as public securities transactions. The hostile corporate takeovers typical of the decade made gaming officials look into the practice of "greenmailing"—buying a casino company's stock in order to drive up the price amid speculation of a possible takeover and then selling the stock for a quick profit after prices rise. But the biggest issue of the decade for Nevada's casino industry was keeping track of and reporting the billions of dollars processed through the casinos each year by gamblers. Officials at the U.S. Treasury Department, planning new cash reporting rules for banking institutions to follow to prevent money laundering, regarded casinos as banks and aimed at imposing the new rules in Nevada. The state's congressional representatives and other Nevada authorities were able to persuade federal officials to exempt the state from the new banking rules by requiring casinos to obey new state cash reporting procedures and paperwork requirements seen as even more stringent than the U.S. government's. Also in the 1980s, the legislature gave the Gaming Commission licensing authority over persons providing various services to casinos, such as operators of gambling tournaments and junket representatives (paid by casinos to arrange travel for high-rolling gamblers). The state also required that financial and other information provided to the Gaming Control Board by licensees remain confidential, permitted public corporations in foreign lands to be licensed, and set up procedures for granting applicants the right to disseminate the live broadcasts of horse and dog races in other states to race and sports books in Nevada. The new age of the megaresort in Las Vegas began in 1989 with the opening of the Mirage, the vision of casino mogul Steve Wynn and his Mirage Resorts, Inc., on the Strip.

In the 1990s, Nevada gaming regulators encountered fewer contentious issues than before. Three new megaresorts opened on the Strip in 1993. New jurisdictions allowing legalized gaming in the United States used Nevada's

regulatory scheme as a model. Encouraged by the effectiveness of strong controls over gaming in Nevada and even stricter legal constraints in New Jersey,
casino gambling became acceptable in other communities across the country.
Gaming boards from the various states, including Iowa, Louisiana, Missouri,
and Mississippi, provided information to one another on the backgrounds of
gaming license applicants and known gambling cheaters. As casino gaming
expanded, the industry matured as more applicants with good backgrounds
were licensed.

In 1997, amid concerns about the spread of legalized casinos and political pressure from social and religious conservatives opposed to gambling
on moral grounds, Congress created the National Gambling Impact Study
Commission to probe the industry and its effects on American society and to
present recommendations for legislation by mid-1999. Fearing that the nine-
member commission might place restrictions or levy new taxes on the industry, Nevada gaming interests succeeded in encouraging the appointments of
three people considered sympathetic to the trade: State Gaming Control Board
chairman Bill Bible; MGM Grand chief executive officer J. Terrence Lanni,
whose company operated the MGM Grand hotel-casino in Las Vegas; and John
Wilhelm, general president of the Hotel Employees and Restaurant Employees International Union, which then represented employees of 32 major Las
Vegas hotel-casinos. When its report was released in June 1999, the commission recommended that states consider a "pause" in approving casinos. It also
called for tighter regulations on Indian and Internet gaming. But to most observers, the report was not harmful to the gaming industry. Congress seemed
to pay little attention to it.

The Gaming Control Board announced in early 1999 that Nevada casinos
had won $8 billion in 1998, a jump of 3.2 percent over 1997, with 65 percent of
the total win coming from slot machines. Casinos on the Las Vegas Strip accounted for $3.8 billion of the total, an increase of only 0.1 percent over the pre-
vious year. The modest gain in Las Vegas was a topic of concern, as four new
Strip resorts—planned during the more optimistic mid-1990s—were built
from 1998 to 1999: the 3,000-room, $1.6 billion Bellagio (opened in October
1998); the 3,700-room, $900 million Mandalay Bay (debuted in March 1999);
the 3,036-room Venetian (May 1999); and the 2,916-room, $785 million Paris re-
sort (September 1999). By the end of 1999, 18 of the 20 largest hotels in the the
United States would be centered in Las Vegas.

How far the Las Vegas casino gaming industry could go and remain profitable, beyond the good times of the early to mid-1990s, was an open question
as the decade neared an end. Some wondered about the town's ability to attract enough visitors to fill its approximately 120,000 hotel rooms or whether

1999 would be the end of a decade-long boom for Las Vegas. But the Las Vegas Convention and Visitors Authority reported that the number of visitors to Las Vegas had increased each month from September 1998 to June 1999, along with the addition of the Bellagio, Mandalay Bay, and the Venetian. Another boom period had occurred. Once again, the naysayers in Las Vegas would have to wait.

Chapter One

Cheating and Murder
The American Coin Caper

At 7:50 P.M., on October 1, 1990, Larry Volk, a 49-year-old former computer programmer for the American Coin Machine Company, was working on his car in the covered carport of his modest mobile home at 5514 Petaca Road in northeastern Las Vegas. A bullet from a gun fired from behind a wooden fence in Volk's backyard slammed into the top of his head and exited through the rear of his skull. He collapsed on the lawn next to the driveway. His wife, LaVerne, called for an ambulance, but Volk was mortally wounded. He died before paramedics reached him. Neighbors reported hearing a motorcycle start up and flee immediately after the gunfire, but the shooter fled the scene without a trace.[1]

To Las Vegas Metropolitan Police detectives and other local observers, Volk's death appeared to be linked to a pending criminal investigation by the Clark County district attorney's office in which Volk was the prime witness. Thirteen months before he was killed, Volk admitted to Nevada State Gaming Control Board agents that he designed cheating, or "gaffed," programs placed into at least 500 of the 1,106 computerized video poker and keno machines owned by two slot route firms, American Coin Machine Company and American Coin Enterprises, Inc. The machines operated in 93 cocktail lounges and other locations throughout the Las Vegas valley. The programs prevented the award of some jackpots when players bet the maximum number of coins in the machines, a felony cheating crime under Nevada law. Volk said he drew up the cheating programs under the orders of two of American Coin's three partners—Rudolph LaVecchia and LaVecchia's son, Rudolph "Rudy" M. LaVecchia—and feared he would be fired if he did not comply.[2] The board discovered later that American Coin had used the cheating feature for more than three years without detection. The Gaming Control Board estimated that during 1986 to 1989, the programs blocked from $10 million to $20 million worth of jackpots, money that was instead pocketed by American Coin's partners.[3]

The American Coin scandal rocked the Nevada gaming industry. Slot and video machines were the most popular gambling games among both tourists and local players. Gaming machines had surpassed table games in 1983 as the state's largest revenue producer. To cynics the scam confirmed the common belief that the machines were unfairly rigged against players. In the American Coin case at least, the cynics were proved right. But even though the Gaming Control Board finally won and learned from the experience, the American Coin debacle called into question Nevada's ability to regulate its gaming industry. The case would later prompt the Gaming Control Board to order each of the 145,000 machines in the state to be tested for cheating devices.[4]

The true story about what happened the night of Volk's assassination would not come out until more than seven years after the slaying. The confessed shooter of Volk revealed it was a murder-for-hire involving him and two others, including a close friend of Rudolph LaVecchia and LaVecchia's wife. But the damage was done. The Clark County district attorney's office had prepared a case with the potential of hundreds of felony cheating at gaming charges against Rudolph and Rudy LaVecchia—one count per gaffed machine—before a grand jury. However, with the key witness dead, the office decided to drop all the cheating charges. The Gaming Control Board had videotaped testimony from Volk about the cheating plan, but the district attorney and the Nevada attorney general's office, which could also have prosecuted the criminal case, decided the tape would not be enough to convince a jury to convict the defendants.

"Larry Volk was the only way to prove the case," said Eric Jorgenson, chief deputy district attorney for Clark County. "I still needed his testimony to prove the case. I didn't figure there was any way to bring it in."[5]

While felony-cheating litigation arising out of the American Coin caper fizzled, the Gaming Control Board and the Nevada Gaming Commission at last permanently ended an ongoing cheating enterprise throughout Las Vegas. In 1989, the board and the commission revoked the gaming licenses of the American Coin partners and fined them a total of $1 million. The company was forced to shut down and file for bankruptcy.

American Coin was once one of the largest slot route operators in Nevada, operating and servicing machines in the Las Vegas area. For nearly 10 years, the company operated without any reported problems. But even before the Gaming Control Board and the Gaming Commission licensed the company, there were indications the firm might run into trouble someday. Transcripts of board and commission licensing hearings show that Rudolph LaVecchia had a history of poor bookkeeping in his business dealings and did not file his 1978 corporate income tax return until the state required him to do so in 1979 in order to receive a nonrestricted gaming license. Further, the Gaming Control Board found out that as late as 1983, the company's owners were paying themselves by literally grabbing some of the cash won by their slots before the rest was deposited in the bank. Still, with its agendas crowded with applicants for entry into the expanding Las Vegas gaming industry of the 1980s, the board and the commission licensed LaVecchia and his partners each time with little or no discussion before moving along to the next item.

Rudolph LaVecchia launched the American Coin Machine Company in 1979, when he moved from New York to Las Vegas. That year he applied for a nonrestricted license to be a slot machine route operator and 100 percent owner of the company. By then most gaming machine manufacturers had switched from making electromechanical pull slots in favor of computerized reeled slot machines and video poker.

At the Gaming Control Board's meeting on May 9, 1979, LaVecchia was represented by his attorney, Paul Carelli, of the Las Vegas law firm Bilbray & Carelli. Board members asked only a few questions of LaVecchia, who proved to be a man of few words. The board's queries amounted to little more than a mild public scolding, a common occurrence at board hearings. Board member John H. Stratton commented on the fact that the state had required LaVecchia to file amended federal tax returns with the board because of "unsatisfactory" record keeping. "If you are issued a gaming license here, we will expect you to maintain records, adequate records and satisfactory records for our auditors," Stratton said.[6]

Board chairman Roger Trounday sounded almost paternal. "It's bad enough when people don't keep good business records," he told LaVecchia, "but when you get into the gaming business, they have to be extra tight, and with the history that you have of not keeping very good business records, we have a concern about how well you are going to keep them now that you are applying for a license."[7]

Carelli replied that LaVecchia intended to use a certified public accountant "to set up a bookkeeping system and to maintain and oversee control in that area as to the records of this business."[8]

Board member Richard Bunker asked LaVecchia about what other businesses he was starting, to which LaVecchia simply said, "A vending business, amusements."

Trounday inquired as to why LaVecchia failed to file corporate tax returns for two companies he owned: House of Tables and American Vending.

"The accountant that was taking care of it, he went back to Minnesota," LaVecchia explained. "His father had cancer. In '78, he went. The accountant that I have, he filed my personal. Since there was no money made and I did lose money anyway, he said, 'We will pick it up next year.' But I did file my '78 personal."

"Did you file your '78 corporate return?" Trounday asked.

"That's being filed now," LaVecchia said. "He has records. No."

"I believe there's been an extension on that, Mr. Chairman," attorney Carelli said.[9]

With no further questions, board members Trounday, Stratton, and Bunker quickly recommended LaVecchia for what would be his first Nevada gaming license. When the matter came up at the commission hearing on May 17, 1979, Stratton informed commission chairman Harry Reid (later elected to represent Nevada in the U.S. Senate) of the board's recommendation. With LaVecchia and Carelli looking on, the commission approved LaVecchia's license in a matter of seconds without discussion.[10] The nonrestricted license meant sole-owner LaVecchia could own and provide slot machines to cocktail lounges and other business on a slot route. The deals with his customers worked one of two ways: Either he leased space for his machines and collected the winnings, or he installed the machines for free and shared the proceeds with the businesses.

More than two years later, in 1981, Frank Romano, who operated a car rental and leasing company in Las Vegas, entered the picture. Romano had married Rudolph LaVecchia's daughter, and his new father-in-law offered him a piece of the family slot route business. Rudolph LaVecchia asked the board to change American Coin Machine Company from a sole proprietorship to a general partnership, with son-in-law Romano to receive a 5 percent interest.

At the board meeting of November 10, 1981, Romano appeared with La-Vecchia's attorney, Carelli, in what would prove to be a brief hearing on Romano's application for a gaming license. Board members questioned Romano about his past association with the late Charles Carol, a one-time hairpiece salesman from Dallas whose criminal activities in that city were investigated by the FBI.

Romano testified he had known Carol "over a period of many years" while Romano sold advertising space for *American Hairdresser Magazine,* based in New York. Under questioning by board member Stratton, Romano admitted that Carol once loaned him money "in connection with a television show."[11]

Romano's association with Carol was treated with little more than the verbal equivalent of waving a finger at the applicant. "Just a point that, of course, when he [Carol] was alive the background of the individual wasn't that of someone which we'd appreciate you associating with," board member Stratton said.

Speaking for Romano, attorney Carelli said that "for the record I would point out that the first time that Mr. Romano learned of any criminal activity on behalf of Mr. Carol was when he talked to the FBI agents that were investigating Mr. Carol, and that was after any business association occurred between the two of them."

"Yes," Stratton said. "He was cooperative. I realize that."

With that, Romano got his recommendation for a license from the board. On November 19, 1981, the commission questioned him a bit more, again with Carelli by his side. The questions elicited a few minor facts about his association with Carol, but not much else. Chairman Carl Dodge asked Romano whether American Coin was to become a family-type business, but Carelli again interrupted.

"This is contemplated in the future that Mr. [LaVecchia's] son [Rudy], when he reached majority, will also, if he wishes, be involved in the business," Carelli said.[12]

Romano, responding to questions from Commissioner Richard Avansino, said he had lived in Las Vegas since May 1978. He met Charles Carol in Dallas while working for the hairdresser magazine out of Las Vegas. Romano was then asked about the extent of his association with Carol.

"Primarily business in the area of manufacturing wigs, advertising wigs and selling wigs. Professional beauty industry," he answered.

Carelli interrupted again. "Mr. Commissioner, there was a time subsequent thereto where a loan did occur, which I believe Mr. Romano has explained to the Control Board, when he was involved in TEV Production in Los Angeles, which was then repaid."

Addressing Romano, chairman Dodge asked whether he had any type of business or social relationships with Carol "or was he just an acquaintance in the same type of business that you were in?" Again Carelli answered for his client.

"Other than the loan that was made by Mr. Carol when Mr. Romano was involved in the television production, that would have been that, plus the sale of advertising that he has explained would have been the only real type of connection between the two. There was no personal relationship."

Answering a couple more questions from Avansino, Romano mentioned that he still owned a rental car company in Las Vegas. Apparently satisfied, the commission voted 5 to 0 to license him.

American Coin came before the Gaming Control Board two years later, this time to make it more of a family affair. Rudolph LaVecchia, his son Rudy, and Romano each applied to hold a 33.3 percent interest in a new company called American Coin Enterprises. The company would serve as a slot route operator, manufacturer, and distributor of slot machines. If licensed, the trio could repair, alter, and even build their own machines, then put them on a route and collect or share the winnings. During that year, 1983, "stepper motors" were introduced, enabling gaming machine makers to directly control the stops of slot reels with computer software. The computerized machines overtook table games in statewide revenues and began to reign over the Nevada gaming industry, from casinos to gas stations.

On October 12, 1983, the board recommended licenses for the three American Coin applicants. Members expressed concern that American Coin had been paying its key employees and owners directly from the "drop"—the hard cash obtained from slot machines. The board, including chairman James Avance and members Richard Hyte and Patricia Becker, voted to place a condition on the company's license requiring that salaries be paid only by check.[13]

The commission considered the applications on October 20, 1983. The executive secretary, Irene Morros, remarked that appearances by Romano and the elder LaVecchia had been waived. Only Rudy M. LaVecchia and attorney Carelli were present. The hearing on the item lasted all of a couple minutes. Commissioners showed little concern about the partners paying themselves from the drop. Commissioner Jack Walsh asked Rudy LaVecchia and Carelli why the company did it that way.

"When it is a small closely held business, that sometimes happens," Carelli replied for his client.

"Sometimes," Commissioner Jerry Lockhart responded.

"Jerry, you knew the answer to that question before you asked it," chairman Paul Bible quipped. "In case you don't know it, Mr. Lockhart spent many years with the Internal Revenue Service."[14]

A potential cause for concern was instead turned into a reason for levity. There was no disquiet about the company's cash dipping on this commission. Lockhart made a motion to approve the application, and all five commissioners voted for it. American Coin Enterprises was ready to take on the leading slot route operators in the Nevada. By 1989, the year it lost its license, American Coin had grown to be the fourth-largest route operator in the state. It got there not only by cheating slot players out of thousands of jackpots over more than three years but by cheating on its bookkeeping as well.

American Coin rose along with a small group of other companies in the 1980s specializing in servicing slot routes. Slot route operators in Nevada provide gaming machines mainly to small businesses with restricted gaming licenses that permit a maximum of 15 machines and no casino-type games. Route operators work two ways: They rent or lease space for gaming machines from businesses and collect all the machines' winnings, or they simply provide the machines and share a percentage of the proceeds with the locations. While it had a state license to manufacture gaming machines, American Coin did not actually construct them. The company's partners bought major brand-name machines assembled by other manufacturers, then rebuilt and maintained the devices for their clients. Each day American Coin would send employees to the lounges and other restricted locations to remove the nickels and quarters and the dollar tokens from the machines, place the money in bags, and bring them to the home office for counting and deposit.

Since the explosion of slot licenses issued to small businesses in Las Vegas that began around the end of World War II, gaming machines have been a standard part of doing business in scores of cocktail lounges, supermarkets, drugstores, car washes, laundries, and other local outlets, providing an entirely separate source of income. American Coin's success in the 1980s was due in large measure to the rapid growth in population and development—including new lounges, stores, and other businesses with slots—that took place in Las Vegas during the decade. Most of American Coin's clients were small lounges that served low-priced drinks and food 24 hours a day to keep their gaming customers happy. By reason of the sheer number and relative lack of surveillance capabilities at restricted license locations, the Gaming Control Board could not monitor or police the lounges nearly as well as they could the casinos.

By 1989, American Coin's operation involved two slot route companies, each with a separate list of clients. The smaller of the two was the American Coin Machine Company, with Rudolph LaVecchia and Romano licensed as owners, officers, directors, and shareholders. In 1983, Rudolph LaVecchia had held 95 percent of the firm and Romano 5 percent, but Rudolph LaVecchia bought Romano out in 1988. The larger company, American Coin Enterprises, was licensed to manufacture and distribute machines and to serve as a slot route operator, with the LaVecchias and Romano serving as equal partners.

In mid-1989, American Coin had business deals with 93 businesses, mainly lounges, throughout Las Vegas, including one small casino. Of the 1,106 gaming machines it owned and operated, American Coin's two slot route firms together collected all the slot proceeds from 33 of the businesses and shared the money at the other 60.[15]

In addition to reaping gaming revenue, American Coin and its percentage share clients were responsible for paying the jackpots awarded by the machines. For instance, a royal flush jackpot on a quarter video poker machine with the maximum five coins wagered was about $1,000; in dollar machines it was $4,000. When patrons won a jackpot at a restricted license location, the route company was phoned and asked to send a technician over to pay the winner in currency and reset the machine. But paying jackpots, which cut into profits, was something American Coin clearly wanted to avoid.

The Gaming Control Board's eventual discovery of the company's cheating scam in the summer of 1989 started not with the late Larry Volk but with a different, unnamed informant.[16] In June 1989, the informant requested an interview with board member Gerald Cunningham, a former Las Vegas police captain who served as the board's law enforcement representative.

Cunningham was already close to completing an entirely separate, six-month probe of American Coin and was preparing to file a complaint with the Gaming Commission against the company. That investigation began in December 1988, after a Gaming Control Board agent read a newspaper advertisement offering slot machines for sale. According to board records, when the undercover agent phoned the number, he learned it was for the offices of American Coin. A man identifying himself as "Tony LaVecchia" answered. The agent, posing as a buyer, asked to purchase some gaming machines. He said he intended to ship them to Minnesota and Colorado, where interstate transport of slots was a felony crime under federal and state laws at the time. Tony LaVecchia told him video poker machines could be viewed at a company warehouse at 3110 Polaris Avenue, about a mile west of the Las Vegas Strip, and video keno machines at the firm's offices nearby at 1919 Industrial Road. After the agent told LaVecchia that he would buy the machines, LaVecchia said he would remove the serial numbers from the machines and have the devices ready at the warehouse on Polaris. LaVecchia said he was an employee of American Coin and the brother of partner Rudy M. LaVecchia.[17]

Gaming agents continued the investigation and found more improprieties by the slot route company. On July 30, 1987, American Coin shipped several video keno machines to Montana that were illegal in the state. The company also assisted at least one gaming licensee with a "dual accounting system," showing revenue figures that differed from the actual money received, so that the altered figures were reported to the IRS. Rudy M. LaVecchia, the board claimed, told a prospective buyer of a restricted gaming location not to include the name of a partner with a criminal record on the state gaming license application, knowing that the partner would be involved in direct decision making for the business.[18]

American Coin also kept inaccurate accounting records. Rudy M. LaVecchia, who directed training of company technicians on filling and removing money from the slot machines, showed them how to skim money from the machines as well, according to board investigators. He instructed company employees to shift coins out of each machine's hopper and drop compartments when the machine was full. He then told them to place the coins in bags inside the machine without documenting the money. They were then told to fill the machines with less money than the "fill slip" accounting documents would indicate, such as putting in $200 worth of coins instead of the $300 written on the slip, permitting the company to keep $100 more than the documentation suggested. The board also alleged the company failed to fill out federal W-G4 forms—IRS tax withholding reports—for some of the jackpots it awarded.

All of that was more than enough for a major complaint by the board, requesting as punishment a fine, suspension, or revocation of the company's gaming license or a combination of the penalties. But the informant's comments about American Coin's video poker machines made Cunningham take a closer look.

The informant explained that the low prices American Coin charged for its leases and contracts on its slot route "were financially impossible to accomplish unless there was something wrong with their machines," Cunningham recalled. "And the way [the informant] described it was that he believed they must have taken face cards out of the deck, because they were guaranteeing that they would pay all royal flushes. And, in conjunction with the percentage that they were getting with whom that American Coin was participating, it seemed in [the informant's] mind you couldn't do it and make money unless there was something wrong with the EPROMS [erasable programmable read-only-memory computer chips in the machines]. Prior to the issuing of the complaint, it was felt that the board should probably send people out to check the EPROMS just to see if there were any irregularities developed. And as a result of that process, they found EPROMS which didn't match those masters that were on file with the board." [19]

On June 28, 1989, board agents were dispatched to six Las Vegas cocktail lounges on American Coin's route: Runway 21, Pete's Place, Skinny Dugan's, West Hill Pub, Gateway Lounge, and Rum Runner. The agents, with the help of American Coin technicians, removed the EPROM chips from the machines and replaced them with other chips so the machines could operate. Board lab personnel looked into the mathematical source codes and the programs in the extracted computer chips and found they differed from the programs American Coin had submitted to the board.

But not until Volk made his confession to Gaming Control Board investigators Ronald Harris and Randy Heaton on July 14, 1989, did the board learn the chips contained programs that cheated gamblers. Gaming Control Board officials admitted the cheating devices in the programs were too difficult for state technicians to find and probably would not have been discovered without someone telling them both of their existence and how the programs worked.

"The questioning of some areas of those source documents led to people in the laboratory and the investigators confronting Mr. Volk and Mr. Volk ultimately cooperating with the board by advising them as to what in fact had been done," Cunningham said. "A high percentage of [the American Coin machines] had EPROMS that had been unapproved or gaffed." [20]

Volk said he learned that in early 1986 American Coin partners Rudolph LaVecchia and Rudy LaVecchia conspired to hoodwink the board's computer technicians by turning in clean versions of the computer programs for inspection. Once they obtained board approval, they had the jackpot-blocking feature placed into the computer chips before installing them in the machines. The LaVecchias told Volk their reason for resorting to the program was that owners of some locations with American Coin machines had complained that jackpots were being awarded too frequently. Volk said he was ordered under pressure of losing his job to draw up the cheating programs for insertion into the EPROM chips. The programmed chips were simple to duplicate and could be placed inside the machines quickly and easily. Volk explained that the jackpot-blocking device in the video poker games would cancel the draw of a certain number of royal flushes when the player had wagered five or more coins.[21] The cancellation occurred after the player had discarded and drew a new card or cards. Another program Volk devised used the computer monitor chip that displayed the video poker cards to the player. The monitor chip program would "read" the five cards of a potential royal flush and cancel certain cards on the basis of the outcome and the number of coins played.

"Royal flushes wouldn't come up as often as you would expect through random selection," said former board member Dennis Amerine, who participated in one of the interviews Volk had with Gaming Control Board investigators. "They basically eliminated a number of the royal flushes. Say it hit once, it would go ahead and stay. If it hit like a second, third or fourth time, maybe it would not come up. It would show some other outcome. So, it wouldn't eliminate every royal flush, but it would eliminate a good portion of them as they came up."[22]

Volk also claimed he was ordered to produce a program that would halt jackpots on video keno machines. The program prevented players from maximum wins, such as 10 spots hit out of the 10 selected by the player or 7 spots hit of the 9 spots chosen. Volk "was scared to death" during his conversations with board officials, Amerine said. "He really was. I don't recall if he felt he was afraid for his life, but I know he was a very, very scared individual when we talked to him. Very nervous. Certainly he seemed to be afraid of something at the time."

On learning of the programs, board chairman Bill Bible on July 14, 1989, authorized state gaming agents to seal all the company's machines in the 33 locations with lease agreements. American Coin technicians were enlisted to remove the EPROM chips for the board so agents could examine them for cheating programs. Again new chips were put in, and the machines were allowed to operate. The board then repeated the process at the other 60 businesses where American Coin shared slot revenues with business owners.

The next day, having found cheating devices in both video poker and keno machines, the board compelled the LaVecchias and partner Frank Romano to sign an agreement to cooperate with the board's investigation, refrain from altering or replacing EPROM in their gaming machines, and pay for the cost of testing the chips.

On July 26, 1989, the board announced its plans to issue a disciplinary complaint to the Gaming Commission against American Coin. The board also requested the commission issue an emergency order to immediately suspend the licenses of the American Coin partners during the commission's scheduled meeting July 27 in Carson City. The commission granted the request the next day, and American Coin was out of business, never to return. Gaming agents shut off and then removed the company's machines and placed them in warehouses to examine them for cheating devices.

American Coin's cheating scheme happened as the Gaming Control Board was still new to understanding the implications of the computerized gaming industry. By the late 1980s, the old electromechanical, "pull" slot machines of the 1950s and 1960s—like the mechanical one-armed bandits invented in the late 19th century before them—were history. Starting in 1976, most gaming machines were manufactured with microprocessors storing programs with the information used to determine game outcomes. Bally Gaming, Inc., which made a fortune building the pull slots once seen in virtually every casino in Nevada, stopped making them in 1979, the year American Coin was licensed. Computerized games had taken over the industry, but the Gaming Control Board was not ready to regulate them. While Nevada's gaming agency had employed computer experts since the early 1980s to examine the random number generators and other programs in gaming machines, the Nevada legislature did not officially authorize the creation of the board's Electronic Services Division, with a small staff specializing in examining slots, until 1987.

In early 1989, the board and the commission wrapped up an investigation of the "near miss" controversy involving reeled slot machines operated by Universal Distributing of Nevada, Inc., the Las Vegas–based subsidiary of Universal Company, a Japanese slot manufacturer detailed in chapter 4. Universal's popular reeled slot machine, introduced in the early 1980s, used an innovative computer program developed in Japan that altered the reel stops in a losing game to a combination that appeared the player was close to winning a jackpot. Universal insisted that it did nothing wrong and that the program met state standards when it was approved. But the Gaming Commission ruled the feature was not acceptable and made Universal remove it from its machines in Nevada.

In 1988, while examining Universal's case, the board conducted a series of hearings that soon led to new rules and minimum standards for computerized gaming machines. The changes were to become part of Nevada Gaming Commission Regulation 14, up to then geared toward the obsolete electromechanical machines. State officials admitted that Regulation 14, without standards for computerized devices, was about 15 years out of date. The commission approved amendments to the regulation in 1988, but additional ones were being prepared and scheduled for approval in July 1989, the month the American Coin cheating scam broke.

Meanwhile, that summer the board and the attorney general's office were preparing the complaint against American Coin for the alleged blocking of jackpots. But there were problems. Since the amendments to Regulation 14 were not yet approved, Deputy Attorneys General Lisa Miller and Ellen Whittemore had to draft the complaint using the rules of the old Regulation 14.[23] One provision of it they cited in the complaint was the requirement that licensed gaming machine manufacturers report all changes or modifications to their machines to the board. Miller and Whittemore claimed American Coin had violated the regulation when the company altered the state-approved program by inserting the cheating device. The unamended Regulation 14 gave the board the right to seal and seize machines that violated that requirement. Miller and Whittemore also said the alleged alterations were violations of Nevada criminal laws against cheating at gaming, punishable by 1 to 10 years in state prison, a fine of up to $10,000, or both. But because the Gaming Commission served as "judge" in complaint proceedings, Miller and Whittemore were in an awkward position. They could not inform commissioners about the American Coin complaint before it was issued since to do so would technically constitute "ex parte" communications.[24]

The complaint, formally issued by the attorney general's office and signed by board members on August 1, 1989, listed 27 allegations against the LaVecchias and Romano. The document also requested that the partners' licenses be revoked and that they be fined $100,000 per count, or about $2.7 million. The proposed fine would have been the second-largest imposed in state history since the $3.5 million levied in 1984 against former Stardust Hotel operators Al Sachs and Herb Tobman for failing to prevent skimming at the hotel.

After the complaint was announced, the Clark County district attorney's office said it would pursue the felony cheating case against the LaVecchias, with charges that could equal one count per gaffed machine. An estimated 500 machines had the cheating device.

On August 4, 1989, American Coin filed for protection under Chapter 11 of the U.S. Bankruptcy Code. The company listed assets of $2.6 million and its largest debt, the potential $2.7 million fine proposed by the state.[25] The judge in the bankruptcy case granted the company's request for a temporary restraining order, halting the board's seizure of the machines. The company's attorney, William Urga (himself later appointed to the Gaming Commission), listed the seized slot machines as assets and asked the federal judge to force the state to return them. The machines, Urga argued, were the company's most valuable possessions. Bar owners on the company's slot routes were signing contracts with other route operators because the Gaming Control Board had seized American Coin's machines, Urga said. If the machines were kept in place, the bars would not seek out other route operators, he added.

But Deputy Attorney General Scott Scherer argued that the seizure was an effort to obtain evidence, and the longer the machines were kept in the field, the more likely the EPROM chips would be damaged or lost. The board ultimately won its case after the bankruptcy judge decided the seizure was a police function and the basis of an investigation into whether the machines had the cheating programs.

Now seeking to dismiss the board complaint, in late August 1989 American Coin attorneys filed a brief with the commission, alleging that the board failed to serve the complaint in a timely manner and that board agents themselves were responsible for inserting the cheating devices into the computer chips. Deputy Attorney General Miller denied the allegations in a response.[26] The complaint, she said, was delivered to the partners or their attorneys within the legally required five working days after it was issued. Board agents discovered the cheating devices within the video monitor chips left in the machines after they had removed and replaced the EPROM chips with the help of American Coin technicians, Miller said. For that reason, it was impossible for the agents to have created a cheating device by removing and replacing the EPROMS, she reasoned. The commission brushed the company's motion aside.

Finally, on February 22, 1990, the board's case against American Coin came to end at a commission hearing in Las Vegas. In a signed stipulation, the LaVecchias and Romano agreed to pay a collective fine of $1 million.[27] The LaVecchias agreed to allow the state to revoke their gaming licenses. They also agreed, in words written by the attorney general's office, "to never again come into the gaming industry either by way of ownership interest, employment, or any type of licensure or application for licensure." Romano, who professed to have known nothing about the cheating devices, also agreed to relinquish his gaming license and stay out of the gaming industry in Nevada.

By the early fall of 1991, almost a year had passed since Volk's murder, and still no one was charged. At one point, Las Vegas police assured inquiring producers of the Los Angeles–based television show *Unsolved Mysteries* that the Volk killing was about to be solved, and the show dropped plans to film a segment on it.

Then, in September 1991, Las Vegas police homicide detectives Tom Dillard and R. D. Leonard filed an affidavit, nearly 400 pages long, charging David Lemons, a former employee of American Coin, with being the lookout for the shooting.[28] The detectives said the slaying involved two co-conspirators, Vito

Bruno (also known as John Sipes) and Soni Beckman, whom the officers did not charge with a criminal offense in the affidavit. Beckman and her husband, Richard Beckman, were described as close friends of Rudolph LaVecchia and his wife, Diana LaVecchia. Police said Richard Beckman had a permit to carry explosive materials, although he was not charged. Police alleged the conspirators intended to silence Volk from testifying in a possible grand jury investigation of the American Coin criminal cheating case. After the slaying, Volk's spouse, LaVerne Volk, told police she believed that someone associated with American Coin was involved in the murder. Homicide detectives investigated the LaVecchias and Romano, but the three men were not charged in the case.

In the affidavit, the detectives said Volk reported having received threatening phone calls as early as December 1989. In one, the voice on the phone told Volk, "How'd you like a bird in your mouth, you squealer, you're gonna die."[29] On September 17, 1990, two weeks before the shooting, a homemade bomb was thrown into Volk's home. The assailant came by shortly after midnight and tossed two sticks of dynamite with an orange safety fuse and blasting caps affixed to a brick through the window of a bedroom. The Volks, however, were on vacation in Hawaii at the time. The bomb caused considerable damage to the room. A family friend, who was housesitting in another room, was shaken but unhurt.

The detectives went on to say that on September 26, 1990, four days before the shooting, two uniformed officers on patrol saw a blue 280SL Mercedes on a dirt shoulder on Cabana Drive in an area of eastern Las Vegas associated with burglaries and car thefts.[30] The car appeared to be camouflaged by nearby bushes. The officers became suspicious because thieves had hidden behind bushes in the area to strip stolen cars. But before the officers could investigate, the Mercedes drove away.

Later that same day, however, they spotted the car again. They saw it make an illegal U-turn and stop at a curb on Cabana Drive, facing Valley View Drive, less than a block from Volk's home. The officers, suspecting the car was stolen, stopped to investigate and reported seeing Lemons, 22, and Bruno, 30, slouching down inside as if to hide from view. Police noticed that the shirtless Lemons was wearing on his chest a series of large, so-called homemade jailhouse tattoos. Under questioning, police found that both Lemons and Bruno were ex-felons from Arizona, Lemons for possession of stolen property and Bruno for burglary. Both had different explanations as to why they were there. Bruno told one officer they were waiting for a friend and pointed to the Winterwood Trailer Estates complex opposite Volk's neighborhood. Lemons, however, said that their friend lived at Desert Inn Estates, Volk's neighborhood.

Lemons, the officers discovered, had recently moved from an earlier residence in Las Vegas but did not file a change of address with police as was required of ex-felons. One officer noticed a 12-gauge shotgun shell and a box of shells inside the car. Bruno then admitted he had a shotgun in the backseat. It had five rounds loaded in a tubular magazine, each round with number 1 shot, which, police said, was not the type used by hunters or target shooters. Police also found a loaded and unregistered .22-caliber derringer under the passenger floorboard where Lemons sat. The 1981 Mercedes was registered to a leasing company in California. Lemons and Bruno were arrested on weapons charges, and police had the Mercedes impounded.

The next day, the Mercedes was claimed from impound by Richard Beckman, whose explosives permit listed the Mercedes as his car. According to the police affidavit, in the early evening of September 30, 1990, a day before Volk was killed, Lemons was issued three traffic citations for driving an unregistered motorcycle in the area of Vegas Valley and Nellis Boulevard in eastern Las Vegas, less than half a mile from Volk's residence. Police later learned that collect calls were made to Bruno's home phone from a pay phone at a 7-11 store at Valley View and Nellis on September 4, 5, and 30, including two calls on the 30th. Volk's neighbors had told police of hearing a motorcycle drive away after the shooting.

With a search warrant, police entered the Bruno and the Beckman homes on November 17, 1990. Checks made out to Bruno were found in the Beckman home, as was an address book with Volk's home address, the license number of Volk's car, a presentencing report on Lemons, and bail release slips for Lemons and Bruno. Blank checks signed by Diana LaVecchia were discovered as well. Police also ran across something more interesting—a piece of paper sent by fax machine with a stick figure drawing with the message, "Good Ole Larry." The figure was hanging by a noose with blood dripping from its head. The drawing was taken from Soni Beckman's desk. Bruno's fingerprints were found on the stick drawing, which included a note that stated, "Burn this as soon as done reading this." Nonelectric blasting caps were located inside a drawer of the desk.

In Bruno's home, police found receipts with Lemons's name on them; a photocopy of a local newspaper article on the Volk shooting; a news clipping of the September 17, 1990, bombing; and a note with directions to a home owned by Beckman in Helendale, California. A safe was found with Gaming Control Board seal tape that had been broken through. Dye stamps—used to make coin tokens—belonging to American Coin also were recovered there. Police recovered an orange safety fuse in Bruno's backyard as well.

With no eyewitness to the murder, police had to file a case on the basis of the circumstantial evidence. Lemons was arraigned in Clark County District Court on September 9, 1992, charged with the bombing of Volk's home, conspiracy to commit murder, and murder with the use of a deadly weapon.

Police alleged that Lemons either did the shooting or aided in it by serving as the lookout.

At the preliminary hearing on September 24, 1992, a former metropolitan police officer and acquaintance of Soni Beckman testified that the woman had asked him in mid-August 1990 to obtain Volk's street address through the Department of Motor Vehicles because she was "having a party or something."[31] An agent of the Bureau of Alcohol, Tobacco, and Firearms told the court that the bomb thrown into Volk's home included an orange safety fuse and was probably ignited by a nonelectric blasting cap. Bruno successfully fought against testifying after his attorney told prosecutors his client would invoke the Fifth Amendment on the stand.

But the strangest part of the case came when David Westmoreland, a prison inmate with Lemons, testified. The prosecution regarded Westmoreland as its key witness. Westmoreland, acquainted with LaVerne Volk through a friend of hers, said that after the murder Mrs. Volk came to visit him in the Southern Desert Correctional Center in Indian Springs, Nevada, and asked whether he would talk to Lemons about her husband's slaying. The 49-year-old Westmoreland, serving time for second-degree murder, claimed he later confronted Lemons, whom he said confessed involvement in the murder, but that he had watched the shooting from a car and that the shooter was a woman. It was Westmoreland's statement earlier to police that had led to the arrest of Lemons on September 5, 1992.

During the trial, the judge instructed the jurors to consider the circumstantial evidence with the same importance as direct evidence.[32] Clark County prosecutor Mel Harmon argued that the LaVecchias had a motive to kill Volk, adding, however, that it appeared Lemons was hired to participate in it. Lemons and Bruno, Harmon said, had planned to kill Volk the night they were arrested outside Volk's neighborhood and then returned four days later to do the job.

Lemons's attorney, Anthony Sgro, countered that the state's case was weak and that police merely used Lemons to fill out their theory of what happened. Lemons, he said, had no motive to kill Volk, but "numerous other individuals connected to this case have a far greater motive."[33] One was Frank Romano, Sgro suggested, despite the fact that police had eliminated Romano as a suspect after he had passed a polygraph test saying he was not involved. Sgro offered his own theory on Volk's killing to the jury. He said that Volk's 23-year-old stepson, Robert D'Addario, was irate because Volk refused to let him live at his home and that D'Addario moved in after Volk's death. D'Addario, who used to sleep in cars, once had been arrested for arson and resented the fact that the spare room where the bomb was thrown was used as a "shrine," always with a lighted candle, for Volk's 10-year-old son, who died of a heart ailment. Also, Sgro said a man in a $2.1 million copyright infringement case, against whom Volk was to testify and so might have had a motive to kill him, settled the case for only $40,000 after Volk died. And Westmoreland, Sgro pointed out, had failed two polygraph tests on his statements about Lemons.

Four days after the case went to the jury, the verdict on April 7, 1993, was not guilty. Jurors said they discounted Westmoreland's testimony. Some of the jurors appeared to be happy for Lemons. One of them shook Lemons's hand and said, "Be more selective when you pick friends." [34]

The Volk murder case was over, at least for the moment. Lemons, meanwhile, was arrested less than a month after the verdict in Las Vegas on felony burglary and home violation charges. [35] But the march toward justice in the Volk case continued. In 1997, while serving time in a state prison in Jean, Nevada, about 20 miles west of Las Vegas, Lemons had an epiphany. Thanks to his newfound Christian religious faith, he decided to come clean about the Volk murder. He sent a letter to Nevada Attorney General Frankie Sue Del Papa in which he admitted he murdered Volk and wanted to speak to law enforcement officers. [36] He later confessed to Las Vegas police that he pulled the trigger (although because of his earlier acquittal, he could not be charged in the murder). Lemons also implicated Bruno and Beckman in the plot. He said they hired him to kill Volk and paid him $5,000 in installments. Bruno went with him several times to case Volk's home, said Lemons, who also admitted that he threw the bomb into Volk's home. Bruno, Lemons added, had assisted him the night of the bombing and had picked him up after the shooting to take him to a place where the gun was thrown away. Immediately following Volk's death, Bruno paid him between $1,500 and $1,700, and a few days later Beckman and Bruno paid him the rest, Lemons said. Police arrested Bruno and Soni Beckman. Bruno remained in custody, but Beckman was released after posting $200,000 bail.

On February 6, 1998, a grand jury in Las Vegas indicted Bruno and Beckman on charges of murder with a deadly weapon. Investigators said that it was Romano who had revealed that Beckman and her husband were close friends of Rudolph and Diana LaVecchia. Detectives also disclosed other facts in the case. In Soni Beckman's house, they found 11 nonelectric blasting caps, similar to the caps used in the bombing, and a fax transmission containing handwritten directions to Volk's home and his physical description, including "glasses, dirty blond." [37] In addition, many items showed a close relationship between the Beckmans and the LaVecchias, including numerous blank checks on the LaVecchias' bank account and a fax mentioning their friendship. Soni Beckman also kept a file with the LaVecchias's name on it that included news articles in the *Las Vegas Sun* on the bombing and slaying. [38]

Even more intriguing to investigators was that the Beckmans' phone bill revealed a long-distance fax to Rudolph and Diana LaVecchia's fax number in Hawaii. The fax was transmitted at 11:08 P.M. on October 1, 1990, three hours after Volk was shot and when news first broke of it on local television. Soni Beckman had also filled out a check for $1,700 in cash the day of the murder.

From wiretaps on phones used by Bruno and Beckman, police listened in on a conversation the two had after police, to stimulate conversation, called Lemons on March 21, 1991, at the Clark County Detention Center and told him he would be charged with murdering Volk. Lemons informed Bruno, who then almost immediately called Soni Beckman, according to Las Vegas police. The following conversation then took place:

BRUNO: Are you leaving town?
BECKMAN: Pardon?
BRUNO: You leaving town?
BECKMAN: No.
BRUNO: Oh.
BECKMAN: Why? You think I would be?
BRUNO: I don't know.
BECKMAN: No, I'm not concerned about, uh, anything that he, he's going to say. What, you know the only thing that really bothers me is what you might say to him on the phone that they might hear, that's the only thing.
BRUNO: Oh, okay.[39]

In another conversation the same day, Bruno told Soni Beckman that his attorney recommended he stay away from Lemons. Beckman then replied, "Isn't it more dangerous to avoid him?" The next day, March 22, 1991, Tony Sgro, Beckman's attorney, visited Lemons at the detention center, and soon thereafter Beckman delivered a cash retainer to Sgro. A couple of days later, from intercepted phone conversations, police detectives stated that Beckman "was diligently transferring ownership of numerous homes to other individuals. She also spoke of depleting bank accounts because of possible arrest."[40]

During an investigation in Las Vegas led by Chief Deputy District Attorney David Roger, prosecutors found that Soni Beckman had ties to two properties damaged in arson fires.[41] One was a 1992 fire that destroyed the former home of the late entertainer Louis Prima in Las Vegas. No one was charged. Soni Beckman and her husband, who held an interest in the home and had tried unsuccessfully to sell it, received more than $250,000 from an insurance company.[42] In 1994, an arson fire damaged a bed-and-breakfast hotel in South Carolina for which Soni Beckman held a business license. Again no one was arrested. In mid-1998, Soni Beckman remained out on bail and Bruno in the Clark County jail for the murder charges. Following procedural delays by their attorneys, their trial in Las Vegas was scheduled to begin January 1999. The main reason for the delay was that Soni Beckman had been diagnosed at a hospital in Loma Linda, California, with cervical cancer and required radical hysterectomy surgery.[43]

Meanwhile, not much was seen or heard of Rudolph and Rudy M. La-Vecchia in the years following the revocation of their gaming licenses. Because of the bankruptcy filing, the Gaming Control Board was hard-pressed to obtain the $362,500 each partner was fined. It was revealed in federal court in Las Vegas in 1995 that the two had traveled to California and Hawaii that year with nearly $1 million in cash and certificates.[44] Rudolph LaVecchia was later found living in Florida, his son Rudy in Hawaii. In 1998, both men were charged with criminal contempt for failing to show up for hearings in Las Vegas into their own bankruptcy filings.[45]

Frank Romano took his former partners to court and won. In May 1995, a U.S. bankruptcy court judge ruled he had the right to recover as much as $13 million, including interest, after Romano's attorneys argued the LaVecchias placed the cheating devices into American Coin machines without his knowledge.[46] The scheme resulted in millions in lost future revenue, ruined his ability to borrow money from banks, and caused him emotional distress, the lawyers said. Judge Clive Jones said he believed Romano's contention that he did not know of the cheating devices.

A year later, Romano, feeling vindicated by the favorable ruling in the bankruptcy case, filed a motion with the Gaming Commission, asking that it set aside the stipulation he signed that revoked his license and fined him $275,000. He alleged that board member Cunningham had colluded with a slot company, United Gaming, to investigate American Coin and that state gaming agents withheld evidence pointing to his innocence in the cheating scheme. Cunningham denied the charges. The former board member said that in 1989 United Gaming had offered to put up $200,000 for a sting operation on suspicious gaming machine firms but that he rejected it "because I thought it would compromise the integrity of the board."[47]

The state attorney general's office insisted in court that Romano should not be released from the settlement, saying that lack of knowledge of the cheating alone did not absolve him of wrongdoing. Romano agreed to the settlement willingly and waived his right to reviews before the commission and in court, the office said. In July 1996, the commission voted unanimously against Romano's request, stating it had no authority to reenter the issue of whether Romano took part in the cheating.[48]

In 1997, Romano appeared on a segment of the ABC television series *Prime-Time Live* about allegations that slot machines in Nevada were deceptive. Romano indicated that the allegations were true.

The legacy of the American Coin case continues. Starting in November 1991, out of concern that other companies might be cheating the same way, the Gaming Control Board launched a program that sent agents to inspect all the 145,000 gaming machines then in Nevada, focusing mainly on 125,000 computerized machines.[49] Two teams of three agents, using laptop computers, each were assigned to inspect the machines inside casinos, lounges, and other sites. The agents would attempt to determine whether the programs in the machines were the same ones approved by the board.

No other cheating devices were found. Ironically, however, those very agents unwittingly created cheating devices themselves at the behest of a computer technician employed by the board's Electronic Services Division. In 1992, Ronald Harris, one of two board employees present when Volk confessed to having rigged American Coin's machines, began developing cheating programs of his own (see chapter 7). Harris fixed it so that the board's laptops transferred a cheating device into some of the machines tested by agents. He also discovered how to cheat gaming machines by using computers to predict future payoffs. Harris's case was profiled in the same *PrimeTime Live* story that Romano also appeared in. The television show, and the Harris matter, would mortify Nevada gaming regulators.

1. Michael Rumbolz during the Nevada State Gaming Control Board meeting on February 15, 1991. Rumbolz was appointed to the board on January 1, 1985, by Governor Richard Bryan to serve as its legal and law enforcement member. He served as chairman from May 29, 1987, to January 1, 1989. (Courtesy *Las Vegas Sun*)

2. Gerald Cunningham during the Gaming Control Board meeting on January 1, 1991. Cunningham was a board member from June 8, 1987, to February 15, 1991. (Courtesy *Las Vegas Sun*)

3. Dennis Amerine during the Gaming Control Board meeting on February 15, 1991. Amerine was a board member from February 1, 1987, to October 31, 1989. (Courtesy *Las Vegas Sun*)

4. Ralph Engelstad, proprietor and operator of the Imperial Palace Hotel and Casino, during an interview with the *Las Vegas Sun* on January 5, 1981. (Courtesy *Las Vegas Sun*)

5. Two unidentified employees of the Royal Casino demonstrate against Royal owner Joe Slyman in the casino's driveway before the place was scheduled to close at midnight, October 20, 1988. (Courtesy *Las Vegas Sun*)

6. Joe Slyman, owner of the Royal Casino, raises his framed state gaming license during his raucous closing party on the casino floor the night of October 20, 1988. Slyman had vowed to turn over his license to Nevada State Gaming Control Board agents himself when they appeared at midnight to shut the casino down. The author, a *Las Vegas Sun* reporter at the time, can be seen at the far left. (Courtesy *Las Vegas Sun*)

8. Sheldon Adelson, owner of the Interface Group, who bought the Sands Hotel and built the Venetian Casino Resort in Las Vegas, in a 1995 photograph. (Courtesy *Las Vegas Sun*)

9. Henri Lewin in August 1981. At the time, Lewin was executive vice president of the Hilton Hotels chain, in charge of the company's 12-hotel western division— including all of Nevada—and its hotel operations in New Jersey. (Courtesy *Las Vegas Sun*)

7. (opposite) The marquee of the venerable Sands Hotel on the Las Vegas Strip as it appeared on the night of June 30, 1996, when the hotel closed forever. Owned solely by Sheldon Adelson, the Sands was destroyed later that year in a televised implosion to make way for Adelson's planned $1.5 billion Venetian Casino Resort. (Courtesy *Las Vegas Sun*)

10. The former Sport of Kings race and sports book, at the corner of Convention Center Drive and Paradise Road, shown here on March 29, 1995, the day before a foreclosure auction produced a winning bid of $3.5 million. (Courtesy *Las Vegas Sun*)

11. Robert N. Peccole served on the Nevada Gaming Commission from February 1, 1985, to April 27, 1989. (Courtesy Robert N. Peccole)

12. Thomas Roche served on the Nevada State Gaming Control Board from December 11, 1989, to September 30, 1993. (Photograph by Tony Scodwell, courtesy Thomas Roche)

13. John F. O'Reilly served on the Nevada Gaming Commission from February 1, 1987, to April 27, 1991. He was chairman of the commission from May 29, 1987, to January 1, 1989. (Courtesy *Las Vegas Sun*)

14. William R. Urga was a member of the Nevada Gaming Commission from April 28, 1991, to April 27, 1997. (Courtesy William R. Urga)

15. Bill Bible served on the Nevada State Gaming Control Board from January 1, 1989, to September 18, 1998, and was chairman during his entire career with the board. (Courtesy *Las Vegas Sun*)

16. Steve DuCharme has served on the Nevada State Gaming Control Board since January 1, 1991. He became chairman on September 18, 1998. (Courtesy Steve DuCharme)

Chapter Two

To Ralphie from Adolph
Ralph Engelstad and the War Room at the Imperial Palace

On December 14, 1984, James and Joan Scanlon, a pair of tourists from Missouri, were in their guest room at the Imperial Palace, a hotel-casino on the Las Vegas Strip a block north of Flamingo Road. Suddenly, a man dressed in what they later described as a "a hotel service-type" uniform somehow entered the room and attacked them. The assailant, armed with a gun and knife, beat the couple, then bound and gagged them. Over what seemed like a very long time, the man raped Joan Scanlon in front of her husband before fleeing into the hallway. Despite an investigation by Las Vegas police, the suspect was never apprehended.[1]

That same year, Ralph L. Engelstad, the 55-year-old, multimillionaire founder and proprietor of the Imperial Palace, was compiling a collection of rare vehicles, banners, daggers, posters, and assorted memorabilia from Nazi Germany and World War II Axis powers nations, Italy and Japan, for storage at the hotel.

By 1988, Engelstad's zeal as a collector and litigation brought against him by the Scanlons over the 1984 attack would together set in motion one of most infamous political embarrassments for Nevada and its casino industry, always sensitive to how public opinion and bad publicity might discourage tourists and gamblers from coming to Sin City. The controversy would also push the Nevada State Gaming Control Board and the Nevada Gaming Commission to seek the right political solution to restore the state's credibility. But an agreement would not come easily, nor would it come soon enough to avoid the national publicity that made Las Vegas a laughingstock during the fall of 1988.

Engelstad, a proud and headstrong man, was a local success story and a man of contradictions. The grandson of a potato farmer, he was the goalie for his college hockey team at the University of North Dakota. A Catholic of Belgian-Norwegian descent, Engelstad moved to Las Vegas from North

Dakota in the early 1960s and made money developing housing tracts.[2] In 1967, he sold 145 acres in North Las Vegas for $2 million to billionaire Howard Hughes, who used the land to build the North Las Vegas Airport. The funds allowed Engelstad to buy the Kona Kai, a small casino on the Strip south of Tropicana Avenue, which he later sold. In 1971, he bought the old Flamingo Capri—a seedy motel on the Strip across from Caesars Palace—and received a nonrestricted gaming license from the Gaming Commission in 1973. In 1979, on the site of the old motel, he opened the Imperial Palace Casino, fashioned after a Japanese royal residence. Engelstad would earn a reputation as an effective casino operator, and his privately held Imperial Palace became one of the most profitable casinos in the Las Vegas. He promoted the hotel-casino toward the middle-class slot player, with guest rooms priced at about $55 a night. In 1981, he estimated his personal fortune at $300 million. The Imperial Palace won national awards for hiring disabled job applicants, and Engelstad was the first Las Vegas casino operator to open an on-site health clinic for employees. Engelstad, who said his workday started 9:30 A.M. and ended about midnight, was proud of the fact he operated on his own cash flow and had no stock- or bondholders to worry about.

When his troubles of 1988 hit, Engelstad's Imperial Palace had 2,700 guest rooms and 2,000 employees. Entertainment at the casino included outdoor luaus and a long-running indoor production show, with celebrity impersonators, called "Legends in Concert." But the biggest tourist attraction at the Imperial Palace was Engelstad's antique car collection—the third-largest in the United States—including more than 200 fully restored and drivable vintage vehicles on display to the public for a small admission price. His international collection, according to hotel news releases, included one of only two 1905 nine-passenger Rapid buses in existence, a 1917 Ford gasoline truck, a 1931 12-cylinder Cadillac, a 1934 Duesenberg, and dozens of German-designed Mercedes-Benzes built in Detroit before World War II. It also featured a 1939 Mercedes-Benz parade car once owned by Nazi dictator Adolf Hitler—on public display at the Imperial Palace since 1980—and a 1939 Alfa Romeo sedan used by Italian dictator Benito Mussolini.

But Engelstad, a World War II history buff, had other plans for his private compilation of relics from the Axis powers. It would be housed within a private, so-called war room, a large, high-ceilinged chamber a wall away from Engelstad's public car collection built on the fifth floor of the hotel's parking garage. As his Axis powers compilation grew—to include staff cars once used by Nazi Air Force Commander Hermann Göring and SS Chief Heinrich Himmler—Engelstad could not contain his pride and wanted to share it with others. Inside the war room in 1986 and 1988, he held private parties, each time on Hitler's birthday and each with about 100 people in attendance. When news of the parties appeared in the media in September 1988, Engelstad insisted that he did not intend to glorify or sympathize with Hitler. The parties, he said, were tongue-in-cheek fetes held to honor employees who had completed restoration work on his vintage Axis powers vehicles. He was merely showing off the collection to employees and guests and intended to open it to the public as an attraction, he said.

The barrage of local, national, even international news reports about the Hitler parties prompted the Gaming Control Board and the state attorney general's office in December 1988 to hand the commission a two-count complaint against Engelstad, citing state gaming Regulation 5.011, enacted in 1969.[3] The regulation stated that the commission was within its authority to fine and to condition, restrict, revoke, or suspend the gaming license of any licensee who conducted an "unsuitable method of operation." Acts that might be deemed unsuitable included "failure to exercise discretion and sound judgment to prevent incidents which might reflect on the repute of the State of Nevada and act as a detriment to the development of the industry." The Gaming Control Board and the Gaming Commission were also empowered to pass judgment on "any activity on the part of any licensee, his agents or employees, that is inimical to the public health, safety, morals, good order and general welfare of the people of the State of Nevada."[4]

The state had the tools to punish Engelstad it if had to. In the Engelstad case, it did not matter if the casino operator denied honoring Hitler or that his unique Axis collection was merely an offshoot of his antique auto accumulation. The board and a reluctant commission determined that the news coverage of his activities alone had hurt the reputation of Nevada and the gaming industry, vital to the state's economic survival.

"Clearly, if there were no publicity, I don't know if we could have had a case," said former deputy attorney general Scott Scherer, who argued the board's 1988 complaint against Engelstad before the commission. "Engelstad never admitted there was a war room or glorification of Hitler. He claimed the collection was of historical artifacts. I don't think the board necessarily disagreed with that. But we were concerned about how it reflected on the image of gaming in the state of Nevada."[5]

"The public policy the state wanted to convey in the statutes was a strong confidence in the licensees's operations, and when one is allowed to divert into such controversial and repugnant type of expressions, I don't think that lends a great deal to confidence," said former Gaming Control Board member Gerald Cunningham, one of three members who signed the complaint against Engelstad. "We were very concerned about the overall effect such activities might have on the industry and the licensing and regulatory process."[6]

Engelstad and his supporters complained that the media had treated them unfairly and that the controversy was blown out of proportion. His attorneys maintained that his First Amendment rights—to hold the Hitler parties—were being violated. Regulation 5, they argued, was enacted in the early 1960s to rid Nevada casinos of members of organized crime families and did not apply to Engelstad.

"I think they [the Gaming Control Board and the Gaming Commission] employed the statute to meet their own views," said George Dickerson, an Engelstad attorney who was chairman of the Gaming Commission from 1968 to 1969. "Obviously, it offended my view of the constitutional right of freedom of expression. They tried to paint him as a bigot, but he never demonstrated any bigotry to me."[7]

"I think it was political," said Owen Nitz, a lawyer and Engelstad friend who started representing him in Las Vegas in 1962. "I think the commission was a victim of the sensationalism of the press."[8]

The entire dispute would grow out of litigation by the Scanlons against the Imperial Palace. The 1984 assault on the couple, who were injured and humiliated, destroyed their marriage. In December 1986, their Nevada attorney, Joseph Cronin, filed a lawsuit in Clark County District Court in Las Vegas against Imperial Palace owners Ralph Engelstad and Engelstad's wife Betty, alleging that the hotel's failure to provide adequate security contributed to the injuries suffered by the Scanlons. The suit produced tensions within the hotel after Cronin sought out and spoke to high-level hotel employees about hotel security and other policies. Cronin attempted to prove the Scanlon attack was part of a pattern of poor security work at the Imperial Palace. On a number of occasions from July to September 1988, Cronin met with Mick Shindell, the hotel's chief of corporate security, and Shirley Arbury, its human resources director. Shindell told Cronin he was ordered to remove and destroy all documents mentioning that the Imperial Palace's security department needed improvement. Arbury claimed that while the Imperial Palace was responding to requests for documents in the Scanlon suit, she was ordered by hotel executives to expunge negative employment information on security officers that might damage the hotel in the case.[9]

Cronin, in talks with Imperial Palace lawyers, had initially offered to settle the case for $750,000, but the testimony about alleged destruction of evidence prompted him to increase his demand to $5 million. In September 1988, Cronin filed a motion asking the judge to rule in favor of his clients. He alleged the Imperial Palace willfully destroyed damaging evidence, including security incident documents and reports of crimes on the hotel property that were filed before January 1, 1983 (the hotel's report on the Scanlon attack, however, had been preserved). According to Cronin, the hotel shredded its own security reports on robberies, room burglaries, purse snatchings, and other crimes in the casino and hotel.[10] Cronin further claimed the Imperial Palace purged negative job evaluations and other documents from the personnel files of hotel security employees.[11] Cronin used depositions from Shindell, Arbury, and other Imperial Palace employees to support the motion. The Imperial Palace, in an answer, denied that documents were destroyed. Lawyers for the hotel maintained that employees quoted in the depositions had also said copies of the documents still existed. The hotel also filed a motion to disqualify Cronin from representing the Scanlons, alleging that the attorney improperly communicated with hotel management without first seeking permission from Engelstad's lawyers. Cronin, they said, compromised the defendant's attorney-client privilege by talking to Shindell after Shindell had met with Engelstad lawyers to discuss settlement strategies. (In late 1989, the Nevada Supreme Court voted to remove Cronin from the case; the Scanlons ultimately settled for an undisclosed amount with Engelstad, who in the end convinced a Las Vegas judge to seal all court documents in the case.)[12]

Meanwhile, Engelstad ordered Shindell and Arbury placed on administrative leave in September 1988 to punish them for talking to Cronin. Within a week, two other high-level hotel employees were placed on leave for speaking to the attorney. Transcripts of depositions given by the suspended employees were then leaked to the local press. That September, the suspended Imperial Palace employees began talking to the Gaming Control Board and the Las Vegas media about the war room and the Hitler birthday parties. The *Las Vegas Review-Journal* and the rival *Las Vegas Sun* newspapers reported that Engelstad had hosted parties for employees and other guests on or about April 20, 1986, and on April 20, 1988. Among the reported festivities were a cake decorated with a swastika, German food, and German marching music. Bartenders wore T-shirts bearing the words "Adolf Hitler—European Tour 1939–45."[13]

The parties took place inside the private, 3,000-square-foot room, featuring about 30 rare World War II–vintage vehicles along with an assortment of Nazi German knives, propaganda posters, uniforms, swastika banners, and Hitler-themed murals and paintings plus a handful of items from wartime Italy and Japan. Some of the vehicles, including the Göring and Himmler models, were valued at $1 million or more each. A huge World War II, 20-man troop carrier from Germany was worth more than $2 million. A life-size portrait of Hitler, with the inscription "To Ralphie from Adolph, 1939," hung on a wall. Beside it was a second painting, with a likeness of Engelstad in a Nazi uniform and with the message "To Adolph from Ralphie." Murals on the room's large walls depicted Hitler giving a speech to a lighted stadium full of people and Hitler giving the Nazi salute while standing in a car driving on the German Autobahn in the 1930s. On September 27, 1988, Gaming Control Board agents asked to view the war room and the relics inside.

Engelstad friend Owen Nitz said Engelstad saw the collection as an investment. "The big troop carrier was part of a quest of World War II vehicles that
were very valuable," Nitz said. "He wanted to make some money—buy cheap
and sell high." [14]

Articles about the Hitler parties and the war room in the *Review-Journal* and
the *Sun* in the fall of 1988 provoked dozens of irate phone calls to the Gaming
Control Board and outrage from Las Vegas's 30,000-member Jewish community, who objected to the appearance that Engelstad had honored the man responsible for ordering the deaths of millions of Jews during World War II. On
September 30, 1988, Engelstad attempted to explain himself in a lengthy news
release:

> First of all, I want everyone to know that I despise Adolf Hitler and every-
> thing he stood for. Nevertheless, he created his own niche in history, al-
> though it was an infamous one. He and World War II were part of history
> that is within the memories of many of us who are still alive. All of us
> wish it had never happened, but it is reality. I have collected many auto-
> mobiles and items of memorabilia from that period of time that relate to
> all of the World War II powers including the Third Reich and other axis
> powers. This collection, when made available to the public, will provide
> to the public an opportunity for a personal glimpse into an era of history
> that must not be forgotten and must not be repeated.
>
> I am truly sorry that this collection has been interpreted in a manner
> that couldn't be further from the truth. Comments have appeared in the
> press from persons who are or were employees of the Imperial Palace, if
> accurately reported, depict a situation that does not exist.
>
> The Imperial Palace is famous the world over for its fantastic, one of a
> kind auto collection. The collection of the vehicles that is now the center
> of attention is a logical continuation of those automobile and memorabilia
> collection activities. It is merely that, and nothing more. Any suggestion
> that discrimination of any type has a place in my life or in the business of
> the Imperial Palace Hotel and Casino is absolutely untrue. A cross section
> of the employees of the Imperial Palace graphically demonstrates this be-
> yond any doubt. I myself am of Norwegian and Belgian extraction, hav-
> ing moved to Las Vegas from North Dakota nearly thirty years ago. I have
> pursued the American business dream both ethically and honestly at all
> times and as a result of hard work and good luck, I have been able to build
> an important and respected business in this community. I am proud of
> that and will continue to conduct my business in a manner that is above
> board in every respect.
>
> The Hotel is presently defending the litigation that is mentioned in the

newspaper as well as other lawsuits. It is common knowledge in Las Vegas that Strip hotels are frequently sued for a myriad of reasons. We will continue to defend all litigation in the courts and through proper procedures in the course of any such litigation, and I have so instructed all of my employees. Any suggestion that I have instructed anyone to the contrary is totally false.

I have tried to be a good member of the community and return some of my good fortune to deserving causes. I have been responsible for the Annual Senior's Christmas Party that the Imperial Palace has put on free of charge for the Las Vegas Senior Citizens for the last five years. I recently made a substantial contribution to my alma mater, the University of North Dakota, and they honored me by dedicating their ice hockey arena in my name. I am proud of that, too.

I can only tell you that I am a solid law-abiding citizen, and the ugly accusations and innuendoes that have been made in the press that either myself or the Imperial Palace Hotel and Casino would condone discrimination of any type whatsoever is simply and absolutely untrue.[15]

But the controversy continued. In October 1988, things went from bad to worse for Engelstad. News stories appeared across the country, and the case became fodder for radio talk shows. Engelstad and his aides, claiming they were victims of inequitable news reporting, sought help. On the first day of the month, Engelstad hired a man from Dallas and another man from New York, both of whom specialized in "crisis communications," to handle news reporters. Three days later, the *Review-Journal* reported that hundreds of bumper stickers with the message "Hitler Was Right" were allegedly designed and printed at the Imperial Palace's print shop.[16] Gaming Control Board agents, who received one of the stickers, went to the hotel and found a plate used to print them and a job order made out for them, dated July 24, 1986. The board alleged later that 500 of the stickers were printed on or about August 15, 1986, and that Engelstad and Imperial Palace general manager Ed Crispell "were either aware of or approved the printing" of the stickers, which were then distributed "by Engelstad and other employees of the Imperial Palace."[17]

In the next few days that October, Nevada lieutenant governor Bob Miller sent a letter to Engelstad saying that to open the Nazi collection in the war room to the public would be in poor taste and damaging to the image of Las Vegas and Nevada. Nevada governor Richard Bryan predicted the Gaming Control Board would act against the casino owner if the Hitler parties in fact took place.[18] Nevada attorney general Brian McKay was quoted in an October 24, 1988, story in *People* magazine saying that Engelstad's Hitler parties and the war room gave the state a "black eye."[19]

With pressure mounting, Engelstad and his media advisers decided to hold another news conference after which the war room would be opened to the media. A former Engelstad employee who viewed the war room the night before the news conference said relatively few Imperial Palace employees knew of its existence. "I decided to see the room," the ex-employee told the author in 1998. "When they opened that gate, I was astounded. I was floored. I thought, 'Oh my God.' I saw the [Axis] jeeps, the murals, the five-foot by five-foot swastikas on the wall, the shovels and daggers. I saw the mannequin of Hitler, but not the [Hitler and Engelstad] portraits. Instantly, I saw it as a PR disaster."

The war room, as it had appeared during the 1988 Hitler party and had been viewed by Gaming Control Board agents, had been changed. The portraits of Hitler and a uniformed Engelstad had been removed and destroyed. That night, more was done to tone down the room's impact, the former employee said. "They did a lot of camouflage. They painted over the swastikas the night before. They moved the [troop carrier] in front of a mural."

On October 6, 1988, Engelstad, appearing almost shaken, read a seven-page statement to members of the media and allowed them into the war room. In his statement, Engelstad again apologized, saying that Hitler's birthday was merely "a silly excuse" for the parties, which were "not only stupid, but insensitive." He then turned and left without answering questions from reporters.

The former Imperial Palace employee described Engelstad as a little nervous prior to the conference but remaining his reserved self. "He was a man who knew what he wanted," the former worker said. "He was, 'That's the way it's going to be. My way, or no way.' [But] I never heard him make any anti-Semitic remarks."

Engelstad also had published apologies in full-page newspaper advertisements in Las Vegas that appeared the next day. But his efforts fell flat as the local media feast on the war room and the Hitler parties continued. Some Jewish leaders rejected Engelstad's apology. Black community leaders asked that Engelstad disband the Nazi collection. Press accounts reported that Lonnie Hammargren, a prominent Las Vegas neurosurgeon and a member of the state university system's board of regents (who would be elected lieutenant governor of Nevada in 1994), admitted that he attended the 1986 party, which he said was in bad taste. Among attendees of the 1988 gathering, at Engelstad's invitation, was Flamingo Hilton president Horst Dziura, who said he left after only 15 minutes when he discovered the party's theme.[20]

Engelstad continued to try to rehabilitate himself. On October 8, 1988, a group of people from the University of North Dakota, Engelstad's alma mater, to which he donated $5 million for the new hockey arena named after him, came and toured the war room with Engelstad. One group member told the *Review-Journal,* "Well, this is Las Vegas and isn't it supposed to be the world capital of bad taste?"[21] On October 10, 1988, the Anti-Defamation League, a Jewish activist organization, announced it was sending a fact-finding delegation to Las Vegas to investigate alleged anti-Semitism by Engelstad.[22] United States Senator Chic Hecht (R-Nev.), a Jewish-American running for reelection against Governor Bryan, charged Bryan was "dragging his feet" in the Engelstad matter and should have had the man in the governor's office "the next morning."[23]

Also that day, Engelstad began publishing another series of full-page advertisements in the daily papers, this time with the printed signatures of dozens of Imperial Palace employees claiming to "accept his explanation and applaud his courage for his public apology. We're proud to work for him." Engelstad also wrote a letter to the Jewish Federation of Las Vegas offering a "heartfelt and sincere" apology for his "insensitivity."[24]

On October 11, 1988, the *Las Vegas Sun* reported that state gaming agents were investigating allegations that Engelstad and other hotel executives tried to suborn hotel employees to commit perjury in response to questions from law enforcement officers.[25] State Attorney General McKay also told the newspaper he was investigating whether the hotel owner and others violated state discrimination laws by setting up a special "code" to evaluate the physical appearance of prospective employees. The code allegedly included rating cocktail waitresses by their breast sizes. The newspaper also ran a story on its front page stating that an aide to Engelstad once expressed an interest in obtaining souvenirs from Nazi death camps. On October 12, 1988, the paper ran a story quoting Gaming Control Board chairman Michael Rumbolz confirming that the board was investigating allegations about death camp relics. The story also mentioned Engelstad had sent a letter to the Jewish Federation of Las Vegas, denying any such souvenirs were ever sought and stating that the *Sun* had "reached a new depth" in its reporting.

At another news conference at his hotel on October 12, Engelstad announced the war room had been cleared and the murals painted over. He said he would donate the war room's contents to the newly dedicated Holocaust Memorial Museum in Washington, D.C. But Holocaust museum officials later said they would accept only concentration camp–related artifacts, such as crafts made by internees, and turned down his offer.[26]

On October 13, 1988, about 30 representatives of the Jewish Defense League staged a protest on the sidewalk outside the Imperial Palace as hotel security and Las Vegas police officers watched. One member, using a loudspeaker atop a sound truck, drove by the hotel and denounced Engelstad as tourists walked by. League members insisted that Engelstad's gaming license be revoked. The league's regional director, Irv Rubin, described Engelstad as "a classic Nazi."

Earl Krugel, a Jewish Defense League member from Los Angeles, maintained that Engelstad "might say he's sorry, but we don't believe him. He's lionizing Hitler." Meanwhile, about two dozen members of a group called the Las Vegas Skinheads demonstrated in favor of Engelstad on the sidewalk outside the hotel. They held signs with the messages "Gaming Control or Jewish Control" and "Save Christians, Smash Jewish Control."

"They have their JDL [Jewish Defense League]," Case Colcord, a skinhead member, told the *Las Vegas Sun*.[27] "Why can't he have his collection? It's private. It's not open to the public."

Things got tense when the skinheads marched by in Nazi goosestep fashion and made the Nazi salute as the Jewish Defense League members looked on, but police succeeded in keeping the two groups separated, and no one was injured or arrested. Both protests were widely reported by the local print and television media.

On October 15, 1988, more full-page advertisements ran in Las Vegas newspapers supporting Engelstad, this time containing the names of about 90 local construction companies. Officials of some of the companies said afterward that either they did not realize what they had signed or people purporting to represent the companies submitted their signatures for the ads without authorization.

The following day, the Gaming Control Board requested the state attorney general's office prepare a complaint to discipline Engelstad, citing Regulation 5 and the alleged destruction of hotel documents in the Scanlon case.

News stories produced additional embarrassments. On October 19, 1988, the *Las Vegas Sun* reported that the board was investigating whether prostitutes were invited to a private party thrown at the Imperial Palace by Engelstad in May 1988.[28] The *Sun* also reported that 200 members of the San Diego chapter of Na'amat USA, a Jewish organization, had canceled plans to stay at the Imperial Palace amid reports of the war room and Hitler parties. Also in October 1988, an executive for the Jewish Anti-Defamation League in Minneapolis said that part of Engelstad's endowment to the University of North Dakota should be dedicated to studying the Nazi Holocaust and all kinds of bigotry.[29] In addition to *People* magazine, the Engelstad story made other national media outlets, compounding concerns in Nevada about how it would hurt the public's view of the state's gaming industry. The case was reported by Cable News Network and discussed for weeks on a radio talk show in Phoenix. On November 7, 1988, *Newsweek* magazine ran a quote from Engelstad in its Perspective column about the Hitler parties: "Every year I try to find excuses for get-togethers and I always try to give them a theme."[30]

On November 4, 1988, gaming agents interviewed Engelstad, who was accompanied by his attorney Dickerson. Six days later, on November 10, another demonstration took place outside the Imperial Palace, but this time there was some violence. Members of the Jewish community and armed forces veterans groups had gathered in protest when about 50 skinheads showed up. Several skinheads clashed with the demonstrators. One of the demonstrators, beaten by skinheads, suffered non-life-threatening injuries and was taken to a hospital. The skinhead group claimed to support Engelstad. However, Engelstad issued a statement the next day disassociating himself from them.[31]

On November 17, 1988, Cronin, the Scanlons' attorney, went to the state courthouse in Las Vegas and filed depositions by Arbury and two other Imperial Palace managers. The witnesses claimed that Engelstad and hotel general manager Crispell ordered the destruction of thousands of hotel security documents. Further, security department records in the office of the hotel's former chief of hotel security were destroyed, the managers testified. They also claimed Crispell allegedly told them that they would have to perjure themselves if the lawsuit made it to the courtroom.[32]

Cronin filed more depositions on November 28, 1988. A pair of employees of the hotel's personnel department stated that they disposed of hotel security and other records on orders from superiors.[33]

Finally, on December 8, 1988, the Gaming Control Board submitted its two-count complaint against Engelstad to the commission. The complaint asked that his gaming license be revoked and that he be fined $100,000 on each count. Engelstad's attorneys filed a 26-page response with the commission on December 28.[34] Dickerson alleged that the board's attempt to yank Engelstad's license violated Engelstad's constitutional and civil rights. The attorney requested a hearing before the commission so that he could offer a case against the complaint.

Mick Shindell, the former corporate security director of the Imperial Palace who was fired soon after his September 1988 suspension, filed suit against Engelstad and went on the attack. Shindell, in the October 24 *People* magazine article, charged that Engelstad engaged in "name calling and reviling of my Jewish faith." Other Jewish employees at the hotel claimed they were forced to come to the Hitler parties and cut the cake, according to the magazine story. One unnamed party guest was quoted as saying that Engelstad "wanted one Jew to cut the cake, but the person ducked out. Ralph ran around trying to find him."

Still other hotel workers claimed they were pressured to attend the parties. One of them was Joe Dickie, the former body shop manager of Engelstad's antique car collection who filed a wrongful termination suit against the Imperial Palace in federal court after he was fired in March 1988. Dickey told *People* that the Hitler parties featured large cakes "with Hitler's name on them. There was a lot of drinking and German marching ballads, too. It was outrageous, but people [employees] were afraid to blow the whistle on him. We were afraid we wouldn't get jobs elsewhere—that no one would believe us if we told them these things." Engelstad, Dickey stated, once related to him that "I ought to be building ovens up there instead of painting pictures." Engelstad, in the *People* story, denied making that statement. The hotel owner also stated he did not order the "Hitler Was Right" bumper stickers or the "Hitler European Tour" T-shirts. Further, he said he was not anti-Semitic. "I don't hate Jews," he told the magazine. "I think of all people the same way. —Poles, blacks, Orientals. It's the way people are inside that counts."

Bothered by news accounts, Engelstad had his attorneys on November 30, 1988, file a motion to seal the depositions in the Scanlon case and "to restrain council, parties and witnesses from discussing their testimony with members of the news media."[35]

By early 1989, closed-door negotiations among board and commission members and Engelstad's lawyers to settle the complaint were under way. State Attorney General McKay sent a letter to Engelstad attorney Dickerson containing a list of 17 witnesses the state intended to call to bolster its case for punishing Engelstad, including Engelstad himself, Shindell, Arbury, Cronin, Dickey, and 10 current or former managers and other employees of the Imperial Palace.[36]

Meanwhile, the Engelstad side decided to put outside pressure on the state. On February 6, 1989, his legal team filed suit against the board, claiming that its three members met on December 8, 1988, to discuss the board's complaint against the casino man without giving proper legal notice of it or holding a public meeting, as required by Nevada law. The suit asked for an award for attorneys' fees and other unspecified damages.[37]

The special hearing by the Gaming Commission on the board's complaint against Engelstad and the Imperial Palace was held the morning of February 24, 1989, inside the Las Vegas City Council chambers. The hearing, however, was much less eventful than audience members anticipated, given the notoriety of Engelstad's situation. Little did anyone but state gaming officials and Engelstad's lawyers know that a proposed settlement was about to be offered, following lengthy closed-door talks. The proposal, delivered prior to the special meeting and signed by both sides, asked the commission to dismiss the board's complaint, with Engelstad paying the second-largest monetary penalty ever levied on a Nevada gaming licensee.

Commission chairman John O'Reilly opened the proceeding. "The issues that we have before us this morning are perhaps some of the more controversial issues that the Gaming Commission is required to deal with," the chairman said.[38] O'Reilly then reported he had been provided only a few moments earlier with documents signed by Engelstad, Engelstad lawyers Dickerson and

Nitz, and board members Bill Bible (appointed in January 1989 to succeed Rumbolz), Dennis Amerine, and Cunningham. The document, titled "Stipulation for Dismissal with Prejudice of the Complaint for Disciplinary Action and Related Proposed Order," swiftly turned what the news media and others had seen as another chapter in the brewing Engelstad controversy to the beginning of the end. It also made the hearing seem preordained since news of the settlement, unlike many other aspects of the Engelstad saga, had not been released or leaked to news outlets.

With the surprise signed agreement in hand, O'Reilly said the commission's focus had shifted away from an evidentiary hearing and toward "consideration of the adoption of the stipulation and related order." He asked lawyers for Engelstad and the board to explain how they arrived at the stipulation.

Dickerson, the former Gaming Commission chairman who also served as district attorney for Clark County in Las Vegas from 1955 to 1959, spoke first. Using a forceful, argumentative tone, he said he intended to use affidavits and various other statements and exhibits to support Engelstad. Scott Scherer, deputy attorney general, then told the commission that the board had filed a statement of facts in response and "was happy to do so in that it feels . . . that this public document will give the public an overview of the facts uncovered in the board's investigation."

Under questioning by O'Reilly, who appeared well briefed on what had occurred in the settlement negotiations, Dickerson and Scherer agreed that the stipulation had been reached after what O'Reilly described as "numerous" consultations with their clients and "several weeks of rather, in fact, very extensive and serious negotiations relating to these various issues." Dickerson and Scherer also said they were ready to plead their cases to the commission if there had been no settlement.

CHAIRMAN O'REILLY: Do you and each of your respective clients believe that the settlement is in the best interests of your respective clients?

MR. DICKERSON: My client believes it's in his best interests, and I have to join in that.

MR. SCHERER: Yes, we believe that this is in the best interests of the Board and the Board in its capacity as an agency of the State of Nevada believes it is in the best interests of the State of Nevada.

CHAIRMAN O'REILLY: Do you and each of your respective clients believe this is a resolution that will enable the Commission and the community as a whole to put these issues in the form of issues that have been resolved and they're behind us so as we can proceed with other business?

MR. DICKERSON: That was the entire purpose of the extensive negotiations that were entered into.

MR. SCHERER: That's correct.

CHAIRMAN O'REILLY: Do you and your respective clients believe that
this settlement is in the best interests of the people of the State of
Nevada?

MR. DICKERSON: I certainly do, not only in the best interests of the State
of Nevada and the best interests of the industry and the best interests
of Ralph Engelstad.

MR. SCHERER: Yes, we do.[39]

O'Reilly then reviewed the nine stipulations in the settlement, which were
essentially conditions on Engelstad's license to continue to operate a casino in
Nevada. The first, O'Reilly said, was "a prohibition against throwing any parties that would be construed or could be construed as glorifying or otherwise
honoring Adolf Hitler, the Third Reich or Nazi Germany. It also restricts various printed material that would be reasonably construed to provide such a
conclusion."[40]

Other conditions listed by O'Reilly restricted Engelstad's display of certain
vehicles—the vehicles in question were not named—at his auto collection at
the Imperial Palace and defined the process of placing "additional" vehicles
there. Engelstad was required to acknowledge that the murals and other memorabilia in the war room found objectionable and offensive by state gaming
officials had been removed and that he was prohibited from creating a similar
room in the future. Further, the casino owner was required to place an additional sign inside his public auto collection—where Hitler's Mercedes-Benz
staff car and a swastika banner were displayed—disclaiming "of any purpose
to identify with or glorifying or honoring Hitler, the Third Reich or Nazi Germany, or which encourages anyone to draw those conclusions," O'Reilly said.
The settlement further laid out steps to be taken by the board in the event of
any future violations by Engelstad, who also agreed to pay up to $5,000 for any
future investigative costs.

O'Reilly mentioned that the commission, with no public announcement,
had visited the Imperial Palace the night before and viewed Engelstad's auto
collection. Referring to the Hitler staff car, O'Reilly noted that the display included an audio message and a brochure. The recorded message about the
Hitler car had been part of the public exhibit.

The commission further placed restrictions on the travel and display of any
vehicles relating to Hitler, the Third Reich, or Nazi Germany at the Imperial
Palace. Engelstad had admitted sending the Hitler staff car on trips for public
viewing. But Dickerson pointed out that the agreement did not prevent Engel-

stad "from acquiring in any manner not contrary to this stipulation additional vehicles and memorabilia for display in the museum here and before."

Scherer said the settlement restrained Engelstad from obtaining anything "that could reasonably be construed as glorifying Adolf Hitler, the Third Reich or Nazi Germany."[41]

Then came the fine and other monetary damages the board recommended against Engelstad: a total of $1.5 million. It was yet another surprise since the penalty had not only been levied, but part of it had actually been paid, even though the commission had yet to vote on the stipulation.

O'Reilly asked whether the first installment had been paid, and both Dickerson and Scherer said it had: $200,000, which was considered the fine. The remaining $1.3 million was regarded as compensatory damages to the state of Nevada. The payments on the damages would be collected over the next two years; $800,000 due on June 30, 1989; $250,000 on June 30, 1990; and $250,000 on June 30, 1991. At the time, the penalty was the next-highest fine and damage claim ever charged a Nevada gaming licensee, below only the $3.5 million imposed in 1984 on former Stardust hotel partners Sachs and Tobman, accused of failing to prevent the skimming of gaming proceeds.

The entire agreement, O'Reilly said, was the product of discussions "over the past several weeks" by Engelstad, his lawyers, Scherer, and the three Gaming Control Board members. O'Reilly related that since he was advised the Engelstad matter was about to be resolved by the stipulation, he wanted both sides to summarize the facts and evidence of their cases. That morning, copies of documentary evidence from both Dickerson and Scherer were provided to members of the commission but not to the media or the public.

Before allowing them to present their cases, O'Reilly went through the basic facts in counts 1 and 2 in the pleadings of the case with Dickerson and Scherer. Count 1 referred to things having to do with Hitler and the war room, while count 2 concerned allegations that Engelstad ordered destroyed documents relating to the Scanlon case.

CHAIRMAN O'REILLY: Let's begin with Count 1. One of the issues that I believe would be of concern to the commission is the issue of whether or not we're dealing with an individual or circumstances or facts that might be described as a radical view that would be using the gaming license as a [forum] or a platform to advocate certain radical or anti type views. In reviewing your summary, Mr. Scherer, I believe you have indicated in part that you recognize that Mr. Engelstad has said in public forums that he despises Hitler and everything he stands for, and to further clarify, that the issue as the Board perceives it is not that Mr. Engelstad was a Nazi or should be punished for Nazi or white supremacist or other beliefs, but rather for bad judgment, bad taste and the embarrassment and damage that he would have caused to the industry. Is that a fair statement generally?

MR. SCHERER: Yes, that is a fair statement.

CHAIRMAN O'REILLY: The document you filed, I believe you indicated that the Board accepts Mr. Engelstad's statement that he despises Hitler, everything he stood for, and clarified this case as not about Mr. Engelstad's beliefs; is that correct?

MR. SCHERER: That's correct. The case is about his conduct and not his beliefs.

CHAIRMAN O'REILLY: During the course of the board's investigation did they find any evidence or other involvement in Nazi and neo-Nazi or white supremacy groups?

MR. SCHERER: No, Mr. Chairman, the Board did not.

CHAIRMAN O'REILLY: The Board does believe, though, that it has significant evidence concerning lack of judgment and lack of regard for community standards that would be consistent and required of an individual who holds a privileged gaming license?

MR. SCHERER: That's correct.

CHAIRMAN O'REILLY: And that the action was such that he should have known it would reflect or tend to reflect discredit upon the State of Nevada and the gaming industry as a whole?

MR. SCHERER: That's correct.[42]

Under further questioning, Scherer said he was prepared to offer evidence of various Third Reich memorabilia owned by Engelstad and at one time delivered to the Imperial Palace, including portraits and mannequins. Scherer also said he knew of no other Nazi-related objects that, in O'Reilly's words, "generally are different than what's been referred to in the public discussion of these issues." O'Reilly also noted that "the impropriety of the April 20th parties" was mentioned in the statement. Finally, Scherer acknowledged that the statement, as described by the chairman, contained "discussion about the bumper sticker issues" and "discussion about the public knowledge of the United States and the world of this conduct and the difficulties it has created."

O'Reilly then turned to Dickerson. Engelstad, Dickerson agreed, had been a collector of "rare vintage and priceless vehicles" since about 1980, Third Reich and Hitler vehicles had been displayed at the Imperial Palace since then, and "there was a private room that was intended ultimately to be open to the public at some point in the future."[43]

Dickerson said that he was prepared to offer evidence that the purpose of the April 20, 1986, party at the Imperial Palace was to celebrate the completion by Engelstad's crew of a two-year restoration of the Mercedes G4 six-wheel command vehicle once used by Hitler. Similarly, the reason for the April 20, 1988, grouping was to congratulate the restoration crew "and to display to his employees and friends the addition of 19 vehicles to the collection for a total display of 30 vehicles of various descriptions," said O'Reilly, summarizing Dickerson's case during the hearing.

The 1988 gathering, described as a "private party," also was held to celebrate the addition of the Cross-Mafi half-track, a 20-man troop carrier, Dickerson told the commission. The vehicle, he went on to explain, "tows the 88 millimeter antiaircraft gun that requires 16 people for the purpose of its maintenance and operation, and this vehicle accommodated all those 16 people."

The surprises continued. Dickerson told O'Reilly that the Engelstad side could offer witnesses who would say the murals relating to Nazi Germany in the war room "were selected by the painter and not by Mr. Engelstad, from photographs of various books and that the other matters that decorated the room were simply memorabilia that had been collected by Mr. Engelstad and others associated with him through the years." Dickerson added that Imperial Palace executive Richie Clyne "assisted" in the selection of items in the war room, that hotel staffers helped choose the vehicles, and that the wall mural of a 1930s German Autobahn was meant to give the illusion that some of the cars on display had just come off the road.

The Hitler and Engelstad portraits, he added, "were absolutely, totally and completely appropriate to the display of the vehicles." The inscription "To Ralphie from Adolf, 1939" on the Hitler portrait was from a vehicle broker in Phoenix, Arizona, from whom Engelstad had purchased a rare Mercedes 770 K vehicle.

"As a joke and gift to Ralph, he had that portrait commissioned and sent to Ralph. The ludicrous conclusion that it was intended as anything but a joke is contained in the inscription 'To Ralphie from Adolf, 1939,' when Ralph was eight years old in 1939," Dickerson said.[44]

Similarly, Dickerson said the portrait of Engelstad's head on Hitler's body was painted by an employee of the Imperial Palace and given to the hotel operator "as a gift and as a joke to Ralph. She saw the Hitler portrait, and what she did is paint it in reverse and then paint Ralph's head at the top of it." The painting was exhibited only once, at the 1988 party, "and destroyed immediately thereafter," he said.

The Hitler "tour" T-shirt, Dickerson explained, came from Engelstad's auto auctioneer, who had seen them while at a fair in Los Angeles. The shirt "is obviously intended as the purpose of a ridicule," Dickerson said. Engelstad purchased the dagger and knife collection from an auction by the Internal Revenue Service in Albuquerque, New Mexico.

"If it was so improper, how come the federal government was involved?" Dickerson asked.

A German tapestry in Engelstad's war room had been a Christmas gift to Engelstad from his restoration crew, the lawyer said. Dickerson then insisted he was ready to offer testimony that the bumper sticker "Hitler Was Right" had actually started out as reading "Hitler Was Reich" and that when some of the stickers were printed "Hitler Was Right" at the Imperial Palace, Engelstad became upset and ordered them destroyed.

O'Reilly said that in the proposed settlement of the complaint, the two sides agreed that "the problems surrounding these issues" concerning the parties and the war room came to light only after an unnamed Imperial Palace employee was fired and filed suit against Engelstad, more than two years after the first party.

Deputy Attorney General Scherer testified that had there been a full hearing on Engelstad, the board was prepared to present witnesses who "would have refuted many of their explanations" and would have proved Engelstad acted improperly, regardless of the hotel man's political beliefs.

"In reviewing that matter," O'Reilly replied, "I think it is a fair summary to say that this would have been a contested proceeding without a lot of agreement on the facts as those would lead us to ultimate conclusions."

"I would say that is a gross understatement," Dickerson responded.

Scherer said that the underlying facts in count 1 "were admitted [by Dickerson] in answers. The dispute would have been over the characterization of those facts."

"The admission is that the [1986 and 1988] parties were held," Dickerson answered. He added that as part of the settlement, Engelstad also affirmed that the Axis powers memorabilia were displayed at the hotel.

O'Reilly, lapsing into lawyer-speak, said that the debate between the board and Engelstad on count 1 came down to what Engelstad actually intended by having the collection and the Hitler parties. "The parties were held," he said. "Much of the memorabilia was actually displayed. . . . The question seems to get down to arguably whether the intent is relevant or not and the perception that it resulted in has provoked perhaps the perception that it should have resulted in. Those perhaps would be your different respective positions."

Both Dickerson and Scherer answered, "Correct."

The commission chairman then moved onto count 2—whether Engelstad took part, as was charged in the Scanlon suit, in the destruction of documents relevant to that case. O'Reilly, seeming to downplay the serious allegation, said that the Scanlon case merely referred to memos and reports related to the administration of security, specifically regarding hotel guests, at the Imperial Palace but "not any gaming records or any gaming financial records, other matters that would be construed as being required by the accounting regulations or other Gaming Commission regulations."[45]

Both Dickerson and Scherer said they were ready to present depositions from people involved in the Scanlon case, as well as interviews with yet other witnesses, to bolster their sides. Scherer said his witnesses would have testified that selected records had been destroyed and that some witnesses would have said they were ordered to destroy evidentiary documents under Engelstad's orders. Others would have said that the general manager of the Imperial Palace had told them that Engelstad had ordered the records destroyed. The witnesses claimed that Engelstad, Scherer said, "took a personal hand in every decision that was made" on the hotel property and so should have known about the missing records.

But Dickerson claimed his witnesses would say the opposite, that neither Engelstad nor any Imperial Palace executive or officer ever made such an order. Further, he said he was prepared to offer the results of a polygraph examination Engelstad underwent voluntarily and had passed after denying the allegations he authorized or ordered destroyed records relating to the Scanlon suit. Engelstad took the test without the knowledge of his attorneys and signed a waiver permitting the results to be released to the Gaming Control Board, Dickerson said.

Scherer answered that the results of polygraph tests are unreliable and "on the basis of the common rule of evidence [are] not admissible in contested proceedings." He said he would have argued against admitting them as evidence in count 2.

Dickerson said he also was prepared to show evidence of Engelstad's good character, his right to privacy, displays of goodwill to the community, and a 1986 letter from former Gaming Control Board chairman Bart Jacka commending Engelstad's conduct as a gaming licensee and businessman in the years prior to the war room controversy. The commission, in reaching a decision, should have considered all these things, the lawyer said.

Part of Jacka's letter, entered into the commission's record, read, "Ralph, you are to be congratulated for the operation. You're one of the few that we don't have headaches with. We appreciate that."[46]

Dickerson then listed evidence of various good deeds by the casino owner, including donations for church and children's welfare groups, families of deceased police officers, soccer teams, funeral and surgery expenses, and senior citizen parties. He offered to provide statistics showing that the Imperial Palace employed a higher proportion of people of ethnic minority groups than the gaming industry as a whole.

"The purpose of which, of course, is to show if this man is so bigoted, why would his employment record be what it is?" Dickerson asked.

"I believe you also indicate in that regard," O'Reilly said, "that not only does he employ many people who are Jewish, but one of the individuals who was involved in a middle management position was in fact Jewish, his mother was employed, and still is employed and other relatives have been and are employed."

"That is right," Dickerson said.[47]

All the documentation favorable to Engelstad that was entered into the record was "for the interest of not only the commission but for anybody else who is interested in assuring themselves that if this stipulation is resolved, this matter is hopefully to be considered all behind us," O'Reilly said.

Scherer explained why the board approved the stipulation that settled the complaint. The agreement placed nine conditions on the Imperial Palace's casino license "to insure that [Engelstad and his wife as co-owner] never again engage in conduct that could reasonably be construed as glorifying Adolf Hitler, the Third Reich or Nazi Germany" and included the $1.5 million fine. As part of the pact, Engelstad and his wife also agreed to "express their sincere regret for any damage done to the reputation of the State of Nevada and its gaming industry and for any offense taken by any individuals or groups as a result of their conduct."

The Gaming Control Board's objective was to punish the Imperial Palace for "engaging in unsuitable methods of operation and to prevent such conduct in the future," and the members believed that the conditions and fine accomplished that, Scherer said.

"Through this disciplinary action the board had clearly demonstrated that it condemns and will not condone any conduct by Mr. Engelstad or any other licensee that discredits the State of Nevada and its gaming industry," Scherer said. He added that "swift and sure disciplinary action" would ensue if Engelstad were to violate any of the conditions. The board, he said, also retained the right to impose other sanctions on Engelstad if allegations of destruction of evidence were found to be true later in court.

Scherer added that while some observers might think that the penalties were too lenient or too harsh and that others might believe the state had intruded on Engelstad's private life, the board felt that the agreement was "an appropriate measured response to the misconduct that while very serious and offensive, is in this licensee's first disciplinary action not sufficient to justify revocation [of his license] and the attendant disruption of the lives of more than 2,000 employees."

"Gaming in Nevada is a privileged industry," Scherer continued. "The board expects the holders of that privilege to exhibit sound judgment and a

healthy regard for the law and community standards. In this case, Mr. Engelstad's conduct exhibited a severe lack of judgment and the regard for community standards expected of gaming licensees. His conduct by his own admission showed, quote very bad judgment and very bad taste, close quote. That
very bad judgment and very bad taste damaged the reputation of the State of
Nevada and its gaming industry."

Scherer concluded by saying that the Engelstad case set a precedent and a
message "to Nevada's gaming licensees, to the rest of the country, and to the
world. The board cares about Nevada's image and will not hesitate to take future disciplinary action against these or other licensees whose conduct lacks
the sound judgment and regard for law and community standards expected
from those to whom the state has granted the privilege of engaging in licensed
gaming." [48]

In response, Dickerson said the Engelstad case raised issues of free speech
and right to privacy. The Hitler parties were held in private by invitation only
and only to honor the restoration crew, he said. They took place in a "secret
room" so that news of the rare World War II collection would not become public and "accelerate the price of additional vehicles that still remain out there,"
he said. News of the parties was leaked to the press by a disgruntled former
Imperial Palace employee after the individual had filed suit against the casino,
he added.

In a somewhat convoluted way, Dickerson then asked how the commission
could "accept what was just stated as conduct on the part of Mr. Engelstad
when the dissemination of this news was not the result of what he did but
rather the result of what was done by a discharged employee and his communication to the press, the press taking that connotation to be placed upon both
the example of the collection, the room and the parties? And it was not, in my
opinion, a report of news, but rather, the making of news." [49]

Engelstad, Dickerson said, concluded that it was not in the best interests of
the state to "go through a protracted hearing here in which there would be, of
course, considerable dissemination of additional news." The casino owner
also decided that it would be too costly and too time consuming for the case to
go through the courts.

"Ralph had to make a pragmatic decision, a judgment, a businessman's decision," the lawyer said. "Cut your losses. Go forward. Put this behind the state
of Nevada. Put this behind me. Put this behind all in the industry. Let us now
go forward."

Scherer, in a brief rebuttal, said that even if Engelstad intended to keep the
parties private, he showed poor judgment in whom he chose to invite and
should have known that of the 100 people at each party "someone was going
to blow the whistle on him." In addition, Scherer maintained that many man-

agers and other employees still working at the Imperial Palace were told "that this was a party for Hitler" and that there was no announcement the restoration workers would be recognized.

O'Reilly finally turned the proposed settlement over to the commission and asked someone to make a motion to accept it. The other commissioners were skeptical about it. Commissioner Ken Gragson said, "This entire thing had kind of been blown out of proportion . . . by a disgruntled employee." Although Engelstad and the casino showed "bad judgment and poor taste" regarding the parties, bumper stickers, and T-shirts, the war room was there to show off the collection and not to memorialize or glorify Hitler, Gragson said. However, he offered a motion to accept the settlement in the best interests of the state and the gaming industry.[50]

O'Reilly, who clearly favored the settlement, immediately asked for a roll call. The vote was 4 to 1 in favor, with Commissioner Bob Lewis opposed. Commissioner Betty Vogler indicated that she thought the settlement might be "too harsh" and asked O'Reilly whether they could deliberate on separate aspects of it. O'Reilly replied that the agreement was the result of lengthy discussions and would be difficult to renegotiate. To pick it apart would "involve disturbing a delicate balance that has been created," he said.

Lewis said he voted no because "I cannot in good conscience allow myself to cast a vote in favor of fining a licensee in the magnitude of a million-and-a-half and then go about our business."

Gragson said he agreed with Lewis. Commissioner Bob Peccole expressed reservations about the settlement even though he voted for it. Peccole said he agreed with Lewis that the fine was excessive. The 1983 Stardust skimming case drew the largest fine ever imposed by the commission, and the Engelstad matter "never came close to a skimming case, ever," Peccole said. The Engelstad controversy "comes down to, in my mind, a situation where the right to free speech . . . overbalanced any reputation that the state may have impaired in any way, " Peccole said. In the second count of the complaint, Peccole maintained that the records allegedly destroyed "were not even gaming records, and I question in my own mind whether or not we had jurisdiction in a matter like that."[51]

To O'Reilly, it was realistic to settle. Many people in the state were dependent on the health of the gaming industry, and it was time "to get on about the business life of Nevada . . . but hopefully we will be able to learn from this experience that perhaps what we think we heard or we think we saw may not have been what was said. I hope that we can realize that judgments that we're sometimes prone to make about individuals without all the facts are perhaps unjustified."

Before adjourning the hearing, the chairman said he did not want people to think that the commission was attempting to halt public comment. The commission record on the Engelstad case would remain open for additional letters from the public for 60 days, he said. But O'Reilly made it clear the commission wanted to put an end to the damage the controversy had inflicted on the state. "I would also indicate to you," he said, "that the issues that we are dealing with here charge the emotions of many, many people, and I do not feel that it's appropriate to begin what could become a day long, week long, a month long process of public commentary on these issues."

With that, the commission washed its hands of the Engelstad predicament. Engelstad himself left the hearing room without comment but later in the day issued a statement, saying that the fine was "excessive" and that he agreed to it only because it was "in the best interest" of the state and the gaming industry.

Also that day, Gaming Control Board chairman Bill Bible released copies of letters he sent to the chairmen of two state legislative committees, asking that the $1.5 million assessed Engelstad be used to fund a Holocaust study program for students in Nevada schools. "The board thinks that it is only appropriate that these monies be used to educate Nevada's school children in events that represent the blackest chapter in mankind's history," Bible wrote.[52]

Governor Miller spoke for most politicians and captains of the casino industry when he told the *Review-Journal* he was glad the "unfortunate" situation had been resolved without a hearing.[53] Miller added he hoped some of the money Engelstad paid would be used to fund Holocaust studies. But Rabbi Mel Hecht, a prominent spokesman for Las Vegas's Jewish community, told the newspaper the state did not punish Engelstad enough. "The message has been sent out that if you have money in this town, you can buy your way out of trouble," Hecht said. "Other people have been hurt by the actions of Mr. Engelstad."[54]

Engelstad disbanded his war room collection and had the murals in the room painted over. Under orders by gaming officials, he placed a disclaimer in front of the Hitler staff car in his public auto collection.

Meanwhile, the success story continued at the Imperial Palace, which seemed little affected by the scandal. In December 1989, Engelstad agreed to out-of-court settlements with Shindell, Arbury, the Imperial Palace's former chief of uniformed security Ed Steffen, and ex–hotel personnel manager Maria Chassey, each of whom agreed to drop their wrongful-termination suits.[55] He also succeeded in convincing the court to seal the depositions taken during the case.

For Engelstad, success continued in the years following the controversy. In 1994, he reported his casino business had a cash flow of $50 million a year. At one point in the mid-1990s, his holdings included 4 million square feet of property, much of it in Texas. Among the perks of his success were two Boeing 727s, complete with living rooms, showers, bars, and beds. By the late 1990s, the increasingly reclusive and media-shy Engelstad was still among America's richest men. From 1994 to 1996, Engelstad made the *Forbes* magazine list of the 400 wealthiest, with holdings in 1996 estimated at $425 million and no debt. *Forbes* reported that his now 250-vehicle auto collection was the third largest in the country and included 43 Duesenbergs. He fell off the *Forbes* list in 1997, something the magazine attributed to the slumping gaming industry. But the Imperial Palace remained the largest privately owned hotel-casino in Las Vegas. Engelstad's financial and logistical support helped open the Las Vegas Motor Speedway, a major auto racetrack featuring NASCAR and other events, just north of Las Vegas, in 1996. And despite the influence of the Las Vegas–based Culinary Union Local 226, a powerful labor organization that had organized 40 Las Vegas hotels by the late 1990s, Engelstad's Imperial Palace hotel workers remained nonunion.

But his past remained a problem. In 1994, Engelstad requested approval from Mississippi state gaming authorities to open a $110 million docked riverboat casino, hotel, and movie theater complex in the southern coast resort town of Biloxi. *Forbes* magazine and the news media in Mississippi made hay of the Hitler parties and the $1.5 million penalty. Engelstad was "Lying low since [the fine], refuses most interviews," *Forbes* wrote in 1996. In late 1997, following squabbles with local officials and frustrating delays in construction, Engelstad opened his riverboat casino complex in Biloxi. But by mid-1998, Engelstad, at 67 years old, decided it was time to get out of the demanding gaming business and offered his private gaming company up for sale.

More than a decade after it broke, the Engelstad scandal still provokes strong opinion. "Ralph was always a target because he was an influential person," said lawyer and Engelstad friend Owen Nitz in 1998. "If there is something unusual about someone, people want to read about it. The public really likes gossip. And Ralph is absolutely not anti-Semitic. He has done business with people of the Jewish faith and people of many faiths. Business is business, and that's the end of that. He didn't realize that some people would take such an offense at such a tongue-in-cheek thing [as the Hitler parties]. He learned it later. His regrets were sincere." [56]

Robert Peccole, who left the commission soon after the hearing and worked for Engelstad briefly before turning to developing Las Vegas real estate in the 1990s, said that he still believed it was wrong to fine Engelstad. Besides, Peccole said, the scandal had "absolutely no effect" on the local gaming industry. "I think that a lot of pressure was brought to bear by the community, especially the Jewish community," Peccole said. "Regulation 5 was used as a major catch-all. If you didn't have a valid case, you use the shotgun approach. We went in and saw the [war] room. It was a spoof, not open to the public. It was a joke. At the time, we [the commission] didn't see it as embarrassing. But there were certain groups that said it was out of line."[57]

To former Gaming Control Board member Gerald Cunningham, the financial punishment was more appropriate than revoking Engelstad's license. "If a fine corrects the action, and we leave everything else intact, I would say the outcome and the sanction we imposed was perfect," he told the author in 1996. "What you're only trying to do in disciplinary actions generally—unless it's so grievous that it's unacceptable no matter what happens—is to correct the attitude. You're trying to impose a sanction great enough so that people remember it and won't repeat it. And I think that's what we were doing [with Engelstad]."

"There was a great deal of outcry over that, especially from the Jewish community," Cunningham added. "They wanted his license revoked. There were several thousand people's jobs at stake. It was a very serious situation. Mr. Engelstad runs a very profitable business. It's good, actually, for the economy. But he had done something which we felt was wrong and we felt he needed to be sanctioned in some way that was proportionate to the seriousness of what he had done."[58]

Chapter Three

Who's Minding the Casino Cage?
Joe Slyman and Regulation 6A

The Royal Nevada Hotel opened near the Las Vegas Strip in 1955, the same year as the better-known Riviera and Dunes hotel-casinos. It was the peak of the first wave of Las Vegas Strip casinos that began with the completion of the Flamingo in 1946. But the Royal, on Convention Center Drive about a half block east of Las Vegas Boulevard, never amounted to much and became what could fairly be called a jinxed property. The small casino quickly earned the distinction of being the first on the Strip to lose its bankroll and close down— bankrupted the same year it opened. In 1960, the Royal was acquired by the Dalitz Desert Inn Group, a list of investors headed by one-time Cleveland mob associate Moe Dalitz, who also owned the Stardust on the Strip. In the early 1960s, the Royal was converted into an auditorium, where the Reverend Richard Anthony Crowley, once a nationally famous evangelist, conducted 4:30 A.M. services for a few years.[1]

Always on the fringe of the action on the Strip, the Royal got a new lease on life in 1977, when Joseph G. Slyman, formerly of Cleveland, decided to make a go of the unsuccessful gambling hall. The state granted Slyman an unlimited gaming license, and he became, at the tender age of 27, the casino's new owner. Slyman, however, lacked money to make major improvements. Despite its proximity to the popular Strip, the Royal was a no-frills gaming business without the space and foot traffic of its celebrated neighbors. By 1982, the casino operation consisted of only 75 slot machines and a dozen table games. Slyman oversaw the gaming, and his general manager, Paul R. Dottore, handled food and beverage. The casino was in the lobby of the Royal Americana Hotel, operated by a separate owner.

But more was going on than met the eye at the Royal Casino, according to law enforcement officers from three separate federal agencies. During an undercover investigation from 1982 to 1983, federal agents alleged that hundreds of thousands and perhaps millions of dollars had been laundered through the Royal's petite casino cage from offshore bank accounts by drug traffickers and other professional criminals.[2] Slyman and Dottore would soon face federal fraud charges.

The federal investigation of the Royal came as other U.S. government authorities uncovered an even bigger caper in Las Vegas, one that would draw national attention. In October 1983, Chicago organized crime chiefs Joey Aiuppa, Jackie Cerone, and 13 others were indicted by a federal grand jury in Kansas City in connection with a mob-run skimming operation that took place in 1982 at the Stardust Hotel on the Strip, just a block west of the Royal. In December 1983, the Nevada State Gaming Control Board reported finding 222 gaming code violations at the Stardust from January to November 1982, when the Stardust passed fake fill slips—used to account for casino chips delivered to gaming tables—to hide $1.5 million from taxation.[3] The fill slips taken to the Stardust's tables made it appear as if the casino had lost money to gamblers when the cash was actually removed from the casino cage by the conspirators.

The casino scandals set the feds into action on the legalized gaming industry. In 1985, as Slyman and Dottore stood trial in federal court on tax fraud charges related to cash transactions at the Royal, the U.S. Treasury Department decided to broaden the scope of the 1970 federal Bank Secrecy Act—part of the department's Title 31 regulations—to include casinos.[4] The new rules would require casinos, then only in Nevada and New Jersey, to follow the same cash disclosure rules as banks, reporting to Washington the names of all individuals who exchanged more than $10,000 at the businesses. The rules were enacted specifically to prevent money laundering in casinos.

In Nevada, casino operators feared the stringent new reporting requirements would offend and discourage high-stakes gamblers who enjoyed privacy and did not want their names sent to the U.S. government. Nevada's congressional representatives, state officials, and casino industry worked together to convince the federal government to make Nevada the only state exempted from the more than $10,000 disclosure requirement. To obtain the exemption, federal officials required the Nevada Gaming Commission to approve cash-reporting rules as strict or more strict than federal banking regulations in the Bank Secrecy Act.[5] Nevada did it, in May 1985, by enacting state gaming Regulation 6A, its own anti-money-laundering statute.[6]

Regulation 6A mandated new cash-reporting and bookkeeping procedures. To satisfy federal authorities, Regulation 6A required that casinos file a "Cash Transaction Report" (CTR) with the Gaming Control Board each time a customer exchanged more than $10,000. The name of the customer had to appear in the report. The state regulation also required that whenever a casino received $2,500 or more in cash from a patron, the casino had to give it back in the same bill denominations (such as $100 bills for $100 bills) when the patron wanted the money returned or else be deemed guilty of a "prohibited transaction."[7] Gamblers who cashed in chips totaling more than $10,000 at gaming tables were not required to sign a cash transaction report as long as the casinos could prove the chips were from winnings and not a bid to launder money. Regulation 6A also required casinos to file a "Cash Transaction Incident Report" each time a gambler cashed in $3,000 or more to make sure multiple transactions did not exceed $10,000. The casinos, however, could choose to write down only a physical description, not the name, of the gambler on the incident form.

Some casino operators complained bitterly about the increased expense and paperwork wrought by the new state rules. But Regulation 6A and the exemption deal with the U.S. government at least helped Nevada hold off additional federal scrutiny of casino operations. The state had spared its premiere industry a lot of grief, and only a few years after federal officials had determined that major money launderers were having their way with casinos in Las Vegas. According to federal authorities, one of them was the Royal Casino.

As early as 1980, the Gaming Control Board discovered bookkeeping problems at the Royal, problems that owner Slyman had pledged to correct. But the Royal was apparently seen by some state officials in almost sentimental terms as one of the last small, individually owned casinos in Las Vegas. The board and the commission continually bent over backward to save the Royal from itself. By the late 1980s, however, with Regulation 6A firmly in place, the casino and owner Slyman would become a royal headache for Nevada gaming regulators. Gaming agents watched Slyman's casino closely and carefully logged dozens of alleged Regulation 6A violations from 1986 to 1988. The Royal was perhaps the worst-ever violator of Regulation 6A. And pressure to keep the troubled casino in line was mounting. In 1988, as the board and the commission held hearings on the Royal's violations, the Treasury Department and the IRS were considering imposing new and more extensive cash-reporting requirements on casinos.[8]

The federal investigation that would eventually include Slyman, Dottore, and the Royal Casino began on May 20, 1982, when undercover agents from the Drug Enforcement Agency (DEA), the IRS's Criminal Division, and the FBI met with two men, Charles W. Broun, Jr., and Jack M. Dubard in Sarasota, Florida.[9] The agents masqueraded as members of a Chicago-based cocaine smuggling ring, attempting to organize a money-laundering scheme with the DEA agent posing as a cocaine trafficker. In a statement filed in federal court in Tampa, Florida, on March 9, 1983, the agents alleged that during the sting operation, Broun and Dubard admitted to being "professional money launderers" who had provided their financial services to drug smugglers in the past. Broun and Dubard offered to arrange to launder the proceeds of illegal drug sales in the United States "and claimed to have personally perfected a method of smuggling cash on board commercial airlines to fly to off-shore islands," the government agents said.[10]

The laundering operation involved the use of a variety of international trusts, corporations, and bank accounts where the drug money could be deposited and disguised as nontaxable, offshore loans. The men offered to sell the agents a "Luxembourg Trust" that would administer assets owned by a "Panamanian Corporation" that maintained a bank account in the Cayman Islands, a British-run country in the Caribbean Sea northwest of Jamaica. After smuggling the agents' narcotics sales money from the United States to the Cayman bank account, Broun and Dubard said they would convert the funds into nontaxable loans to themselves. The loans would then be transferred into the accounts of phony U.S. corporations or into assets that would be controlled by the undercover agents.

Broun informed the agents that "for several years he has been exchanging small denomination 'street bills' into $100 bills for narcotics traffickers at several Las Vegas casinos and will provide the undercover agents with introductions to the casino owners/managers who launder money." [11] The U.S. agents said Broun claimed to have previously laundered $4 million worth of drug money through the Las Vegas casinos and that the exchange of cash was done "with the knowledge and consent of the owners and managers of [the] several casinos." The casino owners and managers, Broun explained, "assisted him by intentionally falsifying official casino records to prevent the government from detecting the large cash transactions. The casino owners/ managers are fully aware of the fact that they are laundering illegal profits and assisting drug dealers to anonymously maintain casino accounts. Additionally, Broun's casino sources afford Broun's customers anonymity by recording their transactions in phony names. In return for anonymously exchanging large amounts of currency, Broun's Las Vegas sources charge a four percent fee, and Broun and Dubard charge an additional two percent fee on all amounts exchanged." [12]

Broun, Dubard, and the agents met a second time the same day at a financial services company in Sarasota, where Broun and Dubard showed them records of previous money-laundering transactions with clients. A deal was about to be struck. On September 21, 1982, the agents had another rendezvous with their two targets. Broun and Dubard promised to exchange $100,000 in street bills for $100 bills at the Royal Casino in Las Vegas for the agents. They said the agents would be dealing directly with Slyman, described as the sole owner of the Royal.

"The man [Slyman] says if we can get there Thursday before banking hours are over, that we can be out of there Friday before banking hours are . . . over with, the deal done," the agents quoted Broun as saying. "And you can see, as the finance man, you can do whatever you see fit with the hundreds but your money will be in hundreds, with no hitches and no observation by anybody."

To reassure the agents, Broun said that Slyman himself would perform the transaction from the Royal's casino cage and "alert them if authorities were snooping about trying to secure information on the undercover agents' activities at the Royal Casino. Broun said, 'That's part of the reason for doing business with the damn owner. At the first ripple, if there was the first ripple, we would know it.'"

Broun told the agents that if he were caught with the $100,000 on the way to the casino, he would say he was going to a real estate closing where the seller wanted to be paid in cash. Broun and Dubard then said they required an "introduction fee" of $15,000 for the laundering, plus a recurring fee of 2 percent of the money exchanged at the casinos. No other casinos in Las Vegas or elsewhere were mentioned in the case aside from the Royal.

On September 23, 1982, the agents met with Broun and Dubard and showed them $100,000 in small-denomination street bills. The two men told them to place the currency into airline carry-on bags to escape detection from airport screening devices. Broun, Dubard, and the undercover IRS agent then flew from Florida to Las Vegas, where they met the DEA agent and went to exchange the money at the Royal. When the four men met with Slyman and Dottore, Slyman told them that "he has been very successful in helping his friends hide money from the IRS," government investigators stated. Slyman described a scheme to exchange the agents' money at the casino "without detection from the IRS, the Nevada Gaming Commission, or any other agency." The $100,000 would be laundered at the casino cage, and the agents would receive a receipt bearing a bogus name, "Robert Mender." Slyman explained that if government authorities ever asked him about it, he would respond, "Who is Robert Mender?" He told the undercover agents he wanted a commission of 4 percent of the money exchanged. Agreeing to the terms, the agents handed Dottore an envelope with the $100,000 in small bills and another envelope with the 4 percent commission. Dottore gave one of the agents a receipt with the name "Robert Mender."

The undercover agents informed Slyman of their intention to open offshore bank accounts where money would be deposited and sent back in phony loans to the United States and that the money was unreported illegal income. Slyman then complained that the commission payment he received was only $3,500 instead of $4,000 but that he would not make an issue of it. He told the agents to give him as much advance notice as possible about future currency transactions "because he is handling cash for a lot of other people who are also hiding their money from the government."[13]

The following day, September 24, 1982, Dottore met with the undercover IRS agent and repeated the complaint about the $500 owed Slyman. Dottore also said he knew Slyman intended to destroy deposit and withdrawal receipts involved in the "Robert Mender" transaction. Slyman met the same agent later in the day at Slyman's office at the Royal. Slyman gave the agent $100,000 in $100 bills and destroyed the receipts bearing the name "Robert Mender."

That transaction over, the agents sought to arrange another one at the Royal. On October 4, 1982, the undercover IRS agent phoned Dottore to say he would be back at the Royal on October 6 to exchange another $100,000 in small bills. Dottore promised to reserve hotel rooms under the name "Robert Mender" and set up another trade for $100 bills on October 7.

Meanwhile, back in Sarasota, Broun and Dubard, still unaware of the government sting, told the IRS agent on October 5, 1982, how they had repeatedly smuggled cash out of the United States on airplanes to the Caymans. They told the undercover agent that for $10,000 he could buy a corporation in the Netherlands Antilles islands in the Caribbean to use to launder cash back to the United States. The men claimed to have done the same for other clients without detection by government officials. They then set up a meeting with another man, Bruce J. Perlowin, a California-based marijuana trafficker who owned two Luxembourg trusts started by Broun and Dubard used to launder illegal drug profits through offshore loans. Broun, Dubard, and Perlowin offered to sell the trusts to the agent for $10,000 each. Perlowin remarked that he found the Royal and other Las Vegas casinos "to be tremendously helpful in handling cash generated from his narcotics business." Perlowin said he used the casinos to launder "large volumes" of $20 bills for $100 bills and as his "operations bank."

A few weeks later, the IRS agent learned from Broun that Perlowin had successfully hidden from taxation $16 million in illegal drug money he earned in 1980 alone. Meeting with Perlowin in early November in San Francisco, the IRS, DEA, and FBI agents gave him $10,000 for one of the Luxembourg trusts. While counting the $10,000, Perlowin told the agents he had "exchanged millions of dollars in $20 bills for $100 bills at the Royal Casino with the assistance of Joe Slyman" during numerous visits to the casino.[14]

In late November 1982, the DEA agent boarded an airplane bound for the Caymans with Broun so the agent could purchase Broun's business account in a bank there. Broun told the agent to bring $4,900 in $1 bills for Broun to carry as a "test run" to see if it got through customs. Broun knew the $4,900 was below the $5,000 limit the U.S. government set on transporting currency outside the country, so they could proceed if discovered. Broun said that if the $1 bills got through, then $490,000 in $100 bills could as well. The ploy worked, as both men made it to the Caymans without being asked about the cash Broun carried. The two went to the Washington International Bank & Trust on the islands, talked to two bank officials, and set up the offshore account with the $4,900. Broun told the bank officials the agent would deposit about $500,000 later. The bank's treasurer mentioned that Broun had made half-million-dollar deposits there "many, many times." The federal agent and Broun then left the bank and immediately flew back to the United States.

When the U.S. agents finally decided to put an end to the sting, the alleged money-laundering conspiracy involving Slyman, Dottore, Broun, Dubard, and Perlowin had exchanged $390,000 through the Royal. The group had also planned to send another $500,000 through the Royal for the agents within a few weeks.[15]

Slyman and Dottore were indicted by a federal grand jury in Florida in 1983 along with Broun, Dubard, and Perlowin. Slyman and Dottore, however, were named in only one charge in the four-count indictment. They were accused with the other three defendants of conspiring to commit income tax fraud in connection with the alleged laundering scheme, involving the exchange of "small denomination bills for $100 bills" at the Royal.[16] Broun, Dubard, and Perlowin were also charged with conspiring to conceal Perlowin's millions in marijuana trafficking profits in the Caymans, conspiring to sell illegal drugs, and dealing in excess of 1,000 pounds of marijuana.

Broun, Dubard, and Perlowin entered guilty pleas in the case. Slyman and Dottore pleaded not guilty. But lawyers for Slyman and Dottore convinced the federal judge in Florida to try their clients separately from the others, arguing that the two Royal men were not involved in the alleged drug conspiracy. In November 1983, the attorneys also succeeded in getting the trial for Slyman and Dottore transferred to federal court in Las Vegas.

The eight-day jury trial in Las Vegas ended on September 27, 1984, with a not-guilty verdict for Slyman and Dottore. Jurors who were questioned by the media afterward said the federal prosecutor sent from Florida simply failed to prove the government's case.[17] Oscar Goodman, Slyman's lawyer, said that Slyman and Dottore did nothing wrong in exchanging the small bills for the $100s and that the Florida prosecutors "don't understand how Nevada works. Money exchanging is not a crime."[18]

Soon afterward, Dottore resigned from the Royal. Dottore had already given up his gaming license rather than face a 10-count complaint filed by the Gaming Control Board against him and Slyman almost a year earlier, in August 1983. The complaint said the two conspired to commit tax fraud by laundering money at the Royal, as laid out in the federal criminal case. The complaint also said that Slyman did not notify the state that he had loaned the Royal money 14 times from 1982 to 1983 to keep it afloat and that he had appointed his wife, Marcia, secretary-treasurer of the Royal's casino parent company.[19] However, the Gaming Commission allowed Slyman to own the casino and operate an office there, with a one-year limited gaming license, during which he was not allowed to directly manage the casino, which would be monitored by board agents.

Gaming officials, however, said they would have closed the casino if he were convicted on the federal charge.[20] After the trial, Slyman held onto the casino with the limited license, hoping to somehow convince the state to grant him a permanent license. In 1985, the same year the state adopted Regulation 6A, the commission fined him $30,000 but still allowed him to remain owner for another year. The board required him to keep a minimum bankroll to pay gamblers and prohibited him from doing business with so-called unsavory individuals.

Then, in April 1986, the board lodged another 10-count complaint against the Royal, claiming casino operators violated the new Regulation 6A requirements relating to cash transactions. The board and the commission spent a year with Slyman trying to work out his problems without forcing the casino to close and put his 100 employees out of work. One concern the board had was that Slyman allowed gamblers to use aliases in filling out casino paperwork. The board voted 2 to 1 to recommend that Slyman receive a one-year limited license and another chance to correct his problems. When it expired in April 1987, the commission granted Slyman another one-year limited license and yet again ordered him to correct money-handling violations. Slyman pledged that he would. The board, meanwhile, continued to closely observe how money was processed at the Royal's table games, count rooms, and casino cage, at times sending agents to work undercover at the casino.

In 1988, after more than five years of negotiations with gaming officials, Slyman was still intent on arguing his case for an unlimited, nonrestricted gaming license to own and operate the Royal. But evidence of new gaming regulation violations looked devastating. The board's yearlong investigation had produced 37 separate concerns, covering scores of alleged violations related to cash handling and loans at the Royal, including virtually the same missteps listed in the 1986 board complaint that the commission ordered Slyman to correct in April 1987.

By the summer of 1988, Slyman had filed for protection under Chapter 11 of the U.S. Bankruptcy Code from $3 million the Royal owed to creditors. He was also operating under the one-year limited license. From the spring to the summer of 1988, the commission had agreed to extend his license month by month after hearing his pleas for more time to get his casino out of bankruptcy and comply with state regulations.

In August 1988, the board was ready to start hearings into Slyman's application for an unlimited gaming license as 100 percent owner of the Royal. The board's chairman was Michael Rumbolz, and the board members were Dennis Amerine and Gerald Cunningham. In April 1987, it was Amerine, former chief of the board's Audit Division, who voted against the limited license for Slyman, with Rumbolz and then-chairman Bart Jacka voting in favor. Tensions were high during the three drawn-out hearings that would take place over the next two months. The sessions were often contentious. Board members appeared frustrated and irritated with the testimony of Slyman and his casino accounting employees and with the length of the proceedings. Slyman and his employees constantly attempted to explain away cash-accounting problems that had persisted in the casino for years.

Slyman was on the agenda for the August 3, 1988, board meeting in Carson City. By this time, his finances were so poor that he told chairman Rumbolz he could not afford to fly in the seven or eight people the board requested to appear for questioning. Slyman, also citing family commitments, asked for another one-month license extension to attend the board's meeting the following month in Las Vegas. An annoyed Rumbolz gave an indication of how the hearings would play out for Slyman: "I want the record very clear that in voting for a one-month limited license, I in no way am indicating to Mr. Slyman or the Royal that I am satisfied that they deserve to continue practicing in the State of Nevada in a privileged industry."[21] The commission extended Slyman's license to expire at midnight after the commission's September 19, 1988, hearing. The board would finally take up the Royal's application at its next meeting in Las Vegas on September 7.

At the September 7 hearing, board members wasted little time dressing Slyman down for not complying with the commission's 1987 conditions. The members complained that Slyman waited almost a year to file a plan of compliance with Regulation 6A procedures instead of 60 days as he had promised. He also failed to hire competent people to handle casino financial reports as required by the regulation. Amerine said the person Slyman employed as an internal auditor was "not an experienced internal auditor, no more than I am a brain surgeon."[22] In fact, "no one had done internal audit work since this condition was put on," he said. Independent audits of the casino's finances, promised by Slyman in 1987, had not been received for the years ending June 30, 1987, and June 30, 1988, and an outside auditor had not even been hired to do them, Amerine added.

Board members further protested that Slyman had loaned himself money from Royal Casino funds without first obtaining required administrative approval from the board. State gaming regulations required him to file a report with the board at least 10 days before any loans or leases were obtained. Royal funds were also used to buy a vehicle for business purposes and to lease a second after the casino was unable to qualify for financing. The transactions, however, were not reported to the board on time. The loan for the first car was acquired March 3, 1988, but not related to the board until April 22, 1988. The lease agreement was signed March 10, 1988, but not reported until May 31, 1988. Also, one of the casino's checks for a lease payment to an auto dealer had bounced. Rumbolz said the problems indicated Slyman did not hire employees competent enough to handle the casino's cash transaction reports.

Board members then grilled Slyman about the Royal's report of assets on Form ER-101, a monthly balance sheet and financial statement Nevada casinos were required to file with the board. In its financial statement, the Royal listed as an asset $490,000 owed the casino by a company, part owned by Slyman, that was in Chapter 7 bankruptcy liquidation. The unpaid bill alone represented 69 percent of the casino's assets. Board auditors said the receivable overstated the casino's actual holdings. Rumbolz and Amerine wanted to know why Royal employees listed the $490,000 bill at face value, given the fact that even a fraction of it would probably never be collected. Slyman explained the bill would come off the books once a review was completed by an outside auditing firm. But the two board members claimed the Royal had misrepresented itself to the state.

> MR. SLYMAN: Mr. Rumbolz, we're not going to a bank and trying to get a loan with this thing. We are not trying to misrepresent anything for any type of—I don't understand.
>
> MEMBER AMERINE: It was misrepresented to us, Mr. Slyman. We are not giving you a loan, I agree. But we want accurate information. This is incorrect, totally incorrect.
>
> MR. SLYMAN: But you know everything about it. If you say this is a 1980 car or a brand new car. I mean, we are not trying to—you know what that receivable is.
>
> CHAIRMAN RUMBOLZ: But Mr. Slyman, the requirement was placed upon you to submit monthly ER-101s. That was supposed to give us an accurate financial snapshot of what was happening in your operation so we can react by having meetings with you or with your audit staff or whatever, to sit down and try and make sure that things like bounced checks to patrons didn't happen. We got instead inflated garbage information. We got garbage information because your people did not take proper steps to give us accurate information. The fact that you submit them every month and they are wrong every single month, in my view, is not complying with the condition, which was to give us a financial snapshot of this company. And it's been violated every single month.[23]

Rumbolz noted that Slyman also violated a condition of his 1987 license by using money left by casino customers for safekeeping at the Royal for his personal use. One customer, Luis Franco, a native of Mexico, wired $42,000 cash for safekeeping to the Royal, which Slyman said the man wanted him to use to buy a $15,000 wristwatch and, later, some head of cattle in Iowa. Franco owed the Royal a $10,000 marker he obtained while gambling at the casino.

Board members wondered why Slyman wrote personal checks off the safe-keeping cash.

MEMBER AMERINE: Was this in fact a loan, Mr. Slyman?

MR. SLYMAN: Absolutely not.

MEMBER AMERINE: Why didn't Mr. Franco use his own account to purchase the cattle, since you both met in Iowa?

MR. SLYMAN: I really don't know. I believe—I don't know if he has—I think he does have a checking account in America. I am not sure.

MEMBER AMERINE: He has an account in El Paso, Texas. That is where the wire came from.

MR. SLYMAN: Okay. I don't know. He says, "I am going to wire the cash up there." It was at no time ever a loan to the casino or to me or to anything like that.[24]

Slyman had used the funds for four months before paying off Franco's $10,000 marker. Franco, Slyman told the board, later decided he could not buy the cattle after losing $200,000 to $300,000 on a "business proposition." Rumbolz observed that the $10,000 transaction kept the cage out of balance for several days because cage staff were unsure how to keep Slyman's transactions on the safekeeping money separate. "It was an unusual transaction," Slyman replied.[25]

Rumbolz also said Slyman did not fulfill his April 1987 promise to submit to the board within 60 days a plan on how the Royal would train employees to meet Regulation 6A cash-handling requirements. The Royal did not turn a plan in until March 1988. During that time, the board discovered several violations of the regulation because Royal employees "had no idea what 6A was all about," Rumbolz told Slyman. "In my view, some of [the violations] rise to the criminal. Some of them are just absolutely outrageous, in my view."[26]

The board chairman then asked the Royal's casino cage manager, Frances Lippe, to testify. Lippe, hired personally by Slyman, had managed the cash that flowed through the Royal for seven years. She had previously worked as a casino cage employee in Las Vegas for 12 years at Binion's Horseshoe casino and for 10 years at the El Cortez casino. The board's Audit Division reported a list of cash-handling violations in the Royal's cage in 1987 and 1988, specifically regarding safekeeping accounts under Lippe's watch. Auditors were unable to reconcile the cash they found in deposit boxes in the Royal's cage with the accounting slips Lippe submitted. Cash was repeatedly moved out of safekeeping and replaced by casino chips, indicating the casino commingled the cash, yet another violation of the April 1987 license agreement. The practice went on from April 1987 to June 1988, during which board agents found cash-for-chip transactions every time they looked. In one case, $2,500 had been withdrawn for chips and was not balanced out for several days. Lippe responded that there were times late at night when the cage was short of $20s or other bill denominations and that she had the consent of Don Garritano, the Royal's casino manager, to order a cashier to replace some of the cash for chips "on an emergency basis." She said she would then go to a banking institution the next day to obtain cash to replace the chips. Board members were incredulous.

CHAIRMAN RUMBOLZ: April 25, 1988. $2,500 deposit in $20 bills [that] were not there. We asked you about it. Asked Mr. Garritano about it. You and Mr. Garritano indicated that he had authorized the previous weekend that that money be taken out of safekeeping and used in the cage funds.

MS. LIPPE: Okay.

CHAIRMAN RUMBOLZ: This is a weekday. You haven't replaced anything.

MS. LIPPE: Maybe I was busy and I forgot.

CHAIRMAN RUMBOLZ: Maybe you don't care.

MS. LIPPE: Yes, I do care.

CHAIRMAN RUMBOLZ: Maybe you have never cared once. Maybe you and Mr. Garritano just consistently used safekeeping money in the cage.

MS. LIPPE: No.

MEMBER AMERINE: Do you understand the implications of what you have done?

MS. LIPPE: The implications?

MEMBER AMERINE: Yes.

MS. LIPPE: No.

MEMBER AMERINE: Do you understand, one, you violated a condition that was put on the license of Mr. Slyman? And believe me, I know you are fully aware of the problems we had with safekeeping because we have gone over this with you in the investigative hearing. . . . You have taken money out and borrowed from a patron. That is a loan. It has not been reported. And you have used it to continue the operations of the Royal. It's totally unacceptable, Mrs. Lippe.

MS. LIPPE: But it is under $2,500.

MEMBER AMERINE: What does that have to do with the loan?

MS. LIPPE: Well, we have never taken more than $2,500 out of safekeeping.

MEMBER AMERINE: What does that have to do with violating the
condition?

MS. LIPPE: I was understanding it was supposed to be over $2,500.

CHAIRMAN RUMBOLZ: That is not even true, Mrs. Lippe. On January 17th [1988], $7,500 in cash was missing from safekeeping that you
had commingled with cage funds.

MS. LIPPE: I don't remember that.

CHAIRMAN RUMBOLZ: I'm not surprised you wouldn't remember it.

MEMBER AMERINE: I don't see any reason to go any further in that area.
I think it is totally unacceptable what was done.[27]

The September 7, 1988, hearing ended with only 15 of the board's concerns
about the Royal covered. Rumbolz set a new hearing for September 28, neces-
sitating yet another one-month extension of Slyman's license by the commission. At the opening of the September 28 session, board members asked
Slyman about loans accepted by the Royal between December 1987 and March
1988 but not reported to the board. One of the loans, for $25,000, came from a
man named Tony Gossett, who was arrested on drug-dealing charges in New
Mexico in 1985 and 1986 and died in June 1988. Gossett, previously known by
Royal employees by the aliases "William Eldridge" and "Robert Davis," had
deposited $29,000 cash in a safekeeping account at the Royal under "William
Eldridge" after meeting and talking to Slyman in late 1987. Slyman said
Gossett had agreed to loan money to the casino. But board members said the
Royal initially did not file cash transaction reports in December 1987 that
identified Gossett by his real name. "We have false reports on file, as far as I
am concerned," Amerine said.[28]

Furthermore, the $29,000 in small bills deposited to the Royal by Gossett
over two days were damp and musty smelling, leading the board to theorize
the cash had been buried for some time and then removed to be exchanged for
other bills. On December 10, 1987, a Royal cage cashier counted out $24,000 in
musty and damp $20 bills that Gossett, using the name "Robert Davis," had re-
moved from plastic bags for safekeeping in a Royal deposit box. The cashier
told the board under oath that Slyman was present in the cage at the time.
Slyman said he was in the casino but not in the cage. On December 13, 1987, a
safekeeping withdrawal for $29,000 was made under the name "Eldridge" by
Gossett, who then loaned the casino $25,000 in his own name. A CTR was filed
for the "Eldridge" withdrawal but not for the loan. Slyman admitted the mistake and said the Regulation 6A paperwork was eventually filed. Board members replied that Slyman nonetheless knew that "Eldridge" and Gossett were
the same person on December 13 but that Slyman still allowed Lippe to file the
CTR on the $29,000 withdrawal bearing Gossett's alias. Lippe then placed the

$25,000 cash from the loan into the casino cage's general operating funds. Lippe testified she was unaware a CTR was required for loans to casinos. She didn't correct the record, however, until seven months later, in June 1988, by placing Gossett's name on a CTR, then backdating the report to December 13, 1987. Slyman eventually paid off the loan, but he used bank checks, yet another violation of Regulation 6A, which required him to use only currency in the same denominations as the original $25,000 he had received.

Amerine said the whole Gossett transaction indicated that money laundering had occurred, and he told Slyman it was "a serious and material violation of Regulation 6A."[29] Slyman stated he thought he had acted properly with the correct paper trail. But Rumbolz claimed Regulation 6A specifically prohibited casinos from exchanging checks for cash. Lippe, Rumbolz said, appeared to be "ignorant" of the regulation. The Royal was the only casino he had ever seen that accepted loans in cash out of safekeeping and then placed it within the cage's operating fund, Rumbolz added.[30]

"But absolutely, you put cash into your cage. It comes out from the cage, or you are in violation of 6A," Rumbolz said. "That is our whole agreement with the feds. If it happened in a bank the same thing would occur. . . . There would be a CTR transaction, currency transaction reports filed."[31]

Rumbolz cited an additional prohibited transaction that occurred on June 12, 1988, when the Royal exchanged $3,000 in $20 bills for $100 bills. He and Amerine also described another transaction involving Gossett that violated Regulation 6A. The Royal made out a $16,000 marker to "Robert Davis" on December 13, 1987, the same day as the Gossett loan. The marker was then transferred to the casino cage. Fifteen minutes later, a man answering Gossett's description deposited $16,000 in chips at the cage for safekeeping, and a few minutes later the cage issued him a check for $16,000. There was no evidence or paperwork to show the person gambled, board agents said. Slyman, who denied that the man was Gossett, said the person must have simply broken even at the gaming tables and then cashed out. But Rumbolz said it appeared as if Slyman wanted the man to take a check for cash so that Slyman could place the money in the cage to supplement the casino's bankroll.

Board members then discussed how the Royal had violated its own internal control system in 1987 when safety deposit boxes in the casino cage were issued to a casino employee and four of Slyman's relatives. Under questioning by the board about safekeeping money deposited in the boxes, Garritano, the Royal's casino manager, admitted forging the name of a personal friend, Jack Delfre, on safekeeping slips. Delfre, Garritano said, had requested he sign the receipts for him so that Garritano could withdraw $600 Delfre owed him. Garritano admitted it was a bad decision but said he needed the money to cover a $600 check he wrote to Delfre and let him cash at the Royal.

MR. GARRITANO: I signed them, sir.

CHAIRMAN RUMBOLZ: So you took the money out, too?

MR. GARRITANO: Yeah. I signed his name.

CHAIRMAN RUMBOLZ: You misspelled his last name when you forged it. You put a p-h instead of an F, for Delfre?

MR. GARRITANO: I am sorry.

CHAIRMAN RUMBOLZ: No, how long did you know him, misspelling his last name?

MR. GARRITANO: He goes by Jackie Dow, he goes by Jack Delfre.

CHAIRMAN RUMBOLZ: But you didn't know how it was spelled, how Delfre was spelled?

MR. GARRITANO: Well, it could be spelled D-e-l-f-r-e or D-e-l-p-h-r-e. I wasn't sure.

CHAIRMAN RUMBOLZ: Actually it is D-e-l-f-r-e, so you are right.

MR. GARRITANO: I still don't know.

MEMBER AMERINE: That is amazing, Mr. Garritano that you have known him that long and you don't know how to spell his last name.

MR. GARRITANO: Mr. Amerine, I have known him all my life.

MEMBER AMERINE: That is incredible. It really is.[32]

Rumbolz discussed other procedural violations. Of 115 safekeeping slips examined by the board at the Royal, board agents found 168 incorrect entries. Further, 20 safekeeping slips made out to the casino's customers in 1987 were missing, meaning there was no record of what happened to the cash.

The board still had 10 additional concerns to review, but it was nearly 7 P.M. After talking to Slyman's attorneys, Rumbolz recessed the meeting to October 11. The commission later agreed to extend Slyman's license through its next meeting, October 19.

After the recess, Slyman told a news reporter that he had "never seen any wet and musty money. I have never seen anyone [exchange] small denominations of money. I don't believe it happened." He said he had accepted responsibility for what happened at the Royal and that the board's concerns "are valid, but they are being blown out of proportion. Things that are going on are infractions, but you could go through any joint and find similar infractions. There are people making mistakes [at the Royal] but not breaking the laws."[33]

On October 11, Rumbolz opened the meeting and said, dryly, "Let me emphasize that this item is the last, final meeting on the matter of the Royal casino."[34] Board members discussed their objections to the "Up and Back" program the Royal ran for selected gamblers, whose buy-in money at blackjack tables was taken by a casino security guard directly to the cage instead of placed into the tables' drop slots. The security guard would buy the chips for the patron at the cage and deliver them to the table. Board auditors said there was no paperwork to show what happened to the money. An undercover agent assigned to the Royal reported spotting a blackjack dealer and a security guard apparently working together to steal money during the program. Amerine said the procedure was "a complete breakdown of internal controls."[35]

Board members also discussed the Royal's failure to assign an accounting employee to watch the count of casino proceeds for months at a time in 1987 and 1988. Amerine said that Lippe, the cage manager, enlisted her own daughter, a part-time Royal employee with no Regulation 6A training, to help her with the count.

The board then grilled Slyman about why he extended $75,000 in credit to a female high roller, known as "Marie Rose," without first checking her credit. The casino had no record verifying she gambled there until July 1987, about eight years after she had started wagering at the Royal. Slyman said the woman was a well-known, high-stakes gambler at other casinos in Las Vegas. She was the Royal's biggest high roller and had lost $400,000 over a six-month period in 1987, he said. During one visit that year, the woman kept losing, Slyman said. She lost $25,000 and wanted to bet more, so the casino accommodated her with $75,000 in markers and other credit. However, the woman was allowed to cash the markers, made out to her alias "Marie Rose," without signing them, in violation of the casino's internal control procedures filed with the board. She then lost the $75,000 on table games, left, and ultimately failed to pay the money back. Garritano, the Royal's casino manager, admitted to the board he had been willing to violate casino procedures to avoid offending the high roller and to ensure that she would continue to wager.

Board members then asked why Royal managers had allowed an 18-year-old male patron to gamble when the legal age for gambling in Nevada is 21. Royal cocktail waitresses served the underage boy drinks (21 is also the legal drinking age in Nevada), and dealers accepted his bets, but no one checked his identification. The teenager, who lost $10,000 over two days playing table games at the Royal, was the grandson of a high roller who gambled regularly at the Royal and had sent him to the casino. Royal managers and other employees insisted the kid was tall and appeared to be over 21. Rumbolz said he was concerned that Garritano "decided not to ask and decided that not knowing was better than knowing" since the teen was losing money.[36] Slyman, who acknowledged that the boy's grandfather had threatened to sue the Royal over the incident and demanded repayment of the money the boy lost, attempted to explain.

MR. SLYMAN: Mr. Rumbolz, I think an important thing is you said did this kid get special treatment because his grandfather called. And prior statements by [the casino manager] said he didn't tell anybody he was there. He was around playing. He stuck [gambled] 1,8-, 1,900, and then we took notice of him. He didn't get no special treatment because his grandfather called.

CHAIRMAN RUMBOLZ: He could have after that, Mr. Slyman.

MR. SLYMAN: I remember them showing me a picture of him, and he had a mustache. I don't know.

CHAIRMAN RUMBOLZ: If you call the seven hairs on his upper lip a mustache, Mr. Slyman, you and I disagree on that definition as well. Mr. [Tom] Pitaro [Slyman's lawyer] has a mustache. You have a mustache. I have a mustache. I don't think this child had a mustache.[37]

Amerine and Rumbolz then reproached Slyman for how he had managed his slot machines. A board analysis showed Slyman did not know the hold percentages—the proportion of the money wagered into them by gamblers and held by the casino—of most of the 75 machines in his casino. Slyman had figured the percentage sort of on the fly, simply by observing the jackpots the machines awarded. Large jackpots, he said, meant that "the hold is going to be out of kilter. It is going to take a while for that machine to get into shape."[38] Rumbolz replied that Slyman's method was "meaningless" and that even the Royal's slot manager and general manager knew nothing about the hold percentages of the machines.

The members further scolded Slyman for having his security guards double as slot floormen, making repairs, and handling jackpot payout slips in addition to watching over the casino's assets. Rumbolz also noted that board agents in November 1987 discovered the weigh scale in the Royal's hard count room, where coins from gaming machines were counted by weight, was missing the lead seal that prevented employees from adjusting the measurements, a trick used to undercount coins in order to skim money to avoid taxes. The lead had been replaced by tape, which could be easily removed, making it simpler for someone in the count room to change how the scale calculated the numbers of coins. The board had notified the Royal about the same problem back in April 1987. Rumbolz said the Royal could not guarantee an accurate coin count with the seal broken.[39]

It was late afternoon. The board's six-hour inquiry was winding down to the final few items on the list of 37. The board discussed how the Royal could not provide records of 10 slot machine jackpots of $1,200 or more won at the casino when federal tax law required jackpot winners to sign W-2G forms that are sent to the IRS. Royal managers claimed the records were lost and that there was no actual proof the jackpots were ever awarded. The board also reported that Slyman had permitted one of his shift bosses to gamble at the Royal, even though the man supervised gaming employees and was considered a "key employee" under state Regulation 5.013, a gaming statute that prohibits certain high-level employees from gambling where they work. The shift boss won a $4,000 jackpot at the Royal in May 1987. Slyman said he thought the law pertained only to table games. Board agents also reported that a low-level Royal employee won a $4,000 jackpot, but a different person's name appeared on the federal tax form. The unnamed employee ended up winning $18,000 at the Royal in 1987. Rumbolz said the board had heard from a person who admitted helping to falsify the form, apparently to help the employee evade taxes. The employee herself told board members she never saw the $4,000 check for one of the jackpots that had been signed in her name. It appeared as if someone forged the check for the jackpot when it was cashed at the Royal's casino cage, the employee had told the board. When board members had asked the employee about the tax forms and whether the jackpots were legitimate, the employee refused to answer without a grant of immunity.

The final concern on the board's list was that Slyman did not keep the pledge he made to the commission in April 1987 to hire a person responsible for day-to-day operations at the Royal. Adding fuel to the fire, Amerine said Slyman was consistently unable to pay state gaming taxes. Amerine pointed to a page-and-a-half list of checks made out by Slyman to the state that had bounced from April 1987 to January 1988. As a result, Slyman had to pay late penalties of more than $10,000. Slyman, Amerine said finally, had not submitted a fully audited financial statement to the board since way back in June 1982.[40]

After a brief recess, Slyman delivered a statement in his behalf. He said he had obtained large loans from his brothers and intended to raise funds from other sources, including a proposed public stock offering for the Royal, to continue operating. He asked the board to allow him to hire an outside supervisor to run the casino to give him time to explore filing for Chapter 7 bankruptcy liquidation, in which he would sell the Royal's assets to pay his debts. The Royal had solved some of the problems it had in 1987, Slyman said, but he admitted others had carried into 1988. Prior to his 1983 indictment, the Royal was doing double the business and employed twice the number of people, he said, adding that he did nothing wrong to deserve the federal government's allegations of money laundering.

"I'm a guy who got indicted for doing something in his business that was— what was happening in our industry," Slyman said. "Whether people want to believe it or not, it was happening in our industry. I wasn't part of any illegal operation. I paid the price. I want to quit paying the price. . . . I need you gentlemen to give me that support, allow me to get out of this Chapter 11, allow me to pay these people their money and allow me to keep my people working. They need to work. I need to work. . . . I have worked so hard. I have got it to a point where solutions are at hand, and we can have a good profitable place, and these problems will go away if I can get out from under this cloud."[41]

Speaking in Slyman's defense, his attorney, Tom Pitaro, told the board that his client was "one of the few small-time operators left in the age of corporations . . . I don't think we should lose sight of the Joe Slymans of the world."

But Amerine said that Slyman had failed to honor his promises to the commission in 1987. "Here we come in October 1988, and, frankly, I don't see a difference in the story," Amerine said. "It's too late, Mr. Slyman. . . . I think the problem is that you do not know how to comply with regulations and you will never know how to comply with regulations. . . . You failed miserably. . . . Your cage is a shambles. Your pit is run improperly. Total breakdowns in internal control. That is how we are assured that taxes are properly paid is proper internal controls, compliance with regulations. You have done neither. . . . If this casino is closed. . . . It's not us that put you out of business. It's you. It's you and your employees. You failed to give them proper direction on how to comply with regulations."[42]

Rumbolz and Cunningham also were unwilling to grant Slyman another extension. Cunningham said he was most concerned about the use of multiple names and the failure to report the loan from Gossett. He also referred to the large number of auditing and other regulatory problems at the Royal, including the altered coin scale in the count room, improper drops at gaming tables, and hiring inexperienced employees.

"In amongst the things that I criticize you for, I find a degree of sincerity," Cunningham said. "But incompetence."[43]

Rumbolz recounted how, in April 1987, then–board chairman Jacka had convinced him to vote for Slyman to give the operator another chance to get out of his financial difficulties even though back then the board had found many of the same problems at the Royal. "I am disappointed that you have not been able to keep promises you made to us," Rumbolz said. "The problem, Mr. Slyman, is not, in my view, that I can look at anything in here and say that you have been skimming or your employees have been skimming from this operation, or that your employees have been embezzling from you. My problem is I can't say that that hasn't happened."[44]

Amerine made a motion that the board recommend the commission deny Slyman's application for a nonrestricted gaming license "based upon the fact that the applicant's prior activities and habits pose a threat to the public interest, the effective regulation of gaming, and enhance the dangers of unsuitable, unfair, or illegal practices, methods and activities in the conduct of gaming and the carrying on of business and financial arrangements incidental thereto, pursuant to NRS 463.170 (2b). Further, that the applicant lacks the adequate business probity and competence in gaming and in general, pursuant to NRS 463.170 (3b)."[45]

The vote was 3 to 0 to recommend denial. The board's marathon sessions on the Royal were over. By the time of the commission hearing on October 19, 1988, the board had submitted a hefty 2,500 pages of material on Slyman for commissioners to read, including the hearings over two-and-a-half days in September and October. Slyman pleaded with commissioners to allow him to stay open. He said he was struggling to get out of bankruptcy, pay back the $3 million he owed, and start a public company to raise funds for the Royal. In an attempt to attract business, he said he had recently resorted to giving out free food at his casino, 16 hours a day. The casino was unprofitable because he lacked control of the restaurants and hotel rooms there and so was unable to distribute complimentaries to table game customers, he said. Because of money shortages, he said he could cash only up to $7,000 worth of employee paychecks at the casino cage on a given day. He also had to deposit between $5,000 and $10,000 a month of his personal funds into the Royal's account to cover the paychecks.

Slyman argued that he could continue to operate the Royal for the 90 days with about $100,000 in loans from family members back in Cleveland. Slyman offered three alternatives. He could convert the property into a slots-only casino, bring in a gaming licensee to operate the place "under an emergency basis," or sell the casino outright. A slot casino would be profitable, bringing in about $20,000 a month, he said. But to do one of the alternatives, Slyman said he needed 90 days, during which he would continue to run the casino without live games and without issuing credit or allowing safekeeping deposits, which he noted were the board's biggest concerns. "We don't want you to ignore the board's recommendation or forgive and forget," Slyman said. "We want you to give us a little bit of time."[46]

But no one seemed willing to consider Slyman's plea. Amerine told the commission the Royal was insolvent. Rumbolz said 90 days "may not be enough time for the board to do anything with any one of the three solutions." Slyman himself reported that most of the Royal's income came from live games, not its 75 slots, Rumbolz added. While the commission under state law could appoint a supervisor until the casino was sold, the Royal was so impoverished that it could not qualify under the regulation, he said.

Commission member Robert Lewis told Slyman the Royal's latest problems were no different from those mentioned by the board in the 1986 complaint. "I have got some real problems with that," Lewis said. "When I was reading this new material, it was like I had already read it. It was the same thing. It was the problems with the cage. It was problems with incompetent employees. It was the fact that you didn't know what was going on, you attempted to correct it when in fact it really wasn't corrected. And things go on and on." [47]

"I get the feeling," commission member Ken Gragson said, "that we would have probably done you a favor and us a favor if we would have probably pulled the plug on this a year and a half ago, whenever it came before us. To me, it's a hopeless situation. . . . I am one of the last ones that likes to see a casino close. . . . There is nothing I have heard here today to convince me that a great miracle can happen in 90 days." [48]

Slyman responded that in hindsight he wished he had "given up" the Royal back in 1983, seeing as he had spent all his personal assets, borrowed all that he could to stay afloat, and racked up $3 million in debts over the past five years. He said, however, that he had still covered his state gaming taxes, federal income taxes, and employee paychecks. He repeated his request for 90 more days to keep the Royal running before getting out of it.

Amerine testified that from the most recent figures Slyman submitted to the bankruptcy court, the Royal had a negative cash flow in July 1988 with the table games and slots. The Royal would save a lot of money after laying off employees working the table games and operating a slot-only casino, but the board had not analyzed how a slot casino would fair, he said.

Commission chairman John O'Reilly made it clear he was fed up with Slyman and his proposed solutions, including the one to sell stock in the casino. "The last thing I would do in this area would be to unleash this company on the public as a public offering with stockholders and with the problems that it has had to date," he said. "It is not only a bad plan I think, but really no plan at all. The five-and-a-half years that you have been with the board, the problems have not resolved it, they are not going to be resolved today. In my opinion, they are not going to be resolved in 90 days." [49]

O'Reilly suggested the commission offer a motion to follow the board's recommendation, which would close the Royal. The closure would take place at midnight the following day, October 20, the last day of the one-month extension the commission had granted in September. The motion was made and passed unanimously. "Mr. Slyman, our regrets are with you, and hopefully it will work out the best for you," O'Reilly said. Slyman, looking dejected, said nothing and left the hearing room.

With Slyman's license about to expire, board agents made plans to halt all gaming activities at the Royal. The agents would place tape over the coin acceptors of the gaming machines and watch casino clerks take the drop (money from the table games and slots) for final deposit in the casino cage.

Slyman decided to hold a party, open to the public, inside his small casino that final night in honor of his employees, who were about to lose their jobs.

During the party, a bartender next to the casino cage served free drinks to an overflow crowd. News reporters and others played slot machines. A smiling Slyman made a show of displaying his doomed gaming license, which was mounted inside a frame. He vowed to turn the license over himself to gaming agents at the stroke of midnight. At about 11 P.M., as the party grew louder, Slyman stood atop the bar and delivered a brief farewell speech into a microphone to the packed room. He concluded by saying there was "whiskey at the bar" and admonished the crowd to stay. As he was getting down off the bar, a man yelled, "Hey, Joe, you going to pay your debts?" A violent fistfight then ensued involving the heckler and a Royal employee. The room erupted into chaos with several fights going on, like a bar scene out of a western movie. A security guard appeared and hollered for the fighters to stop. He withdrew his pistol, got into a crouch, aimed the gun at the ceiling, and fired off a round. The fighters froze for a moment before continuing. The bloody altercations waned as Las Vegas police finally arrived. Police, who detained the security guard, went to the second floor over the casino and determined the bullet had lodged in the ceiling. By midnight, most of the crowd had left as gaming agents began to quickly shut the casino down. Slyman looked weary and downcast as he made his way to the rear of the cage with the agents. The drop for the night went toward paying Slyman's debts.

With no gaming licensee to take over, the table games and slots at the Royal were removed, and the property became a nongaming hotel. One of the worst and most troublesome gaming operations in Las Vegas was finally gone. Slyman remained in town. The man whose sales pitches had failed in the end to dissuade the commission from closing him down later entered a Las Vegas real estate business. Gaming eventually returned to the Royal under new ownership.

As Slyman faded into obscurity, his former general manager at the Royal, Paul Dottore, made headlines in Las Vegas in April 1996. Dottore was indicted by a federal grand jury along with then–U.S. District Judge Gerald Bongiovanni, whom Dottore considered his closest friend, on racketeering, wire fraud, and conspiracy charges.[50] In 1997, Dottore was convicted of bank fraud in a separate case. Then, in a bargain with prosecutors for a reduced sentence, he pleaded guilty to racketeering in the Bongiovanni case in exchange for testifying against the ex-judge.

Dottore admitted in court that he arranged a number of bribes for the federal judge. In one, Dottore said a friend of his, Terry Salem, convinced him to approach Bongiovanni in 1993 with the offer to pay the judge $3,500 to dismiss a criminal case.[51] Dottore said the judge agreed to accept the money, but Dottore told the friend the judge requested $10,000, of which Dottore admitted under oath he intended to pocket $5,000. The criminal case, however, was assigned to another judge, and the bribe never took place. Salem later became a government informant and testified that he gave $3,500 in bribes to Bongiovanni in 1995, including marked bills allegedly given to the judge by Dottore and found later by investigators in Bongiovanni's home. Dottore said he also served as go-between in a $5,000 bribe to Bongiovanni for a Las Vegas casino entertainment director who had a civil case in the judge's court. Tom Pitaro, a former Slyman attorney who defended Bongiovanni, railed on Dottore in court, calling him "a scammer, an opportunist, a thief, a liar."[52] In the end, Dottore's testimony failed to influence the jury. The panel voted to acquit Bongiovanni of the charges at the end of 1997.

Meanwhile, the gaming board continued to enforce strictly Regulation 6A to police cash handling in casinos and to show that the state was capable of regulating itself. By 1997, using Regulation 6A, the board had assessed more than $2 million in fines against violators and reviewed more than 370,000 cash transaction reports.[53] The U.S. General Accounting Office praised Regulation 6A and advised that the federal government adopt its prohibitions to improve anti-money-laundering regulations. But the Treasury Department later required Nevada to amend Regulation 6A to conform with other states that had since legalized forms of casino gambling. The major change was that customers would have to place their names on a cash transaction report when cashing in more than $10,000 in chips, even if it was from winnings. A gambler wanting to bet over $10,000 would have to provide identification, or the casino could not accept the bet. Nevada also agreed to require casinos to file "suspicious activities reports" to the Gaming Control Board and the IRS if operators believed someone was attempting to make an illegal cash transaction. However, Nevada once again got a few breaks, included within a bill offered by U.S. Senator Richard Bryan (D-Nev.) and passed by Congress. The state convinced the U.S. government that only casinos with more than $10 million in annual gross gambling revenue and $2 million or more in table game revenue need comply with Regulation 6A, unless required by the Gaming Control Board's chairman to do so.[54] Before, all casinos with $1 million or more in annual gross gaming revenue had to comply. Also, under the new Regulation 6A, the amount of currency casinos had to return to gamblers in the same denominations—such as safekeeping deposits—was raised to $3,000 from $2,500.[55]

Gaming Control Board members and representatives of the board's Audit Division met with Las Vegas attorney Bob Faiss and Paul Larsen, a representative of the Nevada Resort Association—a casino-industry lobby group—to discuss revisions to Regulation 6A that would satisfy the Treasury Department. The Gaming Commission passed the revised regulation on January 23,

1997, and it took effect September 1, 1997. After the unanimous vote, commission chairman Bill Curran remarked that the rewritten rules would enable the board and the commission "to maintain control of the activities in the state rather than sending that control to Washington. So I think this is a good day for all of us."[56]

Chapter Four

Near Miss

The Rise and Fall of Slot Machine Innovator Universal Distributing of Nevada

In the early 1980s, two companies dominated the gaming machine trade in Nevada: Bally Manufacturing, Inc., and International Game Technology (IGT). Bally controlled virtually all of the market for spinning reel slots, while IGT dominated the smaller, fledging video side. The most popular gaming machine in Nevada casinos was Bally's E-2000, with three mechanical reels that spun with a pull of the handle. A simple computer logic board inside the device read the reels and paid out players. A savvy gambler could estimate the potential percentage payout of the E-2000 by watching the symbols on each reel as they appeared in the "pay line" at the end of each game.

Casinos could change the frequency of coin payouts large and small on the E-2000 simply by switching around the plastic reel strips—with the bars, cherries, and other symbols painted on them—on the reels. The variety of strips available for the E-2000 gave casinos the flexibility to set up to 50 different payout percentages.[1] Jackpots, however, were rare. A slot with 22 symbols per reel might align three jackpot symbols as infrequently as once every 10,648 games. The E-2000, with its mechanical reels that spun and stopped at random to reveal a game result, operated on virtually the same concept as the first slot machine, invented in San Francisco back in 1899.[2]

But in 1983, a young upstart corporation from Japan, Universal Company, Ltd., owned by wealthy businessman Kazuo Okada and his two brothers, opened an office in Las Vegas and soon revolutionized the slot machine industry. That year, Gary Harris, one of two sales managers of Universal's new Las Vegas–based subsidiary, Universal Distributing of Nevada, Inc., presented the company with a new marketing concept: award smaller jackpots instead of a single large one. Universal became the first gaming machine maker to run slot reels with computerized "stepper motors," technology used in auto manufacturing and appliances, instead of mechanical reels. The company then perfected a way of awarding a 1,000-coin jackpot about once every 4,000 games on a slot with 32 symbols per reel. The machine, called Magnificent 7s, used computer software programmed with more than 200 ways to hit three 7s, and also produced many 100-coin payouts. At first, Las Vegas casino operators did not accept the idea of awarding more money to slot players. Aside from machines, Universal had to sell its clients on a new strategy to operate a casino.[3]

"We preached to the industry that casinos should be real 'loose,'" Harris said. "Casinos then thought people wanted frequent small winners, like every three games. We said it was better to have a winner every 20 games with a higher pay out. But we had to work ten times as hard to convince them."[4]

Universal's sales and marketing approach worked. Casinos tried out and bought the new machines. By the mid-1980s, play on Universal's computerized machines surpassed the action on Bally's machines, which, like other machine companies, also began using stepper motors. At one point, Universal's slots had 16 times higher the volume of coins wagered than Bally machines, according to Harris. "We sold the machines looser. And by having the machines looser, the casinos found that people were not leaving," Harris said. "It led to more traffic. People were in fact standing in line to play our machines. People began winning more than ever. They were taking money home. Las Vegas became the most competitive slot market in the Western Hemisphere. A market that was the low end, Universal took to the high end."[5]

Universal's swift success coincided with a major change in the gaming industry. In mid-1983, revenues from slot machines for the first time surpassed revenues from table games in Nevada casinos.[6] A leading manufacturer of amusement and gaming machines in Japan, Universal started out in 1983 with an ambitious plan to have its machines in most of the major casinos in U.S. legal gambling jurisdictions—then isolated to Nevada and Atlantic City—within 10 years. It took only three years. Harris estimated that about 75 percent of the reel slots sold in Nevada were made by Universal in 1986.

Universal virtually transformed casino gambling in the 1980s. Its innovative computerized slot machines became the most popular among players who thought Universal's were more fun and paid out more often. The higher volume of play translated into higher casino profits. The stepper motor machine used a "random-number generator" to run the reel strips instead of the less-accurate timing schemes in other slots. With the new machine, the player activated the slot, and the computer determined the outcome of the game through the random-number generator. The new motors drove the reels to specific stops during a game, and the reels only displayed the results determined by the computer program inside the machine.

Stepper motors offered a number of advantages over mechanical reels. They detected and prevented a common method of slot cheating—opening the machine and manually turning the reels to form a jackpot. The motors also made it far easier to place a new game inside a machine on the casino floor. While mechanical machines required casino operators to select from dozens of reel strips to modify a machine's payout percentage, with stepper motors operators needed only to replace the machine's three or four reel strips and the computer chip with the game's program on it.

"We could change a game with a small conversion kit, including three pieces of glass, a set of reel strips and the EPROM [computer chip]," Harris said.[7]

The computerized gaming devices also introduced "the concept of volatility" in awarding money, which was more exciting for players, Harris said. "Universal's slot with a 97 percent pay out over a long period of time might pay out up to 120 percent on a given day," he said. "There could be a $4,000, $10,000 loss [to a casino] on a Universal machine somewhere each day. On a daily basis, we were up and down. Over time, the casinos still made money. But it was better for the player than a regular, tame machine that just paid out 97 percent each day."

By the late 1980s, only five years after it came to Nevada, Universal had sold more than 10,000 machines in the state. In 1986, the Nevada company grossed $15 million and had 60 employees. Some major Las Vegas casinos had more Universal machines on the floor than any other brand. The Mirage hotel in Las Vegas had 700 to 800 Universal machines in 1989.[8] A year later, the Excalibur hotel in Las Vegas had 1,600 Universal slots.[9] Universal touted its machines as the biggest revenue producer in the state's casinos. Competing companies scrambled to copy its technology and unique features.

"Universal was the slot of choice and had almost captured the market" by the late 1980s, said Frank Schreck, a Las Vegas attorney and former member of the Nevada Gaming Commission who represented Universal before the Nevada State Gaming Control Board and the commission. "Universal was rivaling IGT. The Universal machine was much, much more popular with the sophisticated slot player."[10]

But in 1988, one of Universal's innovations drew the attention of the Gaming Control Board, thanks in part to objections by Nevada-based IGT. Out of the controversy, the Gaming Commission would for the first time adopt regulations covering computerized slot machines, including the concept of "random" selection of stops on slot reels. The commission's action also stalled the growth of the Japanese company, which would eventually lose most of what it had built in Nevada to its American counterparts.

The debate centered on Universal's so-called near-miss feature, which had been inserted into the computer programs of the company's three- and four-reel slots in Nevada. The Gaming Control Board alleged that the company used near miss in its machines to alter the "random" generation of game results. A losing game of three blanks might be altered to show a near jackpot, such as two jackpot symbols and one blank. The idea of near miss was to add excitement and thus induce players to continue betting in anticipation of an eminent jackpot. The problem for Nevada was that when the Gaming Control Board heard of the near-miss feature in 1988, the state had no written regulation governing the concept of what would become known as "randomness." In the early 1980s, when computerized stepper motor technology was developed, Nevada's gaming rules on slot machines—written in state Regulation 14 in 1969 and amended in 1972—were based on how traditional mechanical slots operated.

When slot machines began using computer components in Nevada in 1976, the new machines were programmed to imitate the old mechanical ones, meaning that near misses would be the natural result of a certain number of games. But despite the new innovations, the commission, instead of amending Regulation 14, chose to approve new games as they came along in consultation with Gaming Control Board technicians.

"Previous administrations have attempted to revise the regulation, but . . . those revisions have never been presented to the commission," board officials wrote in a July 13, 1989, memorandum to the commission. "One reason for this occurrence is the ever-changing technology in this field. In the past, a regulation draft would be circulated, and before it could be adopted, technology would make the draft obsolete."[11]

By the spring of 1988, during the debate over Universal's near-miss feature, the commission and the Gaming Control Board realized that Regulation 14 was inadequate and had to be rewritten to cover new computerized devices in use since the mid-1970s.

The board first learned of Universal's near-miss feature when IGT complained about it in early 1988 at the height of Universal's success. IGT executives said the company was ready to file a petition for declaratory relief, asking the commission to approve IGT's version of a similar program in its machines. Gaming Control Board member Dennis Amerine, who at the time oversaw the board's New Games Lab, thought the near-miss feature was deceptive and led a campaign with state officials to draw up new regulations to ban it and require Universal to remove the feature from the company's slots in Nevada. Universal would argue that near miss was a gimmick that dated back to the first mechanical slot machines produced at the end of the 19th century and utilized in slots produced by other manufacturers.

In the 1980s, computer software programs used by most gaming machine companies were based on how the old-fashioned mechanical machines operated. As the mechanical slot machines had done, the computerized machines increased the chance of near-miss results above and below the pay line by "clustering" blanks above and below the single jackpot symbol on the last of the game's three or more reels. That way, game results showing jackpot symbols on the first two, three, or more reels, followed by a blank on the final reel, would occur "naturally."

But after years of research, Universal's engineers in 1985 produced a computer program that would place a near-miss result directly into the pay line. Without fully understanding the implications, the Gaming Commission approved Universal's new program that year as a "modification" of a previously approved program. The company then started selling machines in Nevada with the feature.

In the mid-1980s, Universal, IGT, and other gaming device companies began producing machines with 32 symbols on a reel strip, which produced a possible 32,768 different game outcomes in the pay line of a three-reel slot (the three-reel machine was the most prevalent model in casinos and the most popular with customers). The stops included jackpot symbols, lower-pay symbols, and blank space.

Universal and its competitors started using computer programs to "randomly" pick out and reveal outcomes of games from tables containing thousands of numbers assigned to specific stops on each reel. But Universal's machines used random selection in a unique way that created a new type of near-miss result.

Universal's slot machine program was based on combinations of reel stops instead of specific reel stops. When a player activated the Universal slot, the random-number generator would almost instantly pick the outcome of all three or more reels at once. The program would then immediately read the results. If the game had a winning combination, the reels would display it in the pay line. But if the game was a losing combination of blanks, the machine's computer would quickly revert to a separate group of six tables of numbers corresponding to "losing" combinations, some of them containing blanks and others containing one or more blanks along with one or two jackpot symbols.[12] The reels could thus be altered in a flash to show the player one or two jackpot symbols in the pay line.

Universal's intent was to maintain player interest by avoiding the display of three blanks, the worst outcome possible. Within the more than 32,000 possible combinations in a complete cycle of plays on three 32-stop reels, a three-blank result was normally expected to show up in the pay line about 5,000 times. The software that contained the losing game combinations in the Universal slot, however, would cause three blanks to show up only 3,000 times. One or two winning symbols would be inserted into the pay line the other

2,000 times, or 40 percent of the time. The table in the software program with the losing combinations became known as the "weighted-loser feature," whereby losing combinations were "weighted" differently than winning ones.

After learning of the feature, the Gaming Control Board complained that Universal had assured state computer engineers that its 32-stop machine had a "physical stop" on its reels to match each stop position written in the machine's software program. Universal submitted at least 461 modifications of its three-reel slot to the board, each time insisting it was a machine with 32 physical stops to match the stop positions in the program. But board technicians said the Universal machine actually had only 22 physical stops on its reels and had used the six tables of losing combinations to alter the outcomes of some of the three-blank games.

The company had also placed the near-miss feature inside its four-reeled slots, which company engineers programmed to catch and prevent all four-blank outcomes from appearing in the pay line. The machines would cause two jackpot symbols to be displayed 50 percent of the time in four-blank games and one symbol the other 50 percent. Universal's engineers had inserted yet another near-miss feature inside the company's so-called buy-a-pay four-reel machines. With the feature, a player would have to have bet the maximum three coins to win a jackpot when three 7s hit the pay line. If the player had wagered only one or two coins, the software caused the row of three 7s to show up more often than mathematically possible. The four-reel machine had reel strips with 22 physical stops and 64 "software stops." Universal, the board determined, also had a five-reel slot programmed with the same near-miss feature.

Universal had introduced the near-miss concept inside its pachinko amusement machines in Japan during the 1980s. The near-miss display was programmed into three slot reels built into the pachinko machines to serve as a side game. The design of the slot reels in Universal's pachinko machine would later be used in its Magnificent 7s slot sold in Nevada and New Jersey, with the number 7 employed as a jackpot symbol. The company also used the near-miss program in tens of thousands of token-awarding slot machines it produced for the Japanese arcade market.

"That's the way they [slot machines] all work in Japan," said Harris, Universal's former sales manager. "No one [in Japan] told Universal the way a slot machine was supposed to work."[13]

Before it entered the American gaming market, Universal made a fortune in the popular pachinko machine and amusement game industry in Japan. The company launched its first product, a Japanese arcade game, in 1970.[14] By the late 1980s, Universal was the number-one producer of pachinko machines and for-amusement-only slot and video poker devices in Japan, controlling 30 percent of the market. Casino gambling was illegal in Japan, and so pachinko machines awarded ball bearings used for replays or to exchange for cigarettes and other prizes, while slot and other gaming machines in Japan paid out tokens redeemed for prizes.

The pachinko machine was Japan's biggest entertainment venue, with three million machines in 14,000 outlets in the mid-1980s.[15] What made the pachinko market even more lucrative for manufacturers was that, by Japanese law, the machines had to be replaced within only four years. In 1986, while Universal was grabbing hold of the Nevada gaming device market, a Universal subsidiary in Japan, the Mikuho Seisakusho Company, introduced the first high-tech, completely electronic pachinko machine.[16] Up to then, pachinko machines operated with purely mechanical parts. In 1987, Universal grossed $165 million from the amusement and gaming machine markets. By then, the company had diversified in Japan, where it owned 20 hotels, a chain of pizza delivery outlets, and office buildings to go with its machine-manufacturing plants and sales offices.[17]

Universal's Nevada-style gaming machines were operating in 23 countries, including Great Britain, Australia, Austria, Turkey, France, Argentina, and Malaysia, in 1987. The company had produced more than 800 different models, including video poker and video blackjack, which sold for approximately $4,000 to $4,500 each. Universal's generic-looking Magnificent 7s offered maximum jackpots of 1,000 coins, awarded when a row of large 7s lined up on the pay line. Some models contained only five ways to win—various combinations of 7s and bars—while others included large and small payouts, including 7s, bars, and fruit symbols. The company's Jokers Wild game featured pictures of jokers in circular jackpot symbols. Both models were sold in Nevada and Atlantic City. Most of the company's machines accepted quarter and dollar bets, but Universal also built machines accepting $100 and $500 coin token wagers for high-end casino clients, such as Caesars Palace in Las Vegas.

Universal owner Kazuo Okada and his brothers, Tomoo and Michiko, were licensed by the Gaming Commission in 1984 to manufacture and distribute machines in Nevada, and the first Japanese-made gaming machines soon appeared in the state. In 1986, Nevada governor Richard Bryan presented Universal president Tomoo Okada with an award recognizing the company as an outstanding business enterprise. Universal executives bragged at the time that all the parts of their machines were made or assembled in the company's plants in Japan.

Slot machines manufactured and sold by Universal and its competitors operated by basically the same principles of producing winning and losing results as the first slots produced in the United States. The three-reel mechanical coin-drop slot machine, known as the Liberty Bell, was invented in 1899 by

Charles A. Fey at his factory at 406 Market Street in San Francisco, where coin-operated gambling machines had been both legal and popular at the time.[18] Fey, who had designed a five-reel poker machine in 1897 and a three-reel poker device in 1898, replaced the poker cards with bells, horseshoes, hearts, and other symbols for the Liberty Bell model. The basic countertop design of Fey's Liberty Bell three-reel machine still survives in casino gambling domains throughout the world. It would become the most popular, enduring, and profitable coin game ever. In 1997, of the $7.8 billion in gaming revenue produced in Nevada, $4.8 billion, or 62.7 percent, came from gaming machines.[19] Most are reeled slots. The firm IGT in 1999 counted 216,000 machines in Nevada, 70,000 of which were video poker games.

The cast-iron Liberty Bell machine and other early slots used a series of metal gears operating three or more turning reels activated by pushing or pulling a metal handle or arm. The Liberty Bell's reels were timed to spin and stop in a 1-2-3 sequence. Each reel had a variety of symbols painted on strips affixed to the reels. The reels stopped at the pay line, where the symbols were seen by the player through a glass window. The probability of hitting a jackpot or another winning combination depended simply on the number of winning symbols placed on the reels. The early machines had only 10 stops per reel, or 1,000 possible combinations: 10 times 10 times 10. Reels were later expanded to 20 stops in the 1930s, 22 in the 1970s, and 25 and 32 stops in the 1980s.

For the operator of the classic three-reel slot, the concept was to place the most jackpot symbols on the first reel, fewer on the second, and then just one on the third. On a machine with 32 stops, for example, a proprietor might place six jackpot symbols on the first reel, four or five on the second, and one on the last. That way, the jackpot symbols would appear more frequently in the pay line on the first two reels but much less often on the third. The idea was obvious—keep people playing by making them believe they nearly won a jackpot. However, the mathematical probability of lining up three jackpot symbols on a mechanical machine with a 6-5-1 configuration on three 32-stop reels is only 1 out of the total 32,768 game combinations.[20]

In Nevada, slots and other forms of casino gaming were legal from the late 19th century until the state banned all forms of gaming in 1909. The mechanically operated slots were allowed in the state again in 1915, but only if they awarded prizes, such as drinks and cigars, worth $2 or less. The state legalized casino games, along with slot machines, in 1931. In the early 1960s, "electro-mechanical" slots were introduced, using electric lights and sounds to make the game more attractive and entertaining.

Electromechanical slots grew in popularity in the late 1960s. Modern slots began in the mid-1970s with Chicago-based Bally Manufacturing's gaming machine that used software in a microprocessor, the brains of a computer. The microprocessor operated the machine, such as directing the number of coins paid out on a winning game. Bally and other slot manufacturers soon halted production of electromechanical slots in favor of the new computerized models. Then came Universal's innovative use of stepper motors, which other machine companies adopted. In 1988, IGT had perfected a machine with 256 software stops on each reel, capable of producing 16 million combinations.

In early 1988, the Gaming Control Board contacted Universal about the near-miss program after IGT officials had said they were ready to ask that the Gaming Commission approve IGT's version of a similar program. In April 1988, the board ordered Universal to halt sales of its slots with the near-miss feature while board members and staff could fashion amendments to Regulation 14. (From 1985 to 1989, the board and the commission had approved 71 new types of gaming machines and more than 10,000 modifications of existing ones on the basis of recommendations from the state's gaming lab.)[21]

The board conducted two lengthy hearings in 1988 and sought input from slot machine manufacturers on the amendments. Meanwhile, the board, acting on the lead of board member Amerine, issued a complaint against Universal to the commission, alleging the near-miss program failed to meet standards set by the gaming lab, even if they were never formally incorporated into Regulation 14. The board further claimed Universal had violated Regulation 14 by misrepresenting the modifications and programs that had the near-miss feature. Universal hired gaming attorney Schreck, himself a member of the Gaming Commission from 1971 to 1975.

Schreck argued that all slot companies used the near-miss concept. There was in fact no standard or mention of "randomness" in state gaming regulations, he said, adding that employees of the state's gaming lab, not the commission, were responsible for determining whether a game was "random."

But his reasoning failed to persuade the commission. Schreck advised Universal executives to settle the board's complaint. Universal consented, signed a stipulation on September 22, 1988, and agreed to pay a fine of $25,000. The company also agreed that its four-reel machines did not meet board standards and that company technicians would retrofit all of its devices in Nevada with new programs without the near-miss feature. Universal also promised to fund a chair at the Engineering Department at the University of Nevada, Las Vegas, to be held by an expert in programming gaming machines who would be available to consult with the board's lab. The Japanese company further agreed to hire an English-speaking employee in Nevada to communicate better with the Gaming Control Board.[22]

However, Schreck decided to take the case back to the commission to help Universal avoid the expense of having to physically remove the near-miss feature from its more than 10,000 machines in Nevada, most of them operating with three reels. He filed a petition for a declaratory ruling in which he asked the commission to acknowledge that the near-miss feature had been used in Universal machines since 1985 and had been approved by the commission. A commission hearing on the petition was set by chairman John O'Reilly for December 1, 1988, in Las Vegas. If Schreck could convince the commission there was nothing wrong with the near-miss feature, Universal might be spared the cost of retrofitting. But even more was at stake. With its sales of new machines halted since April 1988, Universal was rapidly losing market share in Nevada to its competitors. Universal was also concerned about the confusion expressed by casino executives and other Universal clients about machines still operating with the near-miss program.

At the December 1988 hearing, Schreck repeatedly insisted that Universal was not the only slot company to use near miss in its games.[23] Universal had merely taken the old mechanical "natural" near-miss concept and computerized it, he said. Universal's machines still selected both winning and losing combinations randomly. The so-called near miss resulted only after the reel symbols in a losing game were chosen by random selection, he said.

"[T]here is not a single gaming device slot machine that I am aware of that doesn't have some sort of near miss feature," Schreck argued. "We are not dealing with anything novel. . . . [This is] a new technology and a newer way of doing what has been done from the day slot machines first entered the industry in the State of Nevada."[24]

Schreck maintained that the old mechanical three-reel slots had always produced near-miss results by loading more winning symbols onto the first and second reels.[25] Players would see the symbols on the first two reels more often than they would normally expect since many players believed that all three reels had the same number of symbols. The third reel would usually contain only one winning symbol, and blanks or nonwinning symbols were "clustered" around it. The effect on games was that two winners and a loser were common—a near-miss result.

The near-miss concept had remained in gaming machines over the years, from the electromechanical machines to the computerized models, Schreck said. The first Bally Series E computerized machine encountered regulatory problems in Nevada before it was approved, he said.

Schreck then pointed out that the commission, while focusing on Universal's near miss inside the pay line, permitted other slot manufacturers to create near misses above and below the pay line. In the early 1980s, slot manufacturers expanded the window where the slot reels could be seen and used reel strips to make near misses appear above and below the pay line to induce "an increased sense of anticipation" in players, Schreck said. The expanded window became a standard in the slot industry. "Manufacturers took advantage of this feature and began making reel strips that incorporate the strong possibility of displaying winning combinations above and below the pay line," he said.[26]

Modern slot companies, Schreck argued, created the possibility of near-miss results by simply positioning winning symbols around losing combinations, increasing the probability that a winning combination would be displayed within the viewing window above and below, and even appearing to be partially on, the pay line. Near-miss combinations with winning symbols, off the pay line but in view of the player, would appear more frequently than they could possibly appear on the pay line, he said.

From stepper motors came the concept of the "disproportionate reel stop," Schreck said. Instead of working off only 22 physical stops on the reel strip, stepper motors enabled the computer to increase the number of software stops on the same reel to 32, 44, 64, 66, or more stops. Each physical reel stop could be assigned four stops; for instance, one blank on the reel could be assigned four software stops. Underneath that blank, a winning symbol could be made to stop, and under that one stop there could be three or four positions in the software. In this case, winning symbols would appear in the window much more often than they normally appear on the reel strips themselves. The use of these so-called disproportionate reel stops with standard reel strip layouts was the most common near-miss method, Schreck said.

Further, with nonpaying outcomes in modern slot machines, winning symbols "are intentionally placed in the viewing window," he said. Payout calculations might figure 90 percent payback, depending on the combinations of winning symbols. However, the player viewing the entire window above and below the pay lines could calculate a 250 percent payout if the winning combinations were in the center pay line.[27] In the machine with 64 software stops, the player could see a 1,000 percent payback or more by viewing the near misses above and below the pay line, Schreck said. Stepper motor technology enabled slot makers to place three jackpot symbols "right below the pay line," he added.

Schreck displayed for the commission two of Universal's machines: the Magnificent 7s and Double Feature. The reel strips on the machines, he said, were "virtually identical" to those of other slots made by other companies. The Magnificent 7s machine had 22 symbols on each reel, consisting of 11 blanks and 11 winning symbols. With this 11/11 scheme, three winning "bar" symbols tended to line up above and below the pay line. On Double Feature, the outcomes also resulted in near misses, such as two jackpot symbols and a blank in the pay line, with winning symbols shown above and below.

"Near miss has been in slots ever since slots were invented," Schreck said. "We didn't make up near miss. . . . There is no evil or deception with near miss.

We just do it differently. . . . It's a concept that's been in machines since the first day they were introduced into the gaming industry, and every manufacturer, including those that have developed the stepper machine based on Universal's technology, embodies the near miss. We just do it differently." [28]

Reel strips, he said, have "always been used to . . . make it appear that you are more likely to win than you really are." [29]

It was Schreck's position that Universal's slots chose winners on a completely random basis. In Universal slots at the time, losing combinations were determined by the machine's microprocessor. When the machine's computer found that the game's outcome in the random-number generator was a loser, the game would enter the weighted cycle that would randomly select another list of combinations from the losing combinations and display the results on the reels. The losing combinations were located inside a "slice" of the pie including the numbers associated with reel stops. When a loser was detected after random selection, the slot's computer would switch to the "slice" containing the combinations that would usually produce a near miss in the pay line and then choose the reel stops the player sees.

Schreck told the commission that computerized slot machines made by Universal and other companies had no function except for display purposes, in contrast to mechanical machines, in which the strips on the reels do determine the outcome. He argued that in any case, near miss was not prohibited under any state gaming regulation, only gaming policies that "are not standards and they are not enforceable as standards." [30] Regulation 14.040 was the only enforceable standard with respect to slot machines in Nevada, and Universal had satisfied the standard, he said.

In response, chairman O'Reilly said that only winning combinations in the Universal machines were selected randomly. Losers, O'Reilly said, were determined not randomly but by the weighted-loser feature.

Schreck replied that even Universal's losing combinations were selected at random. Besides, the weighted-loser feature on the three-reel machine could be introduced on the reel strips of a mechanical machine and produce the same result.

"You can move the symbols around where you always have a near miss somewhere," he said. Universal's games, he added, were purely computerized, while machines made by other companies were merely computerized versions of electromechanical machines. [31]

But board member Amerine testified that the weighted-loser feature was not actually random. To meet state standards, he said, there should be a direct correlation between the computer stops and the physical stops on the machine.

"What we are saying," Schreck responded, "is yes, in fact, our machine creates entertainment for the playing public by not having lots of blanks . . . not only Universal but every other manufacturer has adopted basically Universal's reel strips because it makes it more exciting for the player. . . . Universal has just created really the new series of slot machines, like the Bally Series E created a new series. . . . Everyone has done it and they have always done it. . . . We should not be penalized."[32]

"Universal's machine pays out more than others," he continued. "That's why it's popular. The casinos say Universal's machine is what players want; there have been no complaints. The public draws the line. They won't pay if they don't win. . . . The final arbiter is the playing public. . . . Other near miss machines made by Universal have bombed. So it's not the magic ingredient."[33]

Amerine warned commissioners that if they approved the near-miss feature, it would "significantly impact future manufacturing of gaming devices and the regulatory process governing such devices. The reason this feature is such a significant departure from any prior approvals of gaming devices can be stated as follows: Never before has the board or commission approved a feature within a gaming device that causes a specific symbol to appear on the pay line more frequently than is mathematically—than its mathematical probability of occurrence."[34]

Because of the complexity of the near-miss issue, chairman O'Reilly asked Amerine to repeat what he had just said twice so commissioners could understand the significance. Amerine then insisted again that losing combinations were not chosen at random by the Universal machine.

"In all other reel-type devices previously approved in Nevada, each specific symbol maintains the same mathematical probability of being selected and displayed to a patron regardless of whether it appears in a winning or losing combination," Amerine said. "Further, in all other devices the same symbols that are initially selected in a losing combination are displayed to the patron."

Amerine had another warning. While Universal was the only company using near miss, other companies were prepared to submit versions of it if the commission approved it. "One manufacturer has submitted a proposal for a near miss feature in a video poker device," he said. "The feature in this video poker device would on losing hands display different cards to the patrons than that which were chosen by the random selection process."[35]

Establishing guidelines for near-miss machines in the future would prove difficult for state gaming officials, Amerine said. If near miss were allowed, "there will be an increased burden upon the board and commission to determine at what is or—at what point a device is or may be perceived as deceptive to the playing public. . . . My question is how will disputes be resolved in the future with patrons? Would it be the outcome of the computer or would it be the outcome that is displayed to the patron?"

Ed Allen, manager of the state's gaming lab, also argued against approving

Universal's near-miss and weighted-loser features. Allen said the lab was unable to test Universal's near-miss machines for randomness the way the lab tested machines made by other manufacturers. In other machines, he said, the state watched the results of games on the "internal reel strip" inside the computer program, not on the actual turning reel. But with Universal's machine, the state could not test to see whether the results were chosen randomly since the machine might make a secondary decision to place a near miss on the internal reel strips of the tested games. The reels on the Universal devices were there only to display game results and were not related to any function in the machine, he said.

"You see, I have no reel strips to gauge the randomness against," Allen said.[36] "When I'm done testing [the Universal machines], I don't really have a concrete set of results that means anything. . . . [W]e're not learning anything new or any piece of information that is going to determine whether the game should be recommended for approval or not by doing that kind of test."[37]

Furthermore, Allen claimed that near-miss machines prevented "sophisticated" slot players from determining the possibility of a payout by watching where the reels stopped in the pay line. The player would see many more winning symbols in the pay line than a machine that operated like a mechanical slot and displayed symbols chosen at random.

"With any conventional type machine, and by conventional, I mean a microprocessor controlled machine which uses the reel strip methodology, you should be able to calculate the pay percentages of the machine based on the outcomes that appear on the pay line," Allen said.[38]

As an example, Allen said Universal's Magnificent 7s machine had awarded a maximum jackpot for three blue-colored 7s in the pay line and lower pays for mixes of blue and red 7s. Universal, with its weighting feature, also produced a greater number of blue 7s appearing on two of the reels after a mixed-7 result had been chosen by the computer. That winning game was not a randomly selected result, he said.

Allen agreed with Amerine that the board and the commission had never before approved a slot machine that caused a specific symbol to emerge in the pay line more frequently than its mathematical probability. With Universal's weighted feature, slot players had no way of calculating what the machine would award in the future, he said.

Commissioner Robert Lewis asked Allen whether, as Universal claimed, all slot machines had a near-miss feature.

Allen acknowledged that other machines did have "naturally occurring" near misses and "have configured their reel strips to produce a given number of near-miss outcomes which will be presented to the player." However, he added, "the Universal machine creates an artificial near-miss situation which goes beyond any type of near miss that you could create . . . on a conventional type machine."

Other conventional machines, using computer software based on the revolutions of old mechanical reel strips, had a standard number of stops and a set number of symbols on each strip, with the program determining the various combinations. However, Universal had no such reel strip and instead used categories of winning and losing combinations of symbols, Allen said.

Slots made by companies other than Universal, Allen testified, did "cluster" blanks above and below jackpot symbols on reel strips, such as placing most of the 12 blanks on a reel above and below a 7 symbol. The practice was done on the disproportionate slots, using software capable of assigning 32 software stops on a reel with 22 physical symbols. That way, players would normally see a 7 or another jackpot symbol above and below the pay line more often in a losing game—a near miss. However, again, Allen said, the individual reel stops on those machines were nonetheless chosen at random, and a jackpot symbol would not appear any more or less often than a blank or any other symbol. Such was not true, he said, of the Universal slot, which in a losing near-miss game would directly assign the jackpot symbols in the pay line, or what Allen termed "an artificial near miss."[39]

Allen admitted, however, it was possible for the Gaming Control Board to come up with a way to test the random selection of the winners and losers in the Universal machine. The test would involve "determining the percentage of time that a machine could produce an artificial near miss," he said. But the commission would then have to decide how often a slot machine would be allowed to depart from the state's standards for randomness. The standard required random selection shown to be within "95 percent confidence limits" on a standard chi-squared test used by mathematicians. Universal's near-miss machine would not pass that test for randomness, he said.[40]

After a brief recess, Schreck was permitted to make a final statement.

"The state of the art slot machine industry is where it is today because Universal developed its slot machine," Schreck said. "It developed stepper motor technology. It developed the reel strips. It developed the whole concept, not just the program that is different from other ones, but it developed what is basically the standard in the industry today. What is left after everything else has been emulated, copied and adopted is the program, the difference between the competitor's copying or replicating of an electro-mechanical machine in software and Universal's true computer."[41]

Universal's unique computer program took years to produce, and it would take additional years of engineering to change the programs in the company's more than 800 models, Schreck said. To do that "would virtually make the company noncompetitive for a number of years before it could change and adopt the electro-mechanical standard that Mr. Amerine and Mr. Allen advocate."

Schreck said that he was "astounded" by Allen's comments that sophisticated slot players were able to calculate whether a machine was going to produce a winning game by watching where the reels stopped. A player at any given machine would not know how many stops there were on the reels since the reels have 22 physical stops but might be programmed for 32, 64, 68, 86, or even 256 software stops. On a four-reel machine, a person would have to watch 100 million games to find out the theoretical payout percentage. To say that someone could do that "is not really explaining the issue in real life," Schreck said.[42]

Besides, so-called sophisticated and high-level players favored Universal's machines over others since some major casinos had chosen them for slot tournaments and $500-per-wager slot carousels, he said. "To say that somehow the sophisticated player needs protection from the Universal machine is not supported by any evidence and any of the play," Schreck said. "Basically, when a player plays a slot machine and he is trying to figure out what it does, he sees how many coins are put in, and how many coins come out. And that's basically [how] he determines whether or not that is going to be a good machine."

The real issue in the whole debate, Schreck said, "is Universal has a sophisticated computerized program that enables it to create a near miss on the pay line and no one else does. That's the whole case in a nutshell. Everybody else creates [near miss] above it and below it because they don't have at least approved yet the technology to do it on the pay line. And that's where the rub comes."

What is the difference, he asked, between producing a near miss above and below the pay line, as Universal's competitors do by clustering blanks around jackpot symbols, since players are influenced in the same way? "I don't think there is anybody in this room, and certainly nobody in the New Games Lab, that can tell you what the difference is. A near miss with three [jackpot symbols] above to me is just—would be more illustrative of almost winning [as] having the pay line show two winners and a loser."

Schreck contended that he had countered the board's statement that the Universal game was deceptive. Slot players were unable to predict their chances of winning by looking at the reel strips of a machine since Universal's competitors also used stepper motors, which permit more software stops on a 22-symbol reel. Further, he said, other companies were able to show more symbols in the pay line window than would naturally appear mathematically by clustering blanks around the symbols.

Besides, Schreck said, the board's gaming lab had at one time verbally approved a competitor's machine that clustered nine blanks in front of and nine blanks behind a jackpot symbol on a reel but withdrew the approval after Universal pointed out the clustering was the same as Universal's computerized near-miss feature. That proved "there is no standard at the lab; it's just what they determine," the lawyer said.

"We have competitors that cluster blanks that show more near miss than our machine shows," he said. "So if we really go back to where this all started with being supposedly some kind of deceptiveness or somehow it was unfair to the player because it causes the player to play more, that's the name of the game. We have always said, that's how gaming has been developed. And we have all tried to continue that."

"Universal had just succeeded at this point in time to a further degree than anybody else," he said. "But we know we have competitors that basically have acquired that same technology and want to use it, and we see no reason why the gaming commission and the state of Nevada would want to hinder that type of progress."

The state should adopt new standards to accommodate Universal's new technology, as it did in the mid-1970s, when slots run on microprocessors were introduced to replace electromechanical devices, Schreck said. Restricting machine manufacturers to "mimicking" electromechanical machines "is a step backwards," he said. "Universal has taken a step forward. . . . What we should be doing is to see how far we can go with new technology, how we can improve machines. . . . Universal does not want to be tied to electromechanical technology. We think that's wrong. We don't think it's the right direction."

Schreck called on the commission to adopt standards that would preserve Universal's popular machines. But the state's gaming lab needed help, he said. There was "a need for high level sophistication in the lab which maybe the state can't afford to pay for," he said, adding that was why Universal agreed to fund a professorship in computer technology at the University of Nevada, Las Vegas.

Universal's machines were responsible for the increase of slot play in Nevada for the past three years, Schreck said. Other machines used Universal technology, and "the only thing that isn't the same is the way we select our losers, and as we have argued before, a loser is a loser. Our winners are determined randomly. The percentage pay out meets chi-squared testing . . . and our losers would meet a chi-squared test. If you tried to relate it to the specific number of stops on losers, it would not [pass] because we don't relate . . . our losing combinations to reel strips because we deal in combinations, not individual stop positions."

Universal's agreement to halt sales of its machines with the near-miss feature at the end of April 1988 had cost the company tens of millions of dollars, and the firm deserved to have the issue resolved in its favor, Schreck said. The company's competitors benefited "because Universal has been basically out of business with respect to its Nevada EPROM machines since May of this year."

Raymond Pike, the in-house legal counsel for slot manufacturer IGT and a former attorney for the Gaming Commission, then asked to address the commission. Pike said IGT had perfected technology to place near misses in the pay line in 1986 but did not use it because the company felt it did not meet state standards. The Gaming Control Board had discussed the near-miss issue back in August 1983 and came to the conclusion it did not want to permit the concept, Pike said.

Because of the popularity of Universal's machines, "we know the customers want the near miss on the pay line," Pike said. "They tell us. Because Universal has been out selling it and has been in the past. If we thought it was not in breach of the policy, of course we would be there because competitively, we would have to be there. We felt that the issue had been decided."[43]

IGT elected to file for declaratory relief with the commission after learning about Universal's use of the near-miss concept, Pike said. Company officials withdrew the filing after the board assured them the state was preparing a complaint against Universal. IGT, he said, wanted the commission "to tell us what the rules are so we can be on the same playing field with Universal. If they are going to have an item or feature like this, that we have abided by your policy on not providing, we are placed at a competitive disadvantage. We are capable of it. . . . I tell you, tomorrow we can do it. We have programs waiting for approval that will do it. But it's just a question of how far you take it. . . . You have to draw a line. You want to draw the line tonight? We would need that. You would have to say how many times we can misrepresent."

Pike said the state should maintain its unwritten standard "that the pay line not reflect something other than what is mathematically in the game, the chances of outcome, rather than go to this weighted loser." Universal, he said, sets up winning symbols in the pay line at a higher degree of probability, equal to a 200 percent payback percentage.

"Yes, [IGT has] had subliminal inducements above and below [the pay line] and people see things peripherally, and they have lights and we have blips and we have bells and we have loud trays and kinds of things that help add to the enjoyments," Pike said. "But we haven't toyed with the pay line."[44]

Commissioner Ken Gragson asked Pike whether it was deceitful to produce near misses above and below the pay line.

"You could argue it is exactly the same," Pike said. "My response to you is we have never allowed the pay line to be played with. And that's what people look at to determine wins. . . . So far the line, and the way in which it's tested and the representation we have had, have not endangered the success of the slot machine as an economic advent in Nevada. There is only one company that's crossed a policy line that's been established for a number of years."

Chairman O'Reilly allowed Schreck to have the last word. Schreck said that he was at the 1983 Gaming Control Board hearing Pike referred to and that Universal did not violate the standards discussed by board members. IGT, he added, had complained Universal was not playing fair. But few players of IGT's Megabucks linked progressive machines have known that the multi-million-dollar jackpots are paid in annual payments spread over 20 years, Schreck said.

The real difference between the two companies, he said, was near miss in the pay line versus above and below. "We have the technology to do it on the pay line. They do it above and below the pay line. They have machines that if you take the calculation above and below the pay line, you get near a thousand percent. I mean, we haven't objected to that. There is a reason to encourage people to play gaming devices. We see the manufacturer's need to create that for the gaming casinos. And that's all we have done. We have just had a little bit better technology."[45]

With Schreck's statement over, it was time for the commission to deliberate. O'Reilly reminded commissioners that Universal's petition for declaratory relief asked them to rule on whether the features in its games, specifically the near-miss feature, were acceptable in Nevada. To rule in favor of the features, the commission would have to find acceptable what Universal admitted in the company's September 1988 stipulation with the board: that Universal's machines contained a program that ensured that after the win or loss of a game was randomly determined, "losing combinations of symbols were weighted so that certain losing combinations appear more frequently than other losing combinations."[46]

Commissioner Lewis said it was true that the near-miss concept was present "in a multitude of gaming devices in one form or another, and we have them in, according to what our lab folks have told us today, in nearly every machine that's on the floor of every casino in the state of Nevada, and it's an accepted process as far as slot machines are concerned. . . . And I would hope that we would not tinker with that. I think the system that we have had works."

However, Lewis said he had a problem with a machine that produced an outcome "not based on randomness." It was best to create a standard "where we have total randomness in losing as well as winning," said Lewis, adding that the type of near miss in mechanical machines could be achieved with random selection.

O'Reilly concurred with Lewis's opposition to Universal's use of near-miss combinations. So did Commissioner Betty Vogler, who said she appreciated

Schreck's arguments but feared the state would not be able to properly regulate Universal's near-miss machines.

Commissioner Gragson acknowledged that Universal's machines were very popular with players. The near-miss concept, he said, thus had merit, and the Gaming Control Board's lab ought to come up with a way to regulate it. Commissioner Robert Peccole said he also supported the near-miss feature. Peccole criticized the board and the commission for having approved it years before and now requiring Universal to spend "maybe a couple million dollars" to retrofit more than 10,000 machines.

"I think declaratory relief should be granted now," Peccole said. "I think that we can cover any problems the other manufacturers have with a meeting on regulations. . . . [The machine] is a proven winner. Why should we now sit back and play Monday morning quarterback and say, well geez, it's not right, it's not a concept that should be out there?"[47]

Peccole also chided Pike for saying that IGT did not alter pay lines. "I can remember the old mechanical machines when you'd load up the first reel and the second reel and have one bar on the end, and if that isn't messing around with the pay line, I don't know what is. I mean you are just as deceptive in that instance as you are with any concept of deception. It will bring those bars up on the first two reels, but nothing shows on the third reel. And people keep coming back because they think they are going to win."

Lewis interrupted Peccole to say that at least two commissioners had said they were not upset about near miss as a concept. Peccole replied that he was prepared to support a machine with the weighted-loser feature, even if it were not based on randomness, and to approve Universal's petition.

O'Reilly told Peccole the evidence clearly showed that some of the losing combinations in the Universal machines were weighted to appear more frequently than other losing combinations and so were not chosen randomly under the board's statistical definition.

The chairman then requested a motion to declare the Universal's near-miss feature unacceptable. When the roll was called, only Peccole voted against the motion. Universal would have to retrofit its near-miss machines. Before adjourning the meeting, O'Reilly said the commission would schedule another hearing to discuss the time frame Universal had to follow.

Schreck later filed another motion asking the commission to reconsider the December 1 decision. Hearings took place on January 26 and February 23, 1989. Schreck tried to argue that retrofitting Universal's 11,000 machines in Nevada to eliminate the near-miss feature would be too expensive. He filed briefs with the commission, pointing out that Universal's machines, including those with the feature, had the highest payback percentages of any other game approved in Nevada.[48] Schreck also filed affidavits signed by representatives of 30 major casinos stating, he said, "that there were never any customer complaints with respect to the machines and they were almost unanimously indicated to be the most popular machines at those locations."[49] Chairman O'Reilly even acknowledged that the near-miss program was not related "to the winning side of the program, but rather, the losing side, and does not affect the randomness on the winning side, of the program. . . ."[50]

Universal company officials claimed that retrofitting each machine would cost $59, and with 11,000 machines, the total cost would be $649,000, plus an extra $30,000 to buy 5,128 new EPROM computer chips.[51] The job would take four people about a year to complete, they said.

By the February 23 hearing, Schreck had more to bolster his case for reconsideration. The Gaming Control Board, in points and authorities filed with the commission, agreed that Universal was not the only slot company to create near miss on the pay line. Other makers of disproportionate slots also created it, the board agreed.[52] Schreck argued that there was nothing in the state's Gaming Control Act or in commission regulations that specifically prohibited a slot's computer program from making certain losing combinations appear more frequently than others after the losing game had been chosen randomly. Schreck then cited affidavits he had filed by a statistician who said the Universal machines chose both the first win-loss and second losing combinations randomly under state standards.[53] Schreck also said the expert had determined that the machines could be tested by state examiners, using a computer program the expert had developed. In a rehearing on the Universal program by the commission, these arguments could be made to refute previous claims about it, he said.

"Primarily the issue is that we can show we are random," he said. "We can show we can be tested, and we can show that we can be regulated."[54]

Deputy Attorney General Ellen Whittemore told the commission that Universal had not offered much new information or evidence since the December hearing. The board, she said, could call forward its own experts and casino executives who did not like the Universal machines.

"But the issue before the commission right now is really a matter of policy," Whittemore said. "Unless the commission believes its policy in the past is incorrect, unless it believes that it should repudiate past standards, there isn't really any reason to rehear or reargue this case."[55]

Whittemore said that the public believed the Universal machine was based on the movement of reel strips when it was based on combinations of stops. She cited an opinion on how slot machines should operate, submitted to the board by Dr. William Eadington of the University of Nevada, Reno. Eadington said slots had three characteristics: The reels must spin, the reels must work independently, and then the machine must relate the result of the game in the pay line. Eadington said Universal's near-miss machines had not met any of those three factors.[56]

"What this means is that if the first reel stops on a seven, that stopping on a seven has no effect on what the second reel will do," Whittemore said. "The second standard that has been applied to slot machines is that the display of a symbol, any symbol, must occur on the pay line in frequency equal to the mathematical probability of their occurrence whether or not that symbol is appearing in a winning or a losing combination. The Universal slots . . . do not meet these standards."[57]

The board, she said, cited another standard that Universal (and disproportionate slots made by some other manufacturers) did not meet: "that the probability of a symbol appearing immediately above or below the pay line is the same as the probability of that same symbol appearing on the pay line."

When the debate went to the commissioners, chairman O'Reilly said that Universal appeared to be the only manufacturer unable to meet state standards and that a rehearing would not accomplish much. Commissioners Lewis, Vogler, and Gragson agreed that a new hearing was not necessary and that they would vote against the motion. Lewis complained that the board should have provided the commission with more information at the December 1 hearing and said he still felt, even without a rehearing, that near miss was acceptable as long as the symbols on the reels were selected at random.

Commissioner Peccole said he still felt that the Universal slot chose winners and losers randomly, that it could be tested, and that the state had no written standards prohibiting Universal's program. Universal was not the only machine maker that put near misses into the pay line, Peccole said.

"Now, why do we allow those then if we are not going to allow Universal?" he said. "Just because they have a different way of getting to the final results?"[58]

The commission voted 4 to 1, with Peccole opposed, against reopening the issue and compelled Universal to remove the near-miss feature from its machines within nine months.

Among the machines Universal had to retrofit was its three-reel machine that caused three 7s to appear in the pay line—a jackpot only with the maximum three coins played—more often when one or two coins were played. Whittemore later estimated there were actually 12,000 to 15,000 Universal machines in the state with the program and that the cost to retrofit was not high compared to the company's income from sales. Universal, which sold the machines for an average of $4,000 each, had made $48 million to $60 million on them, she said. The cost to retrofit was actually relatively low—about $30 per machine, or $360,000 to $450,000, equal to only about 0.75 percent of gross sales, she added.

In July 1989, the commission approved key amendments to Regulation 14. One required that all gaming devices use random selection to determine game outcomes and "meet 95 percent confidence limits using a standard chi-squared test for goodness of fit." Electronic games that simulated live games, such as video craps, had to use computer programs that copied the mathematical probability of the live version of the game. For other machines, "the mathematical probability of a symbol appearing in a position in any game must be constant," the new regulation read. Furthermore, the selection process in gaming machines "must not produce detectable patterns of game elements or detectable dependency upon previous game outcome, the amount wagered, or upon the style or method of play." The games also had to "display an accurate representation of the game outcome" and "must not make a variable secondary decision which affects the result of the player." Also, unrelated to the Universal matter, the commission for the first time in writing obliged gaming machines in Nevada to have a payout percentage of at least 75 percent for each coin wagered.

Universal went about retrofitting its machines in Nevada and continued to sell gaming devices in the state. In 1990, Universal's share of the world's gaming machine market stood at about 17 percent, compared to 26 percent for Bally and 44 percent for IGT. But according to Universal attorney Schreck, the company suffered irrevocably from the April 1988 ban on sales of its near-miss machines.

"Universal went from having the premiere machine in the business to being, for all intents and purposes, out of business," Schreck said.[59]

"All of our resources went to fighting this," said ex–Universal sales manager Harris. "It was very controversial. There was misinformation in the newspapers. We proved beyond a shadow of a doubt that it was random. Near miss came down to how we displayed our losing combinations."[60]

The company suffered other problems followed the near-miss settlement. In September 1989, Universal agreed to stop selling models of a video poker machine to settle a copyright infringement suit filed in federal court in Reno by IGT, which claimed the machines were copies of IGT's Player's Edge machine. The agreement gave Universal the right to submit a new video poker device to Nevada gaming authorities for approval only after IGT had reviewed the model to see whether it duplicated its machines. That same year, Universal stopped producing video gaming machines. By then, IGT was already the number-one manufacturer of gaming machines in the world. In 1988, IGT grossed $140 million. In 1996, IGT had sold 85,300 machines, or nearly 75 percent of the gaming devices purchased worldwide.

Universal's success story faded in the 1990s. The company was hurt both by its waning ability to supply the rapidly expanding American casino market and by a downturn in Japan's economy. In February 1995, Universal's sole owner, Kazuo Okada, who was found guilty of tax evasion in Japan in 1984, agreed to give up daily control of his U.S. subsidiary to a U.S. citizen in exchange for permission to sell only 240 Universal machines, worth $1.2 million, to Harrah's Jazz casino in New Orleans. Gaming control officials in Louisiana demanded the concession after learning of Universal's poor financial state. The company, which had a net worth of just $8 million in 1991, was in the red to the tune of $21 million in 1994 and owed $39.5 million to Kazuo Okada.[61]

In Las Vegas in 1997, Universal launched a new model of slot machine but still had not recovered. The firm's workforce fell from a high of 138 in the late 1980s to only seven in early 1998. A company official told the author that Universal's goal for 1998 was to try to develop a new type of gaming machine.

Chapter Five

Casino Politics
The Gaming Board vs. Sheldon Adelson and the Las Vegas Sands

When the five-member Nevada Gaming Commission was created by the state legislature in 1959, lawmakers gave the commission the power to override the three-member Nevada State Gaming Control Board, created in 1955, on gaming licensing recommendations. If the board voted 2 to 1 to recommend or to deny a license, the commission could overrule it by a simple majority. But if the board voted 3 to 0 against granting an applicant a gaming license, the recommendation would stand unless the commissioners voted unanimously in favor of the applicant.

The unanimity provision has been practically unnecessary. The board and the commission have rarely disagreed over the past four decades. But one time they did in a big way. In 1989, the commission overturned a license denial recommendation by the board for the first time. That year, amid a heavy dose of political pressure, the commission ignored the board's 3-to-0 vote and granted a license to a former hotel executive who had left the industry in disgrace a few years before. The public nature of the arm-twisting to license the man aroused bitterness on the board and tarnished the credibility of Nevada's gaming control process. The overruling left the impression that politics, "juice," and the prospect of a more than $200-million megaresort could influence the state's ability to judge the "suitability" of a gaming license applicant, one of the board's most important functions. Ultimately, the decision would matter little in the case of the executive himself. But it would set in motion a project that a decade later would become one of the most expensive ever in Nevada—the $1.5 billion Venetian Resort Casino.

The battleground for this conflict in February 1989 was the venerable Sands Hotel, by then only a relic of its heyday in the 1950s and 1960s as the famous mobbed-up "Place in the Sun" playground of Frank Sinatra and his Rat Pack group of entertainers. On the gaming-industry side was Sheldon G. Adelson, a 56-year-old trade show man from Boston who had agreed to buy the Sands in 1988 from casino and movie studio wheeler-dealer Kirk Kerkorian for $110 million. After the sale, the board launched a nine-month licensing background investigation of Adelson, his partners, and his management team.

As the leader of this new pack intent on operating the aging Sands, Adelson was already well known in Las Vegas as a man accustomed to using influence to get his way. The barrel-chested, 5-foot-5 Adelson, in interviews with the media, said he grew up poor in the slums of Boston, the son of a cab driver. He studied corporate finance and real estate at City College of New York and developed an ambition to strike it rich on Wall Street during a stint as a court stenographer for the U.S. Army in the 1950s. Adelson, as he once put it, later "made my first million" charging small capital companies a finders fee to help them go public and sell stock.[1] In the 1960s, he became a self-described venture capitalist in Boston, eventually buying up 75 companies. He lost his first fortune after the stock market declined in the late 1960s. He soon recovered by entering the real estate brokerage business, concentrating on arranging condominium conversions for a single client. But that venture failed, too, and Adelson, who still owned a condominium building, lost a second big wad of cash. Adelson's road to ultimate success started in 1971, when he acquired a majority interest in a small publishing company. He read in a magazine about a trade show for the condominium market to be held in Anaheim, California, and decided to attend. While in Anaheim, he learned that the magazine he had read also owned the trade show. The magazine sold exhibition space for the show to its advertisers, and Adelson figured he could do the same with his company's computer industry publication, *Data Communications User.* In 1973, his company produced its first high-tech industry trade show in Dallas. In 1975, Adelson, unable to see eye-to-eye with his partners, sold his share of the publishing firm, but he held on to the trade show. With money raised from the sale of his condominium building, he started Interface Group, Inc. Progress, however, was slow. In 1979, his firm had 21 employees and revenues of only $250,000.

But Adelson and the Interface Group, based in Needham, Massachusetts, finally made it big that same year when he conceived of and produced the annual Computer Dealer Expo, known as COMDEX, geared toward small computer dealers, at the old MGM Grand in Las Vegas. By 1984, Interface was producing some 40 trade shows, and the COMDEX/Fall show in Las Vegas alone grossed $20 million. COMDEX soon became the largest trade show in Las Vegas. Four years later, the gathering attracted 125,000 people, up from 100,000 the previous year. Adelson's company saw its net income reach a hefty $250 million. Interface also put on COMDEX shows in Chicago, Atlanta, and

Anaheim and in Europe and Japan, prompting some companies to complain there were too many shows and too few attendees. Others balked at the high prices for booths, which reached $500,000 each. Adelson, assessed only 15 cents per square foot by the Las Vegas Convention Center for exhibit space, charged his show customers as much as $50 per square foot for the same space.

Interface guaranteed itself a healthy cash flow by requiring COMDEX exhibitors to sign contracts for exhibit space and then pay up front for it a year in advance of the show. The ever-ambitious Adelson, seeking more space to feed the demand for COMDEX, spent $1.8 million of his own money in 1985 to build a new convention hall next to the Las Vegas Convention Center, then sold the new hall to the Las Vegas Convention and Visitors Authority for just a dollar.[2]

But in the late 1980s, Adelson wanted more dollars from Las Vegas, this time from the gaming industry on the Strip. After unsuccessful attempts to purchase the Dunes and Frontier hotels and overtures for the Aladdin Hotel, he landed a deal for the Sands in 1988. By that time, Interface Group owned the convention-meetings firm, a pair of tour and travel companies, and an airline with five Boeing L-1011 aircraft. Adelson's blueprint for the Sands property included flying in guests on the company's charter planes and investing an additional $150 million in a new resort and shopping mall there, featuring 1,300 new guest rooms and a $60 million convention center with a million square feet of exhibit space. He boasted that the center would be the largest single-story convention facility in the world. His overall strategy was to use the Sands as a destination for his tour and travel customers from the eastern United States. He announced the project would start in November 1989 and open about 18 months later.

Adelson also yearned for something else for his Las Vegas project, which would prove difficult and challenging. He wanted former Hilton Hotels Corporation executive Henri Lewin and Lewin's hotel-casino management team to be licensed by Nevada to operate and share in the gaming proceeds of the Sands. Adelson's Interface partners and fellow Bostonians, Irvin Chafetz and Theodore Cutler, had known Lewin since the mid-1960s, when Lewin was an executive at the San Francisco Hilton. They were grateful for his help with the American International Travel Service (AITS), their innovative tour and travel business, which by the late 1960s had become a company worth tens of millions on Wall Street. However, Adelson and his team backed Lewin, knowing that state gaming officials would have problems with the former hotel executive's troubled background.

With that in mind, Adelson went shopping for political clout in Las Vegas. As part of the Sands battle plan, Adelson's team convinced Clark County Sheriff John Moran, former Nevada governor Mike O'Callaghan, Hilton Hotels

Corporation chairman Barron Hilton, and ex–Gaming Control Board agent Dennis Gomes to send letters to state gaming officials praising Lewin and supporting his licensing bid. And, figuring to add more local influence, Adelson hired attorney and former Nevada governor Robert List to argue for the Sands partners during the final licensing showdown before the Gaming Commission.

Adelson's determination was characteristic. The *Boston Globe,* from interviews with his former employees, described Adelson in 1988 as someone who was "dictatorial, moved too fast and has a penchant for suing." One former employee noted that "the problem comes when you stand in the way of Mr. Adelson. He doesn't want anyone to get in his way and that is why he is buying the Sands."[3]

Lewin, once one of the top hotel-casino executives in the country, was ready to reenter the Las Vegas casino fray after a four-year absence. From 1981 to 1985, Lewin was chief executive officer of Las Vegas–based Hilton Nevada Corporation, then the hotel-casino subsidiary of the Hilton chain headquartered in Beverly Hills, California. Hilton Nevada operated the chain's two casinos in Las Vegas and one in Reno. Those four years, during which Lewin presided over major expansions by the Las Vegas Hilton and the Flamingo Hilton, transformed the worldwide hotel company. By the late 1980s, Hilton officials said its Nevada hotel-casinos alone accounted for more than 40 percent of the revenue of the entire Hilton chain. Lewin helped make the Las Vegas Hilton the top-grossing convention hotel in the country. Barron Hilton once dubbed Lewin "the best executive the company ever had."

What made Lewin's rise to the top of the hotel-casino business even more impressive was the story of how he got there. As he described to journalists over the years, Lewin, a native of Potsdam in eastern Germany, was working in his father's hotel in 1937 at age 13 when he and other Jews were arrested and sent to a concentration camp in Spandau. A German policeman who knew Lewin's father helped the young Lewin leave the camp, and he fled to China in 1938. He found work in Shanghai in nightclubs, and in 1940, at age 16, was elected president of the Foreign Hotel Employees Association. But in December 1941, he was arrested and placed into a refugee camp by the occupying Japanese. After the war, in 1947, he said he weighed only 78 pounds when he arrived on a merchant ship at the port of San Francisco. Lewin claimed to have asked a cabbie to take him to the best hotel in town and was driven to the Fairmont, where he soon got a job washing dishes. He moved into food and beverage management at the Fairmont, then joined the San Francisco Hilton in 1964 as food and beverage director. He became a vice president of the Hilton hotel chain only three years later.

In 1980, Hilton made Lewin executive vice president of the chain, in charge of the company's 12-hotel Western Division and its hotel operations in New

Jersey. Lewin was sent to Las Vegas the following year. While ensconced in his expansive office at the Las Vegas Hilton, Lewin was known as a flamboyant and irreverent character, at times arrogant and self-congratulatory. He was also willing to speak his mind to the press on topics avoided by other hotel-casino executives.

But Lewin's days at the helm of the Hilton hotel-casinos in Nevada and New Jersey ended in 1985. That year, a Las Vegas Hilton cocktail waitress alleged in a suit in federal court that he tried to grope her breasts and buttocks in his office. The suit was settled for an undisclosed sum, its contents sealed by the court. But the timing could not have been worse. That same year, the Hilton chain was applying for a license in the only American casino jurisdiction other than Nevada at the time, Atlantic City. In a major embarrassment for the Hilton company, the New Jersey Casino Control Commission, using gaming regulations far more strict than Nevada's, turned down the application. One of the commissioners' concerns had centered on Sidney Korshack, an influential Chicago and Beverly Hills attorney that the Hilton company insisted on retaining despite allegations Korshack had ties to organized crime figures for many years.

There were also questions about Lewin's background. The New Jersey commission's investigation revealed that while senior vice president of the San Francisco Hilton in 1974, Lewin faced federal charges for giving $886 worth of free lodging, entertainment, food, and drink to Rudy Tham, an official of the Teamsters Freight Checkers Local 856 who participated in negotiating labor contracts for hotel employees. That case was moved to federal court in Las Vegas, and in 1980, U.S. District Judge Harry Claiborne dismissed the charges against Lewin and Tham. It was later learned that Lewin had helped arrange, at Claiborne's request, rooms for the judge at a Hilton hotel in Hawaii on two occasions in 1982. (A few years later, Judge Claiborne was charged with tax evasion. A longtime Nevada attorney, Claiborne in 1986 became the first federal jurist to be impeached and forced off the bench by the U.S. Senate. In an unrelated case, Tham was convicted of embezzling Teamster funds in 1982 in connection with an investigation of alleged kickbacks from hotels.)

After hearings on the Hilton application, the New Jersey commissioners voted 2 to 2 (with one seat on the commission vacant), defeating the company's licensing bid. One commissioner who voted against Hilton indicated that Korshack was the problem, not Lewin, and even said he favored licensing Lewin. But the damage was done. Hilton sold its proposed Boardwalk hotel-casino property to casino mogul Donald Trump. Amid the attention in New Jersey and the waitress's suit back in Las Vegas, Barron Hilton asked Lewin to quit. With Lewin out of the picture and Korshack fired, the company reapplied for a license in New Jersey and received one in 1991. Lewin moved to his home in Zephyr Cove, Nevada, on the shore of Lake Tahoe, out of which he operated a consulting business for the hotel industry called Aristocrat Hotels of Nevada, Inc.

Despite the baggage Lewin carried, Sheldon Adelson was determined to have his man, the 65-year-old Lewin, in at the Sands. On February 8, 1989, Adelson, Lewin, and their respective teams appeared at the Gaming Control Board's hearing in the second floor of the board's main office in Carson City, Nevada's capital city, about 400 miles northwest of Las Vegas. The board included members Dennis Amerine, a former chief of the board's Audit Division, who was seated as the board's auditing expert, and Gerald Cunningham, a former captain in the Las Vegas Metropolitan Police Department, serving as the board's law enforcement representative. The chairman was Bill Bible, appointed only two months earlier by Governor Richard Bryan in Democrat Bryan's final act as governor before joining the U.S. Senate. Bible was a former state budget director and had managed Bryan's successful November 1988 election campaign. Bible's father, Alan, was a U.S. senator from Nevada, and his brother, Paul, an attorney in northern Nevada, once served as chairman of the Gaming Commission.

At 9 A.M., the board began the hearing into the application by Las Vegas Sands, Inc.—a Nevada corporation that would own the Sands—and Lewin's Aristocrat Hotels for nonrestricted gaming licenses to operate and partake in the profits at the new Sands. Under state gaming laws, each shareholder in the private companies had to submit to and pay for investigations by the board into their financial backgrounds as well as any arrests, convictions, or civil actions brought against them.

The business deal Adelson crafted had each shareholder of the Interface Group owning the same amount of shares in Las Vegas Sands. Las Vegas Sands listed Adelson as president, director, and 58.8 percent owner; Irwin Chafetz, a director, 14.7 percent; Theodore Cutler, treasurer and director, 14.7 percent; and Dr. Jordan L. Shapiro (Adelson's brother-in-law), secretary and director, 11.8 percent. Las Vegas Sands asked that the gaming license application of a fifth man, Richard A. Katzeff, for director and shareholder, be withdrawn. All five men were Interface partners.[4]

Lewin's Aristocrat Hotels sought to both manage and participate in the hotel's profits. Lewin was listed as president, director, and 25 percent owner; Kenneth S. Scholl as executive vice president and director with 25 percent; Lewin's son, Larry L. Lewin, as secretary, treasurer, and director with 25 percent; and Paul F. Klapper as simply a 25 percent shareholder.

At the start of the hearing, Chairman Bible directed Las Vegas Sands attorney Robert Callaway to provide an overview on how the hotel project would operate, what the relationship would be between the Sands operation and

Interface Group, and how the project would be financed. Bible also wanted details on the backgrounds of the eight applicants and the advisory role of Drexel-Burnham-Lambert, the Wall Street firm of financier Michael Milken, who had recently pleaded guilty to securities fraud charges following an investigation by the Securities and Exchange Commission (SEC). Adelson's Interface Group hired Drexel to raise $75 million worth of unsecured debt to help finance the Sands project, using future cash flow at the Sands to back it.

Addressing the board, Callaway emphasized what the Sands deal would mean for the investors and for Nevada's economy. The purchase of the 716-room Sands by Interface Group "represents the front end of a quarter-billion-dollar investment with the stated purpose of once again placing the Sands in a position of preeminence, both in Las Vegas, Nevada and worldwide."[5]

Callaway then described the expansion plans. Interface Group's experience in convention-related business and the tour and travel business and its fleet of aircraft would allow the company to offer a "fully integrated business" at the Sands, Callaway said. "It presents an unparalleled opportunity for success in the tourism market of Las Vegas and Nevada," he said, adding that even though the buyers were from Boston, "they already have strong ties to the Las Vegas community" because of COMDEX and the CINTEX film festival Adelson had recently organized in the city. He acknowledged eight people in the audience brought in to help answer questions from board members. One was Steve O'Conner, Interface Group's director of taxes and treasury operations. The others included a financial analyst from the Las Vegas office of the Arthur Anderson & Company, three executives from Drexel-Burnham-Lambert in New York, a securities law attorney, a Las Vegas gaming lawyer, and Interface Group's private legal counsel.

O'Conner testified about the complex financial framework that Interface Group and its individual shareholders worked out to back the Sands project. Of the total $128 million Interface spent to purchase the Sands hotel, Adelson and other Interface shareholders planned to loan $12 million interest free to Las Vegas Sands, plus arrange for $46.5 million in interest-free loans from Interface Group company funds—effectively, $58.5 million the partners would loan to themselves. The group also would obtain a $70 million first mortgage loan from outside the company.[6]

For the $87.5 million needed for a first-phase expansion of the Sands, 7 percent would be loaned by the Interface Group partners, 28 percent from a loan from Interface Group as a company (both loans, again, without interest), and the remaining 65 percent from outside financing. The partners used this complicated financing method to accommodate federal income tax rules. Interface designated itself, under U.S. tax laws, an S small business corporation, which permitted company-to-company, interest-free loans under certain conditions.

Shareholders in S corporations paid 6 percent lower federal income taxes than larger C corporations. Interface had wanted Las Vegas Sands to be an S corporation as well. However, under federal rules, Interface could not own 80 percent of the stock of a subsidiary company, in this case Las Vegas Sands. And since S firms also were not allowed to have a corporate shareholder, Las Vegas Sands would likely lose its S status if Interface invested money into it by buying shares. So, to play it safe and stay under the 80 percent investment figure, Interface's individual shareholders would themselves loan just over 20 percent of the funds—about $12 million—for the Sands project, with the remaining 80 percent or so "in the form of paid in kind loans" from the corporate entity, Interface, O'Conner said. An additional $3.5 million would be set aside by the shareholders to help service the debt.

Interface also was in the process of trying to finance $40 million for the proposed convention center. Along with that, "the shareholders through a combination of their equity investments and the loans from the Interface Group will have in excess of $100 million at risk here," O'Conner said.[7]

Chairman Bible attempted to make sense out of the complex deal. "The finance package is a $75 million package, and it looks like there is $16 and-a-half million of the placement that stays with Interface," he said, to no objection from the applicants.

Under additional questioning from Bible, O'Conner agreed the Sands venture would not be able to service its $46.5 million debt after three or four years without income anticipated from the planned expansion of the resort.

Adelson was the first of the Sands applicants to testify. Interface, he said, had three divisions, including the show production company, a tour division consisting of two firms, G W V Travel and International Weekends, and its private airline, Five Star Airlines. Interface was in good financial shape, thanks mostly to its insistence that trade show exhibitors pay their money up front, enabling Interface to use the funds for a year prior to actually putting on the shows, he said.

"Our cash flow is assured because deposits for and contracts for future exhibition space, which is the dominant part of our income, is signed and submitted and paid for a year in advance," Adelson said. "And our system of reserving space for future shows is one that guarantees us future cash flow. . . . Our travel division is also we get paid before anybody goes on a trip. Deposits are made in advance, and nobody goes on their plane or takes a vacation without it being paid in advance. There is vertical integration between all divisions. The tour operation division, the travel division supply passengers to the airline and also provide services to the show division in the form of hotel reservations and airline reservations for both our in-house staff and customers."[8]

The company's strategy was to use Las Vegas as a tour destination and build the convention center to hold its own trade shows. Interface would borrow the money to construct the center, own it, and lease it out for about $8 million a year. The center would pay for itself in five to six years, Adelson said.

Board member Amerine asked Adelson what role Interface would have in managing the Sands with Lewin's team. Adelson replied that Lewin would operate the Sands but that Interface would retain "veto power" over him. Adelson said he had known Lewin for a dozen years, and Interface partners Chafetz and Cutler had known him for 25 years. Apparently anticipating the board's concerns about Lewin, Adelson then put the whole project on the line.

> ADELSON: We have a great deal of respect for Mr. Lewin and Mr. Scholl and Larry Lewin. As a matter of fact, if it wasn't for Mr. Lewin's availability, we probably wouldn't—we wouldn't have gone into this deal at all. We never would have signed the agreement, and the transaction would have no interest for us.

Board member Cunningham then raised a question about what would happen if Lewin were not licensed.[9]

> MEMBER CUNNINGHAM: You pose an interesting proposition. You have heightened the expectations that are coming forth. I hope you are aware that there are some problems that are going to be talked about today with Mr. Lewin, and you have indicated that you may be canceling your interest in this whole project. It depends on the outcome of that.
>
> ADELSON: Correct. If you had the relationship with him like we do, and you had the trust and confidence in him based upon experience with him, you'd feel the same way that we do.
>
> MEMBER CUNNINGHAM: Well, we'll see.[10]

Mark Attanasio, Drexel-Burnham-Lambert's vice president of corporate finance, was sworn in and asked to provide an update on the Wall Street company's legal problems. Drexel, one of the top investment bankers on Wall Street, had put up more than $2.5 billion—mostly in junk bonds—to gaming projects built by major casino companies, such as Golden Nugget, Inc.; Circus Circus Enterprises, Inc.; Caesars World, Inc.; and Bally Manufacturing, Inc., in Nevada, since 1980.[11]

Attanasio told the board that Drexel, which was helping Interface obtain outside financing for the Sands, had only recently entered into an agreement with the U.S. Attorney's office in New York to plead guilty to six counts of mail fraud and securities fraud charges. The deal was contingent on the firm settling a complaint filed by the SEC. None of the criminal charges and none of the 18 violations alleged by the SEC related to financing of Nevada gaming companies, Attanasio said. He offered to give the board a copy of the settlement agreement with the SEC as long it was not released to the public.

Cunningham asked about Milken, the Drexel executive facing sentencing on felony securities fraud charges. Cunningham said he was concerned about Milken's suitability to lend money to gaming firms and that at some point Drexel might have to be called forward for a suitability hearing by the board. But, he added, he did not wish to halt Drexel's financial efforts for the Sands project. Amerine and Bible also favored investigating Drexel's role in financing gaming companies.

"[W]e have to assure ourselves through our own investigation that none of the gaming companies' stock were involved in any of these deeds that may not have been included in a complaint but may have occurred," Amerine said. "I think the only way we can do that is to take a look at Drexel at some point in time." [12]

After Attanasio left the podium, Adelson asked to make another statement for Lewin. He praised Lewin's ability and said his experience in marketing and conventions at the Las Vegas Hilton coincided with Interface's strategies for Las Vegas. "[I]t's all of our money, and we are making over a $103,600,000 wager, so to speak, on Mr. Lewin's ability," Adelson said. [13]

In response, Cunningham repeated that he was concerned about licensing Lewin. "Obviously, my statements were predicated on the fact that there are things that are bothering me," the board member said. "Whether or not you are aware of them, I don't know, but before this meeting is over you will, and I would probably appreciate your comments at directing the issues that are bothering me after we talk to Mr. Lewin."

The board had few concerns about Interface partners Cutler and Shapiro and Aristocrat partners Kenneth Scholl and Larry Lewin. Cunningham questioned Cutler about his association with Henry Vara, a Bostonian and one-time owner of a nationwide string of gay bars who served time in a state prison and was alleged to have had associations with organized crime figures. Cutler said he had met Vara socially over a period of years and took part in some investments with him, including a casino cruise ship in New York in the mid-1970s and an airline in Atlantic City. Cutler said that he and Interface partner Chafetz each put up about $50,000 into the cruise ship, the *USS America*.

The board then called Adelson to come forward to answer questions. He acknowledged that his Massachusetts real estate license was suspended for six months in 1975. He was also was called to testify before a grand jury about two business associates who were subsequently indicted, convicted, and sentenced to prison. Board investigators had also found his name attached to about 100 civil suits, mainly dating back to the 1960s and 1970s. Many of the lawsuits came from companies or people to whom Adelson owed money, including bills for utility and gas station charges, hospital services, private prep school tuition, American Express charges, and service at a restaurant.

> CUNNINGHAM: It is expected of course that you would have a few lawsuits. What bothered me in looking at some of these is that it appears they are ordinary-type bills. It just goes on an on. It is like you never paid a bill.
>
> ADELSON: They are what, sir?
>
> CUNNINGHAM: Ordinary-type bills that you were hesitant or unable to pay. And I'd like to ask you about a couple of those, if I might—
>
> ADELSON: Sure.
>
> CUNNINGHAM: —and if you recall them. There is one in '63. It is the Hawaiian Village Restaurant. Do you remember that one?
>
> ADELSON: 1963?
>
> CUNNINGHAM: Yes.
>
> ADELSON: I don't know what the Hawaiian Village Restaurant is.
>
> CUNNINGHAM: Try a little easier one. There is a 1971 one, the Beth Israel Hospital, a $600 contractual dispute.
>
> ADELSON: That was just—that was just one of a whole series of what I call household or personal kinds of expenses that arose out of a very severe financial reverse that I suffered with the drop in the market in May of 1969.
>
> CUNNINGHAM: Okay. Really that kind of addresses a lot of things that I take into account.[14]

Cunningham listed debts that Adelson had settled, including a $1,000 bill for carpeting reduced to $745 and a bill for $1,500 from a lamp company erased for $1,100. Adelson explained that his financial reversal in 1969 prevented him from paying many of his bills. He said was heavily leveraged and was unable to retrieve funds he loaned to "venture capital-type investments." Other bills arose from an investment with a partner and from a bar owned by his own brother. However, Adelson insisted he paid the bills back completely. Cunningham said it appeared as though Adelson settled the debts for "somewhat less than the amounts charged." Adelson replied that it was "more expedient" and less costly for him to settle some of the smaller bills than hire and pay an attorney to fight them.

"I appreciate that," Cunningham replied. "I think what I'm indicating, it would have probably been more expedient if you had the ability to pay the bill."

The exchange continued. Cunningham asked about years-old disputes over $400, $1,500, and $9,000 that were settled for lower sums. Adelson testified that he could not remember any of them. Cunningham then asked about a conflict over $200,000 Adelson had with man named Philip Sforza.

ADELSON: You know, when that matter came up, I couldn't remember what it was. I know it is a substantial amount of money.

CUNNINGHAM: I was trying to get out of the hundreds and get to something that might trigger your recollection.

ADELSON: Yeah. Frankly, the name evokes a memory, and I think it had something to do with my brother and the bar. But I frankly can't remember.

CUNNINGHAM: Well, I like that. A man that can forget $200,000 is my kind of guy.

ADELSON: Well, I'm glad I am your kind of guy as opposed to not being your kind of guy.

CUNNINGHAM: I am trying to not discuss all these with you, and I am scanning some of them that might have interest to me.

ADELSON: I don't remember what it was. Honestly, I don't.[15]

Adelson also had a $155,000 dispute, later settled, with convicted tax evader Sanford A. Sorrentino over repairs that Sorrentino was to have made on a house in Cape Cod, Massachusetts, that Sorrentino had sold to Adelson in 1983. Sorrentino was sentenced to prison for tax evasion and later fled the country. Chafetz, who had mentioned to Adelson that Sorrentino was going to jail and needed to sell the home, introduced Adelson to Sorrentino.

Board member Amerine said he did not have a problem with Adelson's slew of settlements since "they did arise out of some financial difficulties. . . . I just want to make sure that Mr. Adelson understands the problem that we have with people that do business through litigation."

Cunningham turned to Adelson's relationship with former gay bar owner Henry Vara. Vara was arrested in Boston for tax evasion in connection with skimming money and canceling cash registers at some of the bars he owned. Adelson's partner Chafetz had invested in a number of radio stations in Florida with Vara and socialized with him on occasion. Adelson said he had known Vara for years but not very well, having only had a drink once in a while with him at Chafetz's urging. Adelson added, however, that the Henry Vara he knew "is totally different than his reputation." Vara lost a daughter to leukemia and consoled a friend of Adelson's who also had a child who died of the disease in the early 1980s. The friend "was very, very broken up over his son and still is today," Adelson said. "My friend kept on telling me that Henry kept on trying to console him, and through that I learned about a very sensitive person. And that's the most intimate knowledge I have of Henry Vara."

The subject then turned to Adelson's friendship with Chafetz. Adelson had known Chafetz for more than 45 years, ever since they lived in a poor section of Boston. "I don't know anyone would say anything negative about Irwin," Adelson said. "He's the finest, one of the few finest men in the world I have ever met in my life." When Cunningham said his concern about Chafetz's association with Vara was "extreme," Adelson replied that "Mr. Vara is not the applicant, Mr. Chafetz is. So I can speak of my relationship with Mr. Chafetz, since I have no relationship with Mr. Vara except to say hello." Nothing in his experience with Chafetz, Adelson went on, would lead him to believe that his friend "would do anything illegal, unprincipled, unethical or untoward." The Sands project would be hampered if Chafetz were found unsuitable by the board, he added. The Sands deal was Chafetz's dream because Chafetz was a tour operator for the hotel starting in the mid-1960s, he said. Furthermore, nothing could change his opinion of Chafetz's adherence to principles and values, not even the issues the Gaming Control Board had with Chafetz's business deals and finances, he told Cunningham.

"I mean, that man and I am almost like Siamese twins. We are almost joined physically. There is nothing in the world that can convince me that he would do anything wrong," he said. Chafetz, Adelson went on, should not be punished for the "sins of a friend."

"But associations are of extreme importance to us," Cunningham responded. "And when we have associations that are deemed less than desirable, this member right here is going to have some problems with it."[16]

Amerine echoed Cunningham. "I disagree with you, Mr. Adelson," he said. "Associations do pose a problem. They have influence on an individual, and if that person is unsuitable, in our opinion, then the person he is associating with, that is an applicant that could be unsuitable."

Adelson replied that he saw their point but that he did not believe Chafetz was influenced by Vara. Cunningham then said that the board expected Adelson, as a corporate representative, "to be able to recognize associations of possible notorious and unsavory character, and I am not referring that to anybody in particular, because we ask that you exclude such persons from dealings of a business nature with your hotel if you are approved on this, and various other matters." Cunningham told Adelson he did not have a problem with his application and appreciated Adelson's candor regarding his past debts. But the board member criticized what he described as Adelson's "ability to judge people and character and your inability to find fault with associations that to me at any rate . . . are not desirable and not in the best interests of the State of Nevada. This is a rigidly regulated industry. It is a constant battle to keep them out." Chafetz was one such person Cunningham was concerned with. "I'm unswaying in my attitude, and probably a lot of people wish they'd never put me here, but it is too late for that."

"Generally, I was excited by what I saw your plans were for the Sands," Cunningham continued. "I think the convention center is neat; the expansion of the tower, that's exciting. And I get no particular enjoyment out of going in the direction I'm going. It's the conflict that arises in these summaries that brings us about. I am not always this difficult. And if you categorize what I am doing to you difficult, then you have seen nothing yet. But I don't know, maybe it is right, maybe it is wrong. But I have got to make judgments based on what I perceive the facts."[17]

Adelson replied that Chafetz would be devastated if he failed to be licensed. He suggested the board could simply give his partner a "provisional license" so Chafetz could have time to disassociate himself with Vara. Cunningham responded he wanted to impress on Adelson what was at stake for the state.

"[W]hat this business leads to are large sums of money, and if people don't honor out of integrity and honesty and so forth the rules, regulations, internal controls that we pose to them, it's a great vehicle to skim a lot of money, to bankrupt an organization, to put a lot of people out of work," Cunningham said. "There is no inference there, Mr. Adelson. We run this business to a great extent on trust. We put the rules there. We follow the rules. The rules tell us or give us an indication if you are doing it right. But the integrity in following those rules is the licensee. So it is important that a great deal of concern and recognition of the things that I am concerned about be recognized by you, and I am not saying you don't."

Chafetz then began his testimony. Bible asked him to talk about Vara. Chafetz admitted that Vara "has a very bad reputation," but he added, as Adelson had mentioned, he knew Vara differently, as a family man, a good businessman, and "an excellent friend over the years." Chafetz said he met Vara in 1958, when Vara had taken over some bars owned by Vara's father. He socialized with a group including Vara at a health club, meeting him once or twice a week. Chafetz was introduced to Vara after the collapse of AITS, the tour and travel company Chafetz founded with Cutler in the mid-1960s. Charter tour programs the company put together included three nights in Las Vegas and four in San Francisco and another tour that involved a seven-day stay in Hawaii.

In 1967, AITS really took off after Adelson helped the company get on the stock market, enabling the public firm to raise $1 million. Within a couple of years, the partners raised more than $25 million and started building the Hawaiian Regent Hotel in Honolulu. For a time, the company was sending several planeloads of tourists to Las Vegas, San Francisco, and Hawaii each week. It was in 1965, while working for the fledgling AITS with Paul Klapper, that Chafetz met Lewin at the San Francisco Hilton. Chafetz said the success of AITS forced United Airlines to introduce promotional airfares for the first time. But in 1969, the stock market took a dive, and so did AITS. The stock started at $10 a share in 1967, rose to $104, and then tumbled to $3. It was a disaster for Chafetz, then the second-largest shareholder in AITS. Chafetz said he went from making $175 a week in 1965 to holding stock worth $8 million. He, Adelson, and the other partners were in trouble in 1969 since they had used the value of their shares as security for bank loans.

To survive, Chafetz testified that he was forced to seek loans from relatives and friends. It was at this point that Vara entered the picture and loaned Chafetz about $10,000 without interest or notes. If it were not for Vara and others, Chafetz said he would have had to file for bankruptcy and lose his house. Vara later loaned Chafetz and Cutler $30,000 to start a new charter travel business. At the time, the early 1970s, Vara owned a pair of gay bars in the Bay Village area of Boston. The businesses were then the largest gay-oriented bars in the city. But eventually, the former low-income Bay Village became gentrified, and the new residents began complaining about the bars. The complaints provoked clashes that drew a lot of local media attention, including many news articles in the *Boston Globe* and the *Boston Herald* that were copied and read by the Gaming Control Board. Vara had local business licensing problems and was later charged with tax evasion. In the mid-1970s, Chafetz and Vara invested in the cruise ship in New York. Chafetz then put $17,000 into a gay bar Vara acquired in 1979 in San Francisco. Vara later bought gay bars in other cities, including Atlanta and Fort Lauderdale, Florida. In 1980, Vara loaned Chafetz $125,000 to enable him to run tours to Atlantic City. Still later, Chafetz and Vara together bought the radio stations in Florida, in which Chafetz had invested $700,000. Chafetz had helped Vara raise the $500,000 bail the bar owner needed to be released pending trial on felony tax evasion and other charges. Vara's eight bars were seized because of the charges, and he was forced to pay $220,000 in back meal taxes.

An unnamed witness had reported to the Gaming Control Board that Vara and members of his group went after outside investors by asking for an investment, for instance, $200,000, and then telling them it would be for 49 percent of the bar when it was actually the entire amount needed to open the bar. If the bar were successful, Vara would claim the 51 percent interest in it. If the bar failed, the outside investors would lose all their money, but Vara and members of his group would profit. Chafetz invested in one of the bars and later became the owner of five others. He denied, however, profiting from them and told the board he never got his money back except for his investment in the first bar.

Chafetz had also been called to testify before a grand jury investigating alleged skimming at a Vara-owned gay club in Boston. The questions were about records kept by the business, and Chafetz pleaded the Fifth Amendment for protection against self-incrimination. He did so, he said, under the advice of his attorney. The attorney had said it was the best thing to do because neither he nor Chafetz knew what the prosecutor would ask once Chafetz took the stand. Chafetz told the board he did not take part in anything illegal and that he took the Fifth only because his attorney told him to. He said he realized now that it was a mistake.

Chafetz claimed that Vara was a friend whom he saw face-to-face about three or four times a year while out to dinner with their wives. They talked on the phone, he added, much more often—as many as two to five times a given week. Chafetz said he gave no credence to the bad press Vara received in Boston. "I believe, sure, there might be trouble in his bars and there might be problems in bars. But I don't believe the bad things that they say about him. I don't believe that he is any part of organized crime or anything else." He said that he realized Vara might cause him problems with Nevada regulators and that he had his attorney check into Vara's background before applying for a gaming license.

Bible asked Chafetz whether he, after having to testify before a grand jury about Vara, had any concerns about having Vara as a business partner. Chafetz responded that he was concerned more about the testifying itself, which he said made him nervous. Stating the question differently, Bible asked whether it made him want to rethink his business partnership with Vara. Chafetz said it did not. He insisted again that Vara "was a good friend of mine who helped me get over some real tough times voluntarily, without me asking him, and I guess that was something I couldn't forget."[18]

That response appeared to irk Cunningham, who asked whether Chafetz could divest and disassociate himself from Vara.

"Could you do that? Would you do that? Is this license that valuable to you?" the board member asked. Chafetz said he had already discussed it with Vara, whom he said understood Chafetz's situation in Nevada and would refrain from communicating with him and borrowing money from him.

According to the board's investigation, Vara had been accused of skimming—having cash registers canceled and the money packaged up for him to take away. Illegal drugs also were allegedly sold inside his bars. Cunningham said that several people who had worked in Vara's clubs told him personally that skimming had occurred. "Why he wasn't convicted is beyond me," the board member said, appearing frustrated with Chafetz's defense of Vara.

CUNNINGHAM: I talked to people who know Mr. Vara for what he is, and he is not this righteous, clean individual, good businessman, who got a bad rap from having homosexual bars that evidently you wanted to get involved with. Isn't it a great aspiration on your part in the late

'70s to want to become a gay-bar owner, a place where they sell narcotics and distribute it. What a wonderful person.

CHAFETZ: Mr. Cunningham, let me just say that I didn't really want to be
a gay-bar owner.

CUNNINGHAM: Why did you do it for?

CHAFETZ: I did it because he asked me to make an investment, and I felt
that I owed him that. He had helped me out a great deal. I wasn't interested in being a gay-bar owner. I don't have anything to do with narcotics. I don't even know what narcotics look like, to be honest with
you. That is not my culture. I drink a little.

CUNNINGHAM: You do funny financial transactions, I will say that, too.
You can dispute that if you like.[19]

Cunningham referred to check-for-check swaps made by Chafetz and Vara.
When Chafetz made a check out for $500,000 for Vara's bail, Vara gave him a
check for the same amount. They also swapped checks made out for $70,000 in
1987. Chafetz said that Vara had made payments on his loans to him but still
owed him $15,000.

Chafetz testified that he agreed that some of his own transactions might appear "funny . . . I lend a lot of people a lot of money," often to friends in need
of help. Chafetz added that "in all immodesty I have never hurt anybody. I
have only helped people."

Cunningham asked Chafetz whether he knew of an "improperly clad" male
stripper at a club owed by Vara in Florida once "serving food between his legs
in the area of his groin." Chafetz said he learned of it only from board investigators. He admitted that he still talked by phone to Vara two or three times a
week but that it amounted only to "small talk" about the radio stations in
Florida.

Board members then queried Chafetz about other problem issues. One was
an investor in Vara's bars named Frank Cashman, who was indicted in Boston
for arson in connection with the burning of a competing bar in 1977 and was
later acquitted. Chafetz said he heard of the arson charges eight months after
he had invested in Vara's bar. He made the investment to repay the favor Vara
made when he loaned Chafetz money after AITS collapsed. Chafetz admitted
that he did, however, speak to Cashman only a week before the board meeting. Chafetz had called the Florida home Vara and Cashman shared, seeking
to reach Vara, when Cashman answered the phone.

Chafetz also was associated with Jordan Friedman, one of the original investors in AITS in the 1960s. Friedman and his wife were arrested in 1987 after authorities found gambling paraphernalia in their home in the form of a
cigarette pack with illegal bookmaking information written on it. Another

Chafetz associate, Larry Reservitz, was charged with wire fraud and dealing 3,500 pounds of marijuana. Chafetz knew Reservitz socially for about seven years and loaned him $10,000 for legal fees. Chafetz told the board that he had no relationship with convicted tax evader Sorrentino other than going to the man's house with Varà some years before Adelson bought it while Sorrentino was about to be sent to prison. Cunningham said that to be licensed, Chafetz would have to divorce himself from these people, which Chafetz said, again, he would do.

Next to testify was Henri Lewin, who spoke in a thick German accent. Bible told Lewin that the board had "some difficulty getting straight answers to our questions." He asked Lewin to describe the association he had with former labor official Rudy Tham. Lewin said he met Tham in 1950, when Tham was the son of a Fairmont hotel customer. He renewed that association in 1964, when Lewin was food and beverage director at the San Francisco Hilton and Tham headed the Teamsters local in the city, which represented the hotel's front-desk employees. Lewin claimed Tham received the $886 worth of complimentaries at the Las Vegas Hilton from the casino office, not directly from Lewin, who headed the hotel-casino at the time.[20]

In connection with the Tham incident, Lewin was charged by federal prosecutors with violating the Taft-Hartley Act, a labor relations statute that prohibits labor contract bargaining units from giving compensation to each other. But U.S. Judge Harry Claiborne in Las Vegas ruled that granting comps in Nevada was a standard method of operation, unlike other states, and that the act's prohibition against giving favors to labor officials did not apply to Nevada casinos.

Lewin's problems continued, however, when he was accused of comping Judge Claiborne himself at a Hilton hotel in Hawaii on two occasions in 1982. New Jersey gaming agents investigated the allegations about the free trips.

Lewin told Gaming Control Board members that he did not comp the judge's stays in Hawaii. For the first trip, in January 1982, he said he only helped Claiborne obtain a reservation. The judge paid a $35 daily government rate during his one-week trip. In July 1982, Claiborne paid $130 for lodging at the Hawaii hotel, and Lewin produced a copy of Claiborne's American Express charge slip. Board member Cunningham replied that he was still concerned about the propriety of Lewin sending a thank-you note to Claiborne after one of the trips in light of the judge's favorable ruling in the Tham case.

The board then turned its attention to Lewin's former association with Johnny "Johnny Yak" Yakoobian, a Hawaiian man who arranged tourist packages to Las Vegas in the early 1980s. Lewin was alleged to have agreed to pay Yakoobian $25,000 every six months to bring casino customers from Hawaii to the Las Vegas Hilton. Lewin said he authorized a one-time $25,000 payment by the hotel and considered it as advertising since Yakoobian had agreed to take down a billboard, plugging the Dunes hotel in Las Vegas, from atop a building in Hawaii as part of the deal to promote the Las Vegas Hilton. Yakoobian received $25,000 on June 30, 1983, and took the sign down. The problem was that no one could locate a signed, written agreement to support the payment, leading the board to suspect it was a "side deal" not approved or monitored by the Hilton corporation. Lewin replied that he had requested the money from the hotel's comptroller. Yakoobian reportedly told others that the deal called for him to collect unpaid markers—casino loans to gamblers—from his Hawaiian clients who bet at the Hilton. Cunningham pointed out that Yakoobian was not a licensed junket representative and thus could not collect markers under state gaming regulations. Lewin said Yakoobian was not authorized to collect markers or $25,000 every six months and described the man's claims as "a total fabrication."[21]

But board members did not appear to believe Lewin's story. Cunningham claimed that Lewin was not being entirely truthful, and Amerine said that investigators found a letter from a Hilton manager to Yakoobian that mentioned "$60–70,000," which appeared to refer to markers.

Cunningham, unwavering in his opposition to Lewin's application, saved his most severe criticism of Lewin for the alleged assault on the cocktail waitress at the Las Vegas Hilton in 1985. The charges were included in a federal lawsuit filed by the waitress that was later settled out of court and whose records had been sealed by a judge. Lewin ended up paying half the cost of the settlement himself. However, on his Nevada gaming license application, Lewin had answered "no" to the question, "Have you ever had a civil or criminal record expunged or sealed by court order?"

"I am convinced that you did something very close to what you were accused of doing," Cunningham said. "I contend that you were not truthful with us. That means in fact you lied under oath, in my opinion."[22]

Cunningham disputed Lewin's description to board investigators of what happened to the waitress. Contrary to Lewin's statements, the woman in fact did not want to see Lewin prior to the incident, and it happened not in Lewin's office but Barron Hilton's, where Lewin directed the waitress to go, Cunningham said. The woman was in an emotional state and said Lewin made an obscene remark. Lewin later admitted to having touched her "ass or tits" and had offered her a string of pearls. The waitress passed a polygraph test on what she said occurred. Cunningham said Lewin had asked an aide and other people to lie for him about it and had offered pearls and "made improper advances" to other women at the hotel. The tough-talking Cunningham described the events as "deplorable."

"Those are kind of a summarization of why I believe that you tried to disguise this thing from the onset in your personal history records and you said in the [board's] investigative hearing that if we didn't believe you, we should deny you, and I assure you, Mr. [Lewin], that's exactly what I'm going to do," Cunningham said.[23]

Lewin insisted that he did tell the truth but admitted that the incident was a mistake and that it would not happen again. "I went to a concentration camp. I was a prisoner of war, and I swore to your investigators on the health of my children that I am innocent," he said in a rambling speech during which he appeared to contradict himself. "Never in my life would I ask somebody to lie for me. . . . I am guilty of having people come into my office and stand in front of me and shaking. I done that. . . . I made a mistake. But you know power is a terrible thing. . . . I didn't touch her on the behind or the tits, whatever it is. But I made stupid words which might open up for criticism. . . . My mistake was that I liked to be powerful, that I liked it to have people standing in front of me and saying, 'I'm going to see the big guy up there.' And I'm sorry for that and I ask your forgiveness. . . . I was just so power drunk that I was standing there and misused the privilege which I had with the position I have."[24]

"If you, sir, are a victim, as you indicate," Cunningham said, "I can only say that I'm greatly sorry because the preponderance of what I have before me says that either you're not telling the truth or you are indeed a victim of a mass conspiracy. I see nothing to support the mass conspiracy side of it, and thus, I make that decision. . . . I find no pleasure in this."

With no further questions for Lewin, the board moved onto reviewing the application of Paul Klapper, a shareholder in Lewin's Aristocrat company. Klapper, a San Francisco resident and an original investor with Chafetz and Cutler in AITS in the 1960s, was a longtime associate of Lewin. In fact, Klapper was the person who contacted the Interface Group about having Lewin join the Sands team. The Interface partners included Klapper, who had no background in hotels or the tourism industry, on the application out of gratitude.

But Klapper had many licensing problems. The board's concerns centered on his business judgment, the long list of lawsuits filed against him, and the people he had associated with in the past. He had been subpoenaed in 1983 to appear before a grand jury in Springfield, Massachusetts, investigating tax charges against H. Joel Rahn, an alleged illegal gambler and a partner with Klapper in a building project in San Francisco and in a video company. Klapper, like Chafetz, also had business dealings with Jordan and Gloria Friedman, the Bostonians who were arrested for illegal bookmaking. He was unable to pay a slew of bank loans for real estate deals in San Francisco and was sued over each of them. He had other debts, including $200,000 in real estate taxes in Massachusetts, which he said he was disputing. Klapper blamed all of it on poor legal advice and carelessness on his part. Another issue was his illegal gambling. He admitted he had used a bookmaker in Boston and California for 30 years and lost thousands of dollars on football and World Series baseball games. Yet another problem for Klapper was his own long acquaintance with Henry Vara while living in Boston, although they were never in business together.

Klapper said most of his financial and business problems would be solved within about six months. But the board, tired after the lengthy hearing, was clearly in the mood to reject him.

The discussion then turned back to Lewin. Adelson returned to the podium and said Lewin would simply receive a fee based on the Sands's financial results plus a salary. The implication was that Lewin would not directly share in the hotel's gaming profits. Adelson said that despite all of the questions, he did not feel any differently about him.

"I'm still willing to bet my $100 million on Mr. Lewin. . . . [He is] not an attacker of women," Adelson said. "I still feel the same."[25]

When the board finally began deliberating on the applicants, all three members cited difficulties with Lewin, Chafetz, and Klapper. Cunningham flatly opposed licensing any of the three men. Amerine said he favored a limited license for Chafetz. Bible agreed with Amerine to recommend a limited license for Chafetz. Amerine made a motion to require Interface to submit a financial statement to the board and provide $10,000 to fund future board investigations of the company. Amerine moved to recommend the Gaming Commission approve a limited two-year license for Chafetz, with the condition he disassociate himself within 90 days of Henry Vara, Vara's brother Carmine Vara, Frank Cashman, Jordan and Gloria Friedman, and Larry Reservitz. He said Chafetz was to end the business relationship with them in 90 days and the social relationship immediately.

The vote was 2 to 1 to recommend the limited license for Chafetz. Amerine then moved to recommend denial for both Lewin and Klapper. Klapper, he said, should be denied a license under Nevada Revised Statutes (NRS) 463.1702B for illegal gambling and NRS 463.1703A for lack of business probity. Lewin should be denied under NRS 463.1702A because he lacked good character, honesty, and integrity, the board member said. The vote to recommend denial for both applicants was unanimous.

With that, the marathon meeting was adjourned, at 2:38 A.M., February 9, 1989 (more than 17 hours, including breaks and an eight-hour adjournment, after it started), and to be reconvened only hours later at 9 A.M. that same morning. When the weary board members and applicants returned, the board recommended gaming licenses for Adelson, Cutler, Shapiro, Kenneth Scholl, and Larry Lewin.

The board's recommendation to the commission to deny Lewin was surprising, even bold, given the high political profile Adelson and the Sands team had created. The board had defied the wishes of some of the state's top political figures and the conventional wisdom that political contacts, or "juice," mattered the most in Nevada.

"Sometimes it seems nothing happens in this town unless the local juice-makers want it to happen," *Las Vegas Review-Journal* political columnist Jon Ralston wrote on February 22, 1989. "But the law of juice, like most truths, is not universal. . . . To public officials, the Lewin episode says that juice peddlers may be intimidating and political fallout may be scary, but conscience must be king. To pundits, it says think twice the next time you think that juice always wins and that all officials can be influenced by outside forces. . . . Bible and his colleagues have breathed fresh air into an all too frequently polluted political atmosphere." [26]

But juice would soon win over the commission.

The Gaming Commission took up the Sands applications on February 23, 1989, this time at the Clark County Commission chambers in downtown Las Vegas. The political tension in the room was palpable. Representing the Sands was Robert List, a Republican who served as Nevada governor from 1979 to 1983. The Wall Street firm Drexel was represented at the hearing by Frank Schreck, a powerful Las Vegas gaming attorney, top fund-raiser for the state's Democratic Party, and himself a former member of the Gaming Commission.

The first order of business for the Sands partnership was to announce that Klapper wanted to withdraw his application. The commission immediately moved and voted 5 to 0 to refer Klapper's application back to the board. The Sands team then made its presentation. Sands attorney Callaway again detailed the project. Adelson talked about his production of COMDEX in Las Vegas and repeated his praise of Cutler and Chafetz for providing tour and travel business to Las Vegas and the Sands in the 1960s. "We are the largest independent trade show producer in the world," he said.

Using a drawing of the proposed Sands project, Adelson said that the hotel's casino would be expanded to 60,000 square feet from 25,000 square feet and that 1,300 guest rooms would be added in the first phase of construction to the 716 rooms already there. The million-square-foot proposed convention center would be 50 percent larger than the Las Vegas Convention Center, he said. The Sands would be redeveloped in a style typical of resorts in Palm Springs, California. The improvements would cost $150 million, Adelson said.

"It's a very ambitious and unique undertaking," Adelson said. "I might tell you there is not another hotel-casino property that has a facility of this nature in the entire world." [27]

Commissioner Ken Gragson, the aging former mayor of Las Vegas, avoided the board's big questions about the Sands. Instead, Gragson asked Adelson about parking at the project and how the names of streets next to the Sands would be changed. In an elongated response, Adelson repeated his views on the merits of the casino project.

Commissioner Robert Lewis requested Adelson to again explain the three divisions of Interface. Chairman O'Reilly asked Adelson go over the details of the project's financing.

With that over, attorney Schreck told the commission that Drexel, still assisting with the funding of the Sands, had been suspended by the New Jersey Casino Control Commission because of the Milken scandal but that none of the transactions complained about dealt with financing of Nevada casinos. Board member Amerine assured the commission that the board was satisfied with the financing portion of the Sands deal and with Drexel's involvement.

Turning to Adelson's application, Chairman O'Reilly praised him for being open about his financial setbacks. With Adelson off the hook, Chafetz was called forward. He promised commissioners he would no longer associate with Henry Vara and the other people the board had mentioned in its motion. After a few more questions, O'Reilly suggested a motion to grant a limited license to Chafetz. The license would expire in two years, and Chafetz would have to apply for a new one all over again. O'Reilly said it would be a "relicensing, not a review," meaning a new license would be more difficult to obtain. The chairman then asked Chafetz, Cutler, and Shapiro whether they understood what disassociation meant, and the applicants replied that they did. The commission then voted unanimously to license the four Interface partners for the Sands, including the limited license for Chafetz.

After a brief recess, it was the Lewin team's turn. Former governor List testified that Larry Lewin, not Henri, would be in charge of managing casino operations at the Sands. When O'Reilly asked whether he could "hold [his] own," Larry Lewin said that he could.

List proceeded to deliver a lengthy statement about Henri Lewin. "The matter of the recommended denial by the board to you of Mr. Lewin has been something that has been a major concern to the applicants," he said.

Lewin genuinely regretted the 1985 "incident," said List, referring to but not specifically mentioning the waitress's allegations. The former governor then detailed Lewin's achievements with the Hilton company and noted that 43 percent of the chain's revenue came from the Nevada gaming operations Lewin once headed. List attributed Hilton's success in Nevada squarely on Lewin. Then, as if to contradict himself about Lewin's responsibility for Hilton's success in Nevada, List ended the statement by saying that "Henry Lewin is not a casino operator." List attempted to explain that Lewin would not be involved in running the Sands casino—even though Lewin, as a key employee of the Sands, would still need a Nevada gaming license to work there.[28]

Chafetz then came up to praise Lewin. During a drawn-out tribute, Chafetz twice made a Freudian slip by referring to Henri Lewin as "Henry Vara" before correcting himself. Chafetz described how he met Lewin in 1965 in San Francisco and how grateful they were that Lewin had helped Chafetz and Cutler establish their tour and travel business.

With that introduction, Lewin walked to the podium. O'Reilly remarked that the commission had spent many hours that month going through 1,000 pages of transcripts. The decision on Lewin, O'Reilly said, "has not been made. . . . It will be made in the next few minutes by this commission." That decision, he added, would not be "on the basis of a popularity poll . . . but on the basis of the evidence that's before us by way of the summary materials, by way of your testimony, by way of your responsiveness today."[29]

Lewin assured the commissioners that his son Larry would run the casino. He said he wanted to introduce "Romania violins" and Czechoslovakian folk singers to the Sands. It would "not be a problem" for him to be uninvolved with the casino, Lewin said. He would, however, look over the casino's revenue figures. The Sands would pay his salary to his Aristocrat management company, and he would not have a percentage participation in proceeds from the casino. List, however, interrupted and told the commission that Lewin would actually receive a bonus, depending on how well the Sands hotel-casino performed under Aristocrat's management. That bonus, List added, could be "a fixed amount" instead of based on a percentage of profits.

O'Reilly then indicated that the tide had turned for Lewin. The chairman said he had asked the board to draft an "alternative course of action" regarding Lewin for commissioners to consider. Commissioner Lewis asked Adelson to talk about Lewin's licensing problems. Adelson said he had merely heard "rumors" about him. Adelson added that the Sands's contract with Lewin "has a clause of outs" that would end the agreement if Lewin misbehaved. But, he added, news of Lewin's possible participation in the Sands had helped the project attract financing, and the Sands project would lose $10 million of it if Lewin were denied a license. The Sands would then be forced to "hire a team of people" in his place, and few people were available in the casino industry to do so, he said. The project was also under the gun because the one-year agreement with Kerkorian to buy the Sands was to end within only two months, since the state's background investigation for the gaming licenses had already lasted nine months.

But O'Reilly told Adelson that if the commission were to deny Lewin, "those are the problems that you are going to have to face. . . . It is not going to be swayed one iota by the fact it is going to create a 50-day time frame and problems for you."[30]

The meeting took a strange turn when a man from the audience came forward and spoke of allegations that Lewin was once involved in drugs and prostitution at the Las Vegas Hilton. The man admitted that he was shopping around his story to serve as the basis of a film script. Board chairman Bible said he had received the man's letter and reviewed the allegations. However, the man had no police or other official corroboration. His charges, denied by Lewin, made no impression on the commission.

List returned to the podium and restated that Lewin was "genuinely regretful" about the incident with the cocktail waitress and that "he wishes he had not been there." Lewin would be simply a key employee, not an investor, at the Sands, List said.[31]

O'Reilly then suggested that Lewin receive a two-year limited gaming license. Commissioner Lewis said he would not support an unlimited license for Lewin, adding that Lewin should have no direct responsibility with the Sands casino and nothing to do with the employee payroll if he did end up working for the hotel. Commissioner Betty Vogler described Lewin as "a talented man" but said that he should not be involved with the hotel-casino's personnel matters. Gragson said that Lewin had been "less than truthful" and that he would favor licensing Lewin only in a "non-gaming capacity."

Commissioner Robert Peccole was more emphatic about his support for Lewin. Peccole read a letter written by a member of New Jersey's casino commission, stating that its opposition to the Hilton application in 1985 was due to mob attorney Sidney Korshack and that Lewin got a "raw deal." Peccole said that Lewin deserved the benefit of the doubt in the matter of the cocktail waitress and that he would support granting him an unlimited license.[32]

Commissioner Gragson, retreating from his earlier statement, said he agreed with Peccole about Lewin. O'Reilly said Peccole was right that the New Jersey commissioner had absolved Lewin of wrongdoing. He said that he was impressed with Lewin's candor and that he had no criminal convictions. The chairman repeated his proposal to give Lewin a limited license, with the stipulation that Lewin have no direct or indirect involvement with gaming. O'Reilly also proposed that Lewin could have authority over the hotel-casino's physical plant and budget and planning but not personnel, and he would not be able to share directly in gaming revenue.

The vote on the chairman's motion was 5 to 0 in favor, enough to override the board's recommendation for denial. Lewin had obtained a gaming license, but one that prohibited him from participating in gaming-related revenue and decision making.

The commission's vote to license Lewin and Chafetz infuriated Cunningham, who later vowed he would never attend another commission meeting, which he said was unnecessary for him to do as a board member anyway. He made good on his promise.

"Character suitability was the main issue for me" regarding Lewin, Cunningham said later in an interview. "It was felt he was guilty as charged and that he was not forthright. I felt the evidence was very strong." Cunningham remained convinced that Chafetz was unsuitable as well. Licensing Chafetz with the condition he disassociate and divest from the five people listed "I thought was outrageous," Cunningham added.[33]

Lewin, as the newly licensed president of the Sands, told news reporters after the commission hearing that he was relieved the licensing process was over. At a subsequent news conference at the Sands, Lewin announced plans to build new restaurants and book unusual entertainment acts. He sought to establish "new standards of excellence" for employees to make the Sands "a five-star hotel" with a "sophisticated casino" and the "loosest slots," apparently to be loosened by his son. Also, members of the media would have 50 percent discounts at the Sands, the hotel president said. "We will outshine the whole industry," he said. "I challenge all hotels to prove they have more talent."

In the months that followed, Lewin published an autobiography and sold copies of it in the Sands sundries store. He placed a sign in front of the Sands with a personal message to Steve Wynn, chief executive of the planned Mirage hotel across Las Vegas Boulevard from the Sands. The message said it was all right with Lewin for Wynn to tell people the new Mirage was across the street from the Sands.

But only 10 months after the Sands opened, Lewin was gone, fired by Adelson after the two repeatedly clashed over operating policy at the Sands. Their disagreements centered on money for improvements to guest rooms and other aspects of the 38-year-old Sands that Lewin said the property desperately needed but Adelson would not approve. Lewin then turned around and sued Adelson in Las Vegas, alleging his ex-employer owed him $1.1 million in a termination agreement.[34] He also asked for the balance owed him and for nearly $400,000 in damages. The case was quietly settled out of court. Lewin was again out of the Las Vegas gaming industry. The feud, however, continued.

When Adelson was sued for breach of contract in Las Vegas by an architect he hired in 1989 to design improvements for the Sands, Lewin testified for the plaintiff. At one point, Lewin said on the stand that the Sands's guestrooms needed to be refurbished and that he "had better accommodations when I was a prisoner of war."[35] Attorneys for the architect said that Adelson had "impeached" himself repeatedly while testifying in the case. They portrayed Adelson as "an impossible taskmaster, who kept changing ideas for the project."[36] A jury awarded the architect a judgment of $1.3 million against the Sands in 1993.

Adelson eventually made good on his promise to build what would be called the Sands Exposition Center, with 1 million square feet of exhibit space. The Sands hotel-casino expansion, however, was another story. Those plans were delayed in 1991 after the trade show promoter said it became too difficult to obtain bank financing while other megaresort projects—the Treasure Island by Mirage Resorts, Inc.; the Luxor hotel by Circus Circus Enterprises, Inc.; and the MGM Grand by MGM Grand, Inc.—were being built on the Las Vegas Strip in the early 1990s. Meanwhile, the Sands was a money loser for five straight years, and from 1989 to 1996 the at-times cantankerous and confrontational Adelson hired and fired four management teams.

But the time was right in the mid-1990s. In late 1995, the 65-year-old Adelson hit it really big. He sold off his COMDEX shows and 16 other exhibitions to Softbank, a Japanese software company, for $860 million. The sale enabled Adelson to act on his vision of a new property. He would be sole owner. His old Sands partners, Chafetz, Cutler, and Shapiro, would not be part of the new project.

In 1996, the fading Sands hotel, the recipient of Adelson's relatively minor improvements over the years, was imploded to make way for his planned Venetian megaresort. Adelson settled on the Venetian theme after honeymooning with his wife, Miriam, in Venice, Italy.[37] The hotel-casino project, scheduled to cover more than 11 million square feet of building area, was designed to mimic the architecture of Venice, and would be built in two phases. The $1.5 billion first phase was to feature a 35-story tower containing 3,036 "all-suite" hotel rooms and would debut in April 1999. The first phase also was to have a casino covering 113,000 square feet, a 500,000-square-foot "upscale" shopping mall, and 500,000 square feet of meeting space. It also would feature canals with gondolas and faux Venetian landmarks, such as the Campanile bell tower, Doge's Palace, and Rialto Bridge. Adelson had hoped to market the megaresort to conventioneers, willing to pay higher room rates during midweek, and to visiting gamblers on the weekends. Construction on the second phase—a second hotel tower with 3,036 suites, another 113,000 square feet of casino area, 500,000 square feet of mall space, and 500,000 square feet of meeting space—was set to begin with the completion of the first.

Even with his newfound wealth, Adelson used the tried-and-true method of "other people's money" to finance the Venetian. In 1997, the Wall Street finance companies Goldman, Sachs and Bear, Stearns arranged $425 million in first mortgage notes with a 12.15 percent interest rate and $97 million with a 14.25 percent interest rate to help back the Venetian.[38] The bonds had a catch, as holders would have to stand in line behind bankers to retrieve their share of the collateral if the project failed.

Adelson put up only $95 million of his own funds toward the project, plus the project's land, which Adelson claimed was worth $225 million. He used the renamed Sands Expo and Convention Center as collateral on a $75 million loan from Goldman, Sachs that he used as part of his $95 million cash contribution. Adelson's resort would have to take in $1.2 million a day to break even on debt services and other expenses.[39] Still, in 1998, Adelson stood as owner of the Venetian Casino Resort L.L.C. and of Interface Group–Nevada, the operator of the Sands Convention Center. To Adelson, the Venetian amounted to a temple, of sorts, to his own success, a paean to himself to last for the ages. "Authenticity is so important to us," he told a reporter for the Associated Press about the project in July 1998. "The key factor in my strategy is longevity."[40]

This time around, at least, Nevada gaming officials had few concerns about Adelson. On February 10, 1999, the Gaming Control Board took only an hour to discuss and recommend that the commission grant him a gaming license for the Venetian. Adelson chose not to attend the hearing.[41]

But new troubles awaited Adelson. The first phase of the Venetian opened on May 4, 1999, before its rooms, shops, and restaurants were completed, forcing hundreds of hotel guests—including actress Sophia Loren, invited to the opening—to check into other hotels. Adelson's Las Vegas Sands filed suit against the builder of the project over the unfinished project, and the builder countersued. The builder and dozens of subcontractors said Las Vegas Sands owed them tens of millions in unpaid construction bills. Adelson sued Las Vegas convention officials to block an expansion, funded by tax-exempt bonds, of the Las Vegas Convention Center, which would compete with his Sands Expo Center. And early revenue results from the Venetian were well below projections. It was the most inauspicious debut of any Las Vegas megaresort.

Chapter Six

Fixed Odds and Wise Guys
The Sport of Kings

When Gregory Peters, a Las Vegas man in the international jewelry and furniture business, heard that the two-acre Deville property was for sale in 1987, he soon discovered its unique investment potential. The boarded-up Deville building, about a quarter mile east of the Strip, was constructed at 365 Convention Center Drive and Paradise Road, an intersection shared by the Las Vegas Convention Center and the Landmark hotel-casino. The owner of the Deville started building a race and sports book on the property in February 1973 but ran out of money and never opened one. The site, however, retained a key advantage. It was the only known vacant piece of property in the Las Vegas Valley "grandfathered," or exempted, from a September 1973 law passed by the Clark County Commission requiring all new casinos in the county to have at least 200 hotel rooms, a condition that made it much more expensive to get into the casino business in Las Vegas. The special designation for the Deville meant that Peters could, with permission, put in a race and sports book—requiring a nonrestricted gaming license—on the property without the millions in extra capital needed to build hotel rooms.

Peters sold a jewelry company he owned in Europe to buy the Deville property for $4 million, then placed it as an asset into an electronics company he controlled in Las Vegas, Electronic Specialty Products, Inc. He hired consultants to perform feasibility and market research studies on a licensed bookmaking operation strictly for horse-race wagering and retained the accounting firm Arthur Andersen to do the expense and income projections. County officials granted Peters zoning and building approvals for a race and sports book at the property. Peters sought to run a posh betting parlor for horse-race bettors, whom he believed were ignored by the Las Vegas casinos.[1]

Thus was set in motion a project known as the Sport of Kings, a race and sports book of a type the Nevada gaming industry had never seen. Sport of Kings became the first race and sports bookmaking business to go public, obtaining approval from the Securities and Exchange Commission (SEC) to sell shares on the NASDAQ stock exchange in 1991. Interest in the book from investors caused the company's penny stock to surge to as high as $2.75 per share—nearly 10 times its original value—and at one point have 22 million shares outstanding. When it opened in the fall of 1992, it was the largest book in Nevada. Some of its innovations, such as small-screen color televisions at individual betting stations and off-site telephone wagering for horse bettors, would be copied by race and sports books in casinos throughout Las Vegas.

But the gaming project would take a series of bizarre turns in the early 1990s, beginning with two license applicants from England, Stephen and James Forsyth, whose problems with the Nevada Control Board would ultimately prove insurmountable. A good idea gone bad, Sport of Kings became one of the most disastrous gaming ventures ever in Las Vegas. The Forsyth brothers would lose millions in the deal. A series of mishaps, ranging from bad bets by smart bettors to questionable loans and problems with the Internal Revenue Service, would continue through a succession of operators.

The fate of Sport of Kings also would raise questions about the operations and behind-the-scenes workings of the Gaming Control Board itself. The Forsyths would complain they were the victims of overzealous and overly suspicious board investigators. The Gaming Control Board's lead investigator in the Sport of Kings case would leave to accept a job as president of the Nevada Pari-Mutuel Association, a group representing major Las Vegas race books in competition with Sport of Kings. And a man licensed as president of Sport of Kings, who was also a former Gaming Control Board member and close friend of board chairman Bill Bible, would resign amid concerns about a $2 million loan from a one-time defendant in an illegal computer betting scheme.

In early 1991, Peters was still looking for investors to help transform the deserted Deville building into a legal bookmaking operation. One investor was Peters's longtime associate Samuel Schulman, a well-connected former owner of the Seattle Supersonics professional basketball team who also once owned a Nevada slot machine company. But Peters needed someone else to provide the cash to construct the race book. So he turned to two multi-millionaire business associates, Stephen and James Forsyth. The Forsyths at the time owned 20 low-stakes gaming arcades and billiards clubs in England that gave them control of about 20 percent of the arcade business in their native country.

Three years earlier, in 1988, the brothers had used their modest arcade business to become one of the largest forces on the international gaming scene. They borrowed money and purchased casinos in London, Turkey, Egypt, and Gibraltar; a racetrack in England; and some restaurants for about $280 million. But the pair bought high at a time when business at English gambling casinos had peaked. Within only a year, their casino chain collapsed with the decline in the number of Japanese and Arab high rollers in the late 1980s. The Forsyths were compelled to resign from the casino company, and their businesses were sold at a loss of $150 million in May 1990.

A year after that imbroglio, the Forsyths, living in England with family trust fund money tucked away in foreign tax havens, were shopping for investments in Nevada. They had recently bought Intermark Imagineering, Inc., a Reno, Nevada, firm that at one time attempted to set up a statewide, progressive-linked jackpot keno game called Megakeno. The Forsyths hired Peters and his associate Blas Molto to reorganize the company, enabling the Forsyths to sell it at a profit. Still grateful, the Forsyths agreed to be the deep pockets Peters needed for Sport of Kings. They would later invest $10 million to develop the book and provide its opening bankroll and cash reserve, as required by the Gaming Control Board to back up wagers placed by customers.

What Peters, the Forsyths, and other investors envisioned for Sport of Kings was a 25,000-square-foot luxury race book for the high-stakes horse player. The project was dubbed the Sport of Kings after the popular term for horse racing. Bettors at Sport of Kings would be comped and pampered the way wealthy high rollers were in Las Vegas casinos. Sport of Kings would offer $10,000 "Turf Club" memberships, with 17 wood-paneled boxes inside second-floor balconies for members to sit, eat, and drink while watching races live on eight 70-inch television screens. About $2,500 of the club membership fee would be rebated back to members in scrip to be used for wagering.

There would be free buffets, comped accommodations at Las Vegas hotels, telephone wagering, valet parking, a 300-space parking garage, and ticket runners to collect bets for players. Patrons could place a bet and collect winnings at the same window, which was not done by other books at the time. Information on the bloodlines of horses would be available, as would videotapes of past races at various tracks for private viewing. The latest satellite broadcasting equipment was bought and placed inside the building, permitting the parlor to offer races on television from all over the country. And the first floor of the building, seen from the Turf Club boxes on the second-floor balconies, had 46 betting desks, each with a small-screen color television, for nonmembers. Each of the televisions had 25 channels and individual headphones.

The stated intention of the partners was to treat their race bettors better than the race books in the big casinos and offer more attractive surroundings. Most Las Vegas books at the time were rather plain. Bettors typically sat in smoky rooms at long, bare-wood or Formica betting tables.

To further entice the biggest bettors from the Las Vegas books, Sport of Kings would offer fixed odds on races set by its own bookmaker and always strive for the most attractive odds in town. Wagers of any size would be accepted—no limits. Customers would be able to wager on future books for the annual Breeder's Cup Classic. The man picked to head the race betting operation was an expert in calculating betting liabilities in England, and his business attracted hundreds of millions of British pounds in wagers per year.

Much of what was planned did come to pass when the book opened in the fall of 1992. But from the outset, the very idea of the Sport of Kings project conflicted with evolving Nevada casino market forces and gaming industry policies, which in turn influence state politics, policies, and regulations, including those of the Gaming Control Board.

At the same time Sport of Kings was being designed, a major change in the casino industry's approach to race betting was taking place. Top Las Vegas casinos wanted to drop fixed odds in favor of the more casino-friendly pari-mutuel wagering scheme used by the out-of-state racetracks (there are no racetracks in Nevada). The Sport of Kings project, by using the chancier, fixed-odds wagering and promising the highest betting limits, challenged bettors to get more for their money than pari-mutuel racing. In doing so, the project placed itself against the grain of the gaming industry and put major Las Vegas casinos at risk of losing the business of hardcore race bettors, who frequented the books, to Sport of Kings. Officials for Sport of Kings told the Gaming Control Board that about 70 percent of the horse betting in Las Vegas came from locals.

In 1989, Caesars Palace, Circus Circus, and Hilton Nevada (owner of Hilton casinos in Las Vegas and Reno) decided to find a way to break free from traditional race bookmaking toward almost risk-free, interstate pari-mutuel wagering.[2] Caesars, Circus Circus, and Hilton (and, later, Bally's hotel-casino) together formed the Nevada Pari-Mutuel Association that year to lobby the Gaming Control Board and state lawmakers to allow the state's race and sports books to sign agreements with pari-mutuel racetracks all over the United States. The agreements would permit Nevada race books to accept wagers on out-of-state races, with the books and the tracks sharing the proceeds.

Most large casinos in Nevada had race and sports books in the 1980s, and the casinos dominated the state's race betting industry, which then included only a handful of independent books. Race and sports wagering annually accounted for only a few percent of the total money won each year by gaming licensees in the state when compared to slots and table games. Nonetheless, the books were popular with both high rollers and low-stakes bettors. The books also served as tourist attractions since Nevada-style bookmaking was illegal in nearly all other states (only Nevada and Oregon offer legalized sports betting. It is allowed in Delaware and Montana, but neither state offers it.). Furthermore, Nevada casino operators historically offered books in order to serve as "full service" gaming operations so that customers would not wander off to other casinos to place race or sports wagers.

For years, casinos employed oddsmakers who themselves placed odds on individual horse and dog races held at tracks such as Hollywood Park, Santa Anita, and Del Mar in California. The odds set on a particular horse at the pari-mutuel tracks, such as 2 to 1, 5 to 1, and so on, rise or fall on the basis of the number and amounts of wagers on the horse. The more money bet on a horse, the more likely the tracks would edge the odds on it downward, say, from 10 to 1 to 6 to 1, to reduce the risk of paying too many winning bets at the higher odds.

The problem for the Nevada casino book operators in the late 1980s was that they were responsible for paying the local winners of the out-of-state races. Winning bets, with odds used from either the tracks or a casino's own book-maker, could mean big losses. High odds posted by the tracks on a horse, such as 50 to 1, might have to be adjusted down immediately by a casino book out of fear a rash of winners would produce losses, which the book's manager would then have to explain to casino executives.

Contributing to the situation was that Las Vegas traditionally has had a small but significant group of savvy, well-connected, well-bankrolled, and successful bettors, known as the "wise guys," who could quickly victimize even a good casino handicapper on a run of winning horses, thanks largely to paid out-of-state tipsters, computer know-how, help from computer consul-tants, and educated guesswork.

The casino operators felt the solution was simple—import pari-mutuel bet-ting used by the tracks into the casino books. In pari-mutuel wagering, all money received from bettors at a track is pooled together, with the track knowing it would keep as profit a mandated "commission," typically averag-ing about 17 percent of the bets. The remainder of the money is divvied up among the winners after state taxes are deducted. Casino operators wanted to convince the tracks, as well as state officials in Nevada and the other states, to allow them to place the wagers taken at the casino books into the pools at the tracks. The casinos would pay a fee of about 3 percent of the wagers they re-ceived for races on each track in exchange for the right to join the pool and ex-tract a share of the track's commission.

Pari-mutuel posed virtually none of the hazards or losses suffered when the casinos had to pay winning race bets. The Nevada casino race books could post the same odds as the out-of-state tracks and even offer other wagers— such as choosing winners of more than one race at a time—that Nevada books did not offer.

"The [Pari-Mutuel] Association believed that there were several potential benefits to pari-mutuel wagering," wrote Dennis Amerine, a former Gaming Control Board member, in a policy statement for the association in 1990, weeks after leaving the board to become the association's first president. "One of the benefits of a bi-state merger of race bets would be the elimination of a business risk for Nevada race books. As Nevada race books do not operate on a pari-mutuel basis, patrons bet against the book and not other bettors. In a pari-mutuel system . . . [a] racetrack is not generally exposed to loss no matter which horse wins. A race book which 'books' its wagers can suffer a loss on any race if too much money is bet on winning horses."[3]

New technologies were also helping to boost race and sports books in Nevada. By the late 1980s, the Nevada books had the ability to make betting more attractive by offering live broadcasting of races. Thanks to satellite transmission, pari-mutuel races from California to Florida could be beamed to televisions in the books, allowing patrons in Nevada to place wagers minutes before watching the races live from inside the book. The Gaming Control Board, concerned about how the broadcasts of the races would be sent, held lengthy hearings in 1988 before setting up a licensing and fee structure for Nevada-based "disseminators," who would send closed-circuit television signals of live races from the tracks to the books in Nevada.

Bringing pari-mutuel wagering into Nevada had been discussed by the state's legislators in the early 1980s, but the casinos and the tracks failed to settle on a deal for an interstate pari-mutuel betting pool.[4] When the Nevada Pari-Mutuel Association hired Amerine as president in 1990, his main job was to convince the Gaming Control Board to recommend the move to pari-mutuel to the Nevada Gaming Commission and adopt regulations. Nevada Gaming Commission Regulation 26A was proposed to govern pari-mutuel racing in Nevada, requiring owners of the race books, the out-of-state tracks, and a new entity—computerized betting operations that would transmit wagers from the Nevada books to the tracks, which would then update their pools—to apply for Nevada gaming licenses. The tracks also would have to comply with other Nevada gaming rules. The board and the commission approved Regulation 26A for a one-year test period in March 1990.[5] The commission gave the regulation final approval a year later.

By then, the Sport of Kings partners were well on their way to making their stylized bookmaking operation a reality. Peters's company had privately issued 19.2 million shares to itself for $192,900, or a mere penny per share, in 1990, according to SEC records.[6] By April 1991, stockholders included the Forsyths, an investor from England named J. Sandys, an investor from Ireland named T. Paterson-Brown, and a company in the United Kingdom the Forsyths owned called Priscian Ltd. In a private placement on April 23, 1991, the company sold 1.42 million shares of common stock to the Forsyths, Sandys, and Priscian for $402,700, equivalent to a stock price of $0.28 per share.[7]

On April 25, 1991, the Forsyths greatly increased their stake, with some vaguely reported stock deals. The company told the SEC that shareholders had approved a bid to privately sell 4.2 million shares to an unnamed "certain group of investors" for $1.2 million and to transfer an additional 1 million shares directly to London Image Amusement Ltd., the Forsyths' company in England that operated their low-stakes gaming arcades. The "group of investors" later sold the shares privately to London Image, 1.4 million shares in July and 2.8 million in September 1991.

Also in July 1991, London Image bought up Paterson-Brown's 1.4 million shares and 400,000 shares owned by Peters. The Forsyth brothers, who would soon own 33 percent of Sport of Kings common stock, placed their shares into a company called Caspian Resources Ltd., based in England.

In August 1991, a majority of stockholders voted to change the company's name to Sport of Kings, Inc., and its symbol on the NASDAQ stock exchange became "ODDS." When Sport of Kings launched its stock offering under its new name on NASDAQ that month, it started trading at $.25 per share. The company said it was awaiting licensing approval by Nevada gaming authorities. The price of the stock would rise continually during the following six months.

The next order of business for the Forsyths was obtaining nonrestricted Nevada gaming licenses to operate a race and sports book with slot machines. The Forsyths enlisted the powerful and established Las Vegas–based law firm Lionel, Sawyer & Collins for help. Attorneys from the firm who would counsel them included Grant Sawyer, the former governor of Nevada who was instrumental in establishing the state's modern gaming regulatory framework in the late 1950s and early 1960s; Ellen Whittemore, a former deputy state attorney general for gaming; and law partner Paul Hejmanowski. Amerine, who had recently left the pari-mutuel association, was hired by Sport of Kings as president and chief operating officer. The applicants figured Amerine's association with his former board colleague, Chairman Bill Bible, would help them obtain licenses.

"They [Amerine and Bible] were close friends, and we felt they would work it out," Peters said.[8]

Amerine, former head of the Gaming Control Board's Audit Division, served three years on the board and was one of the last members exempted from the state's "swinging door" law, which prevented board members from taking jobs in the industry they regulated for at least a year after leaving office. He was one of a number of board members and employees—including attorneys, such as Whittemore, who performed the board's legal work in the state attorney general's office—who had left over the years to accept high-paying jobs in either the gaming industry or with Nevada law firms with gaming industry clients.

Amerine became a consultant to Sport of Kings in May 1991 and was elected to the board of directors at the time of the public stock placement in August 1991 "to render consulting services with respect to gaming and compliance with the regulatory requirements of Nevada Gaming Authorities," according to s e c records.[9] In exchange, Amerine received 250,000 shares of common stock, issued in monthly installments of 40,000, and would receive 50,000 when the company obtained a license. By that August, Amerine had received 160,000 shares, then worth about $40,000.

Applying for nonrestricted gaming licenses for Sport of Kings were the Forsyth brothers as shareholders; former Sonics owner Schulman as chairman of the board, secretary, and treasurer; and Amerine as chief operating officer.

The Forsyths acted quickly to advance the project. In October 1991, their London Image company, a subsidiary of Caspian, bought $4 million in convertible notes from Sport of Kings, a loan to enable Sport of Kings to complete the partially built race book. The loan was to last five years, secured by a first mortgage on the Deville property, with 11.5 percent interest paid every three months. The brothers stipulated that the $4 million in notes could be converted to Sport of Kings stock, at a price of $.35 per share the first year, $.50 the second, $2 the third, $3 the fourth, and $5 the fifth. The deal showed the investment community the brothers had a financial stake in getting the project up and running as soon as possible. It was also potentially very lucrative for the Forsyths, who held 7.1 million shares.[10]

Sport of Kings stock continued to sell briskly and rise in value in the months leading up to the Forsyths's licensing hearing before the Gaming Control Board in February 1992. The stock, which was $.25 a share when it hit the market in August 1991, traded at a high of $2.75 per share prior to the board hearing.[11]

But from the end of 1991 to early 1992, the Forsyths' application appeared to be in deep trouble. Peters and the two brothers believed they would obtain swift licensing approval from the board and the commission. But the board probe began to turn up serious questions about the brothers in the minds of board members and investigators.

The Forsyths were born in England and raised in Canada, where they became citizens before their father moved them back to England. The 20 gaming and billiard arcades they owned featured English low-stakes gaming machines, accepting bets equivalent to 20 to 40 cents each, with maximum payouts of just over $5. But the arcades represented only a part of their financial holdings.

After receiving license applications from the Forsyths in the fall of 1991, the board sent a team of six agents overseas to London, Switzerland, Gibraltar, and Cyprus to try to make sense of the brothers' foreign finances, stocks, and trust holdings. One of their investments was in offshore Russian oil drilling operations in the North Sea. Their London Image firm was owned by a company called North Caucasian, which was owned by Caspian Resources. They also held an entity called London Image Amusement Trust. Applications showing the holdings of each had to be filed with the board.

Added to the complexity of the brothers' financial picture were difficulties gaming agents had in untangling information from foreign agencies and financial institutions. The agents' background investigation included research and interviews with various foreigners with knowledge about the Forsyths. Agencies that cooperated with them included the London-based Gaming Board of Great Britain and New Scotland Yard, which had an investigative arm known as the Gaming Squad.

The Nevada gaming agency's investigation uncovered a list of potential licensing problems for the Forsyths. The main problem concerned the Gibraltar-based estate of the brothers' late father, Edward G. Forsyth, that the brothers had inherited. Shortly after signing a trust document transferring his company, Second Time SA, to his sons in 1987, Edward Forsyth died in a car accident in Cyprus.[12]

Board investigators said the Forsyths did not open the family trust to them until seven months into the investigation. The agents also alleged that the Forsyths withheld information on the amount of money in the trust from British tax officials. The tax officials claimed they would have tried harder to tax the estate had they known it contained as much money as it did. Furthermore, Nevada agents also suspected that Stephen Forsyth may have controlled Edward Forsyth's company, Second Time, even before his father died; that profits from it were sent to Switzerland to avoid taxes; and that the company was used to facilitate alleged improper securities dealings through Leisure Investments, the brothers' gaming arcade firm.

The agents learned that a man named Chris Munhall had decided to travel to London during the board's investigation to speak with both Nevada and British officials about the Forsyths. Munhall alleged that Tom Scrase, a Forsyth associate and trustee in Edward Forsyth's offshore family trust, was running questionable "parallel" stock trades for Second Time with Stephen Forsyth. The board also wanted to know how Scrase had deposited profits into the Forsyth trust from the sale of property the trust did not own. Further, the board wanted more explanations from the Forsyths about a settlement deal involving the Russian oil holdings and a bankruptcy case filed in England.

By February 1992, these questions and others were still unresolved. Meanwhile, the Sport of Kings building in Las Vegas was completed and opened to the news media. Stephen Forsyth brought local reporters to the second-floor Turf Club, overlooking the first-floor betting stations, with a sea of small, glowing color televisions. Large projection televisions stood on the other side of the large room. The paint and carpeting was turf green. The interior walls had dark wood paneling and prints depicting English horse races. Stephen Forsyth explained how the $10,000 Turf Club memberships worked and mentioned that some had already been sold, including one to actor Mickey Rooney. The tour included a look into a backroom with satellite-receiving equipment on shelves stacked from floor to ceiling.

The board's regular monthly meeting was in the first week of February, but Sport of Kings, still planning its strategy and holding private discussions with board personnel, was not ready. The board granted the applicants' request for a special hearing in Carson City on February 13, 1992. That meant the board could still recommend licensing in time for the commission's regular meeting February 20.

At the February 13 hearing, Sport of Kings attorney Ellen Whittemore admitted that the board's investigation of the Forsyths, who still owned 33 percent of the company's stock and $8 million of its debts, was incomplete, making it impossible for them to be licensed at that time. Whittemore said the brothers had spent $400,000 on the board investigation. The $4 million Sport of Kings building was ready for occupancy February 14, and to be fair to stockholders, the legal book had to open without the Forsyths, she said.[13]

Whittemore proposed that the Forsyths' Sport of Kings stock and loans be placed in trust until the investigation was completed. The trustee would be Dennis Amerine. The Forsyths would have no control of their Sport of Kings assets and loans and could not direct or manage the book in any way. If the investigation proved the Forsyths unsuitable, they would have to sell out and leave the project. Whittemore said other people without gaming licenses in Nevada had been permitted by the board to guarantee loans to gaming businesses. Additionally, she said, the Forsyths were seeking to reduce their investment by selling off $2 million of their interest in the book.

"They will abrogate total, absolute control over every bit of their investment in the State of Nevada," Whittemore said. "And if they're found unsuitable, they'll go out without harming the company and the other shareholders."[14]

Board members were clearly annoyed by what they said was a lack of cooperation by the Forsyths, specifically with providing records of financial transactions from their late father's trust. Board agents, who had asked to examine the trust's records starting in August 1991, said the trust was only recently opened to them and would take up to several months to sift through. Agents spent a week in Gibraltar and Cyprus, where they said the Forsyths' accountant did not allow them to view trust records.

Board chairman Bible noted that Nevada gaming regulations required the Gaming Commission to determine whether the source of funding for a gaming applicant was from a "suitable" source before granting a license. He told

Whittemore that "from our perspective, by your own admission . . . we've had some delay in having access to the trust. . . . We haven't had an opportunity to take a look at the trust."[15]

Whittemore said that the Forsyths at first had problems convincing the trustee for the family trust to cooperate with the board but that the trust had since been opened for them. In Cyprus, Stephen Forsyth wanted to make sure the accountant released only the Forsyths' holdings and not ones they had sold off.

"The bottom line is, these people are complex," Whittemore said. "They have complex business dealings. They at one point owned a company in the United Kingdom, which was the largest leisure company in the United Kingdom. It's a complex investigation."

Under questioning from Bible, the Forsyths explained their dilemma with their investment in Sport of Kings. Stephen Forsyth said their initial intention was to invest $6 million in Sport of Kings, including $2 million in stocks and a $4 million mortgage. But in December 1991, they learned that $3 million more was needed to open. That required them to find some assets to sell off since the climate for loans from banks in Nevada and abroad in 1992 was tight.

The Anglo-Irish Bank in Ireland was willing to put up the $3 million if the Forsyths deposited $2 million as security. The brothers proposed to raise $1 million from their investments in West Germany and $1 million from the family trust. Also, to reduce the interest rate charged to Sport of Kings on their $4 million loan, the Forsyths said they would change the stock conversion on it, from their planned $.35 per share that would increase to $5.00 per share over five years to a fixed $.50 per share for the full five years. Finally, they agreed to obtain a $1 million letter of credit to serve as a reserve to cover bets at the race and sports book as required by state gaming Regulation 22.

James Forsyth agreed that a "hostile atmosphere" existed when he and his brother met with gaming agents in Gibraltar in August 1991. The agents were to blame for it, he said.

"I think there was a lack of exposure on—there was a lack of two-way dialogue going on between your regulators and ourselves," James Forsyth said. "Their first trip over there, they weren't talking to us. In fact, in the original interview I think we got off on the wrong foot when they all but tried to pin it down as to whether we were responsible for murdering our father. That did not go down very well. There were some heated moments out there in Gibraltar. I felt that I had laid on discussions and interviews which didn't take place. There was almost sort of a shotgun approach put to our head. If you don't show it, we're catching the first plane back. . . . We were not holding things back, but there was this uneasy atmosphere that existed between [us]."[16]

Stephen Forsyth explained that some of the problems were due to "a difference in culture that exists between what we in Europe release [for] information and to that with which you expect to be released as a matter of course. . . . And I think this aspect of confidentiality of the release of information you interpret [is] slightly different to how we interpret it. . . . What we were not able to do is to give authority to people to give information where we did not have that authority to give."

Family trusts in the United Kingdom and throughout Europe have existed for centuries and include funds passed on for generations, Stephen Forsyth told the board. The information in them is considered confidential, and he and his brother were reluctant to reveal it. Releasing family trust information is "not done at all in the United Kingdom," and their agreeing to show it to Nevada "is more so than what we would give to our own professional advisors in the United Kingdom," he said. "There was reluctance on the part of my brother and myself to release that information. That information is confidential."[17]

Amerine then testified that it was important Sport of Kings be licensed soon. Anglo-Irish Bank, he said, was to give Sport of Kings $500,000 in April only if it were licensed, and without a license, the project would be unable to pay its vendors.

But board member Steve DuCharme said he was not prepared to recommend the book's licensing bid since the board had in its confidential summaries "at least 27 pages of unresolved concerns involving the Forsyths. . . . And I would not want, if what's contained in these 27 pages of unresolved areas of concern are even halfway true, I wouldn't want the Forsyths even minutely in Nevada gaming. And I'm not willing to take that chance until these issues are resolved."[18]

Chairman Bible said he had other major reservations about the project, specifically the viability of the book as a business, were it to open. He proposed Sport of Kings return the following week with a new trust agreement ensuring that the Forsyths would be unable to shift away any assets of Sport of Kings while they still held the mortgage and their stock in the project.

Board member Tom Roche, agreeing with Bible, said the intention of a new trust would be to build "a very high Chinese wall" between the book and the Forsyths.

The board decided to recess to 9 A.M., February 19, 1992, a day before the Gaming Commission was to meet. At the board hearing, Whittemore submitted a new proposed trust agreement. Board members wanted to keep the Forsyths from controlling Sport of Kings in any way before the brothers obtained gaming licenses. In the new proposal, the Forsyths agreed to place all their holdings in trust, with Amerine serving as trustee with sole voting power on their 7.1 million shares. The brothers also agreed to obtain approval from the Gaming Commission to sell shares and that all accounting whatsoever involving the trust would have to be done by Amerine—the former chief auditor for the Gaming Control Board—himself.

Whittemore testified that with the trust, "I think that there [are] a couple of things here that I think go to creating this Chinese wall. First of all is the trust documents itself, and the second is the confidence that you hopefully have in Mr. Amerine's integrity."

Whittemore, noting the board needed assurances Sport of Kings would survive as a business, introduced Trevor Beaumont, a race and sports book expert from England hired to operate the Las Vegas book. Beaumont was recruited by Peters and Amerine in England and was seen as integral to the successful operation of Sport of Kings. Peters sought to bring Beaumont's profit-making ability in bookmaking and fixed-odds approach to Las Vegas.

Beaumont testified that he had worked for 20 years in the race and sport betting business and ran Coral's Betting Shops, a network of 1,000 English off-track race and sports books that took in $1.3 billion in wagers a year. Not a handicapper, Beaumont described himself as a "money manager," applying simple risk management—a series of mathematical and statistical formulas used in the insurance business—to move betting lines on horses or sports up or down once the opening lines were given to him by his handicappers.

English books seek to accommodate race bettors with the good betting potential of fixed-odds on horses and then make money with the help of the risk management method, unlike Las Vegas books, Beaumont said.

The odds on a horse or sports event may have to be altered if enough money is bet other than on the favorite to win, he said. If a lot of money is placed by bettors on a given horse, "then my job is to manage the risk of exposure that the company is subjected to." In such a case, "we try to . . . make another horse very attractive, or another two or three or four horses preferably very attractive, and then, attract money against the liability we have. That does not necessarily require an in-depth knowledge of the business in terms of horse racing."[19]

To keep bettors coming back, Beaumont said his company gave them individual attention. A book has to risk losing to keep its bettors and so has to put up its own odds on at least some of the horses in each race above what the pari-mutuel pools provide, he said. From a competitive standpoint, his odds had to be higher to satisfy bettors wanting a bigger payoff than the more conservative pari-mutuel lines. English bettors, he said, overwhelmingly prefer house odds over the pari-mutuel; less than 2 percent of his bettors wager on pari-mutuel races. The reason: Bettors like the feeling of beating a specific betting location, not a pari-mutuel pool.

Beaumont wanted to bring this approach to Sport of Kings once he was able to move his son, suffering from leukemia, to America. His assistant from England would work in his place in Las Vegas in the meantime. He predicted about 50 percent of the bets at Sport of Kings would be placed by phone, a convenience for bettors. The hold, or profit, for the book would be about 23 percent of the money wagered. The 23 percent figure was submitted to the board by Sport of Kings as part of its projections of future profits once it opened.

But board members Roche and DuCharme said the profit projections appeared too high. Roche said Nevada books without pari-mutuel had an average hold of only 9 percent to nearly 14 percent, while books using pari-mutuel had between 15 percent and 17 percent. The Sport of Kings, Roche said, was projecting the highest hold percentage in the state.

Beaumont replied that it was because the Las Vegas books, as well as some books in England with lower profit margins, tended to take on big players "without really understanding how to control the risk, get hit by the big players and then do a complete hundred eighty degree turn and say I am not going to take the big players anymore. That . . . leaves you with a small handle and a small margin."[20]

But Roche and DuCharme remained unconvinced. Roche expressed doubts that the book would be able to reach its projected handle, or cash taken in from all bets—$152 million the first year, which would be the fourth-largest handle for sport books in the state.

Amerine explained that the handle would be high because of the appeal of telephone wagering and aggressive marketing by Sport of Kings. He promised he would "do everything humanly possible to insure that the regulations and statutes are followed and that nothing will taint Nevada's image and reputation."[21]

Chairman Bible, noting his association with Amerine on the board, told Amerine that he trusted him to resist attempts by the Forsyths to influence him while serving as trustee. "[I]t becomes to a large extent a personal integrity issue with you, and I have worked around you for a while, and I have comfort levels in your personal integrity," Bible said.[22]

Sport of Kings was now requesting only a temporary limited license to operate the book for four months, the time the board estimated it needed to complete its licensing probe of the Forsyths. The board hearing was recessed again to the next morning, February 20, but the result was encouraging, if not perfect: a 2 to 1 vote in favor of the temporary license, with the trust run by Amerine. Bible and Roche voted for it, DuCharme against.

The Gaming Commission took the agenda item only a few hours later the same day. Sport of Kings needed a favorable vote to obtain the temporary license.

At the time, about 500 shareholders owned 35 percent of the Sport of Kings, with the Forsyths owning 33 percent and Sam Schulman 24 percent.

During the commission session, James Forsyth testified that if he and his brother withdrew from the project or failed to be licensed, it would "effectively ostracize us from [the] English and the American business financial community."[23] Anything less than an unrestricted gaming license would cause the "ship to run aground on the rocks of Chapter 11 within months." He urged the commission to grant Sport of Kings a full license and let the market punish him and his brother if they themselves failed to be licensed and were forced to sell their shares at a loss.

Amerine put himself on the line as trustee. He said that he had "spent 15 years, 13 of it with the Gaming Control Board and two of it with the Nevada Pari-Mutuel Association, trying to further the interests of Nevada, and I feel that this project will do the same."[24]

But it was not to be. The commission declined the recommendation, citing the incompleteness of the Forsyth investigation. Members voted 5 to 0 to refer the application back to staff. Sport of Kings would have to be considered at an undetermined future hearing.

Commission chairman Bill Curran acknowledged that the project "really does embody a new idea and a new concept" and was "a very positive new use" of the Deville site. But, Curran added, the applicants failed to meet financial requirements under state gaming Regulation 3, which requires that licenses not be granted unless the applicant's financing is "from a suitable source."[25]

Curran said he was "personally uncomfortable how at this time we can go forward given our—the rules that we must operate by until that suitability of those funds [has] been more completely investigated." He also blamed "failure of the cooperation from the Forsyths" in the board investigation.[26]

Meanwhile, in Las Vegas, in the days following the commission hearing, sources close to the board investigation began leaking unflattering news stories about the Forsyths, published by various English newspapers, to the *Las Vegas Review-Journal,* the largest newspaper in Nevada. The *Review-Journal* ran a stream of articles on the brothers in late February and March 1992.

According to the stories, the Forsyths were using some of their English gaming arcades as collateral on a $4 million loan for Sport of Kings from Anglo-Irish Bank.[27] The brothers, to raise additional cash for the project, were in the process of selling two of the arcades to Martin Bromley, an American national and Forsyth rival who then owned about 75 percent of the arcade business in England.

Nevada gaming investigators learned that in 1981, the English government forced Bromley to pay $4.3 million to settle what was regarded as the largest avoidance of value-added taxes in the country's history. Authorities said they had evidence Bromley avoided about $16 million in the taxes from income received at his gaming arcades. The Gaming Board of Great Britain and the Gaming Squad investigated Bromley's private membership in the Aspinall's Casino, while the Forsyth brothers owned the members-only casino in London in 1988. (Bromley was nonetheless approved for licensing by British gaming authorities to own his gaming arcades.)[28]

The Forsyths replied that Bromley was a member of their casino, but they denied knowing or having any dealings with him at the time.

The *Review-Journal* also reported that gaming authorities in England investigated alleged business ties the Forsyths had with Alan Poulton, the manager of two gaming machine companies who was alleged to have been part of a $500 million international securities swindle run by Thomas Quinn, a man sentenced to prison in France for stock fraud. Quinn had been indicted by a federal grand jury in Las Vegas in October 1991 in the Meyer Blinder penny-stock fraud case in which Blinder was sentenced to 46 months in prison on racketeering charges in 1992 from the Las Vegas–based scam. The Forsyths would answer that investigators in England found nothing linking them to Poulton or Quinn, with whom they said they had no business dealings.[29]

The newspaper further reported that investigators turned up questions about the bank the Forsyths were using in Ireland. Anglo-Irish had been rocked by a scandal involving a director at the bank, John Clegg, who resigned in January 1992 amid allegations of money laundering at the bank to benefit the Irish Republican Army terrorist group. Clegg's family was said to own 15 percent of the bank. The Forsyths' attorney answered that Clegg did not participate in day-to-day operations of the bank, that he was no longer with it and had no influence on the brothers' finances.[30]

Issues raised in the news stories, while sparking questions, did not seem to concern the Gaming Control Board. What did was the Forsyths' alleged lack of cooperation with the board's investigators regarding the family trust holdings.

The overseas meetings involving the Forsyths and gaming agents were reportedly tense. The Forsyths complained they were treated unfairly and in a heavy-handed way by board agent Brian Callaghan, the lead investigator. Board agents reported to Chairman Bible that they had doubts the Forsyths released the true extent of their financial holdings and that the brothers were trying to hide them from the board.

The Forsyth brothers said they could not understand why their applications would not be approved in Nevada. They had been forthright with investigators, they said. They produced a report from their attorney in London showing that they had been investigated and licensed by the Gaming Board of Great Britain.

Then, in April 1992, the brothers were faced with yet another big problem.

While a Nevada board agent was in London, talking to investigators at Scotland Yard and the Gaming Board of Great Britain, an anonymous letter was received at the London Stock Exchange, alleging the Forsyths had engaged in stock fraud. A copy of the letter was forwarded to authorities in Nevada.

The Forsyths insisted Gaming Control Board investigators somehow instigated the letter. Peters and the Forsyths further claimed the board had relied heavily on negative information provided by a single law enforcement officer at Scotland Yard whom the Forsyths alleged had once asked them for money while they owned their gaming arcades in England and that they refused to do. The officer, the Forsyths insisted, was biased against them and therefore unreliable.

"One of the biggest things that happened was that the London Stock Exchange received an anonymous letter, saying that the Forsyths were involved in trading and used stock manipulation, and what not," Sport of Kings founder Peters said. "This letter was sent to the Gaming Control Board. Not only was it not true, one of our lawyers said 'How could you possibly accept an anonymous letter as a reason?' [The answer was] 'Well, anonymous letters have some validity.' What is very interesting is that the anonymous letter was sent while the [Nevada] investigators were in England."[31]

The Forsyths and Peters complained privately it appeared as though the Gaming Control Board was, for some reason, deliberately trying to block Sport of Kings. They also blamed pressure from the gaming industry, which they claimed did not want to lose business to them.

"The thing about the licensing procedure was it looked to us like they didn't want the place to open," Peters said.[32]

One of their complaints involved board agent Callaghan himself, who investigated the Forsyths in Europe and was, as early as February 1992— the month of the Gaming Control Board hearing on the Forsyths—negotiating with the Nevada Pari-Mutuel Association to become its new executive director.

Callaghan, a 10-year veteran of the Gaming Control Board, was the choice of a five-member pari-mutuel association committee, made up of high-level casino executives, set up by the association after Amerine left to join the Sport of Kings in August 1991. In the six months while the job was vacant, Las Vegas attorney Whittemore, part of the Sport of Kings legal team, herself served as interim director of the association.

Callaghan assumed the position of executive director for the association on June 1, 1992, when he began a monthlong orientation under the direction of Whittemore, who had by then represented Sport of Kings in a public hearing before the board.

In an interview published in *Sports Form Casino Gaming Weekly,* a race betting industry publication out of Las Vegas, Callaghan said that "I was first approached in February [1992] about the opening, but I was very happy at the gaming board and really wasn't looking for a change. When you spend 10 years with an organization, it's like home and not easy to leave. The board indicated they were sorry to see me leave but they could appreciate my decision and are very supportive."[33]

"The first interview [with the association]," Callaghan continued, "we talked for an hour, discussing all aspects of the NPMA and its concepts for the future. It piqued my interest when I learned they were looking for someone who would be strong in communications while dealing with the race book managers, track managements around the country, and state regulators."

Callaghan told the weekly he felt that with only 18 of the 47 licensed race books in Nevada hooked up to pari-mutuel tracks, the association "has hardly touched the tip of the iceberg." He mentioned that his investigations while on the board "took me to England, Spain, Switzerland, Cyprus, Canada and Japan," countries, with the exception of Japan, he visited during the Forsyth investigation, although Sport of Kings was not mentioned in the *Sports Form* story.

Near the end of the article, Callaghan said that before taking the association post, he "searched inside myself if I could do the job. I got the right answers and feel very comfortable with it. Dan Reichartz [president of Caesars Palace] and Michael Gaughan [a partner in Barbary Coast/Gold Coast casinos] who headed up the search, like the other three members, were extremely helpful in making this transition comparatively easy."

Peters and the Forsyths howled that this was a conflict of interest since the Nevada Pari-Mutuel Association represented Nevada sports books dealing with the owners of out-of-state racetracks with only pari-mutuel waging, and Sport of Kings had no plans to join the pari-mutuel pools.

"We felt that it just didn't seem proper that he would go from investigating the Forsyths and then going to pari-mutuel," Peters said.[34]

The next board hearing on Sport of Kings was another special meeting, on July 23, 1992, in Las Vegas. By that time, the board and the commission had held 23 hours of hearings on the book, mostly on the Forsyths' financial transactions. This time, the Forsyths, who were back in England, essentially agreed they would not be found suitable for licensing and threw in the towel. They requested to withdraw their gaming license applications.

The brothers had by then invested more than $10 million: $5.2 million with the note secured by the mortgage on the Sport of Kings property, $2 million in stock, and an additional $3 million toward the book's opening bankroll and reserves to pay off bettors.

On July 16, 1992, Sport of Kings announced that it had agreed to buy the

Forsyths' shares in the race and sports book and accepted the two men's resignations as company officers. The transactions, however, would have to be approved by the Gaming Commission.[35]

At the July 23, 1992, board hearing, Sport of Kings lawyer Paul Hejmanowski laid out the company's proposal: removing the Forsyths by buying their interests out completely within two years. The stock would be bought at 50 cents per share, the figure included in the original mortgage in 1991, meaning the brothers would realize a profit of 40 percent from the average price they paid per share. The Forsyths' 7.1 million shares in the project were unregistered and not on the open market. The proposal was that for 1.6 million of the brothers' shares, Sport of Kings would pay them $850,000, which would be added to the $5.2 million note, bringing the Sport of Kings's mortgage debt to the Forsyths to more than $6 million. The benefit was to eliminate them as shareholders.[36]

The $6 million note would be placed in escrow in a Nevada bank, and the Forsyths would have no influence on the book's operations. The note, however, would still be convertible to Sport of Kings stock for three years until it was bought, giving the Forsyths the potential of more profits if Sport of Kings stock went up and the book was unable to buy out the loan. Under the plan, the Forsyths' holdings would decline from 33 percent to 5 percent within 90 days. The Forsyths, said their attorney, Hejmanowski, had already lost about $1.5 million on the deal.[37]

At the time, Sport of Kings's balance sheet looked shaky. It had only about $90,000 in cash on hand, $400,000 owed to attorneys, and $700,000 in other bills. The company proposed attempting to raise $4 million in a private stock placement to both keep afloat and open the book without the Forsyths.

But board members remained irritated from previous dealings with the brothers. Bible took issue with the stock sale price of 50 cents, which he said would give the Forsyths a gain of about $4.2 million since the average price the brothers paid was 29.3 cents per share. He complained that "the Forsyths, at least as you have proposed this deal, they come out of this thing very, very well, and they could come out of this thing considerably worse under a number of scenarios."[38]

Hejmanowski argued the 50-cent figure was fair because the Forsyths suffered losses from currency conversions and having to sell off some of their assets at lower than market value to come up with funds for the project. Also, the Forsyths had received no interest on their investments. They deserved the gain because they were the only ones to finance the project initially and "there wouldn't be a project if it weren't for them," the lawyer said.

Board member DuCharme also said he was concerned about the proposed transaction. "[Given] the history of the Forsyths and all their dealings that were questionable that we have spent many days talking about, they have always been two- or three-step transactions that was either through an Aegean Trust 1, 2 or 3 or some other confusing mechanism to where we didn't know who shot Cock Robin, and so, if I read where the Chairman is going, we want to know exactly who is selling and who is buying at all times."[39]

Roche said that "obviously, one of our concerns is that the Forsyths aren't economically advantaged to the detriment of the company through this type of buyout."[40]

Bible asked to hear from John Marshall, a 30-year veteran of the brokerage company Merrill-Lynch and hired by Sport of Kings for advice on the private placement. Marshall told the board he was amazed that Sport of Kings had sold 15 million shares in the first six months of 1992, had 22 million shares outstanding, and was trading from $1.50 to $2 per share. If the Forsyths were to register their 7.1 million shares, they would get about $1.50 per share—more than $10 million—even without obtaining a gaming license, he said. But they would be restricted under SEC rules to selling only 1 percent of the outstanding shares, or 202,000 at the time, every three months, he added.

Under the Sport of Kings's new proposal before the board, however, the brothers would not be able to take advantage of selling stock at the lucrative $1.50 per share, Marshall said, adding that "given a choice to do it all over again, I can assure you the Forsyths wish they never heard of Sport of Kings."[41]

Leaving the Forsyth buyout plan aside, board members quibbled with Amerine over the reserve the book would need to comply with state Regulation 22.040 to pay winning bets once it opened. They said they were not sure that the $500,000 Amerine claimed would be in the reserve at opening was enough. They repeated their doubts about the 23 percent hold percentage the book estimated it would get. Sport of Kings was hoping to profit to the tune of $17 million the first year, mainly through telephone horse wagering.

Amerine said the book expected to earmark some of its profits toward the reserve. Profits would also be used to secure future financing the company would need, he said. Hejmanowski said that Trevor Beaumont's risk management methods would be the key to the hold percentages.

Bible continued to question Amerine. The exchange would presage what would eventually happen to Sport of Kings.

CHAIRMAN BIBLE: What happens if you are wrong?

MR. AMERINE: What happens if we are wrong? It depends on the degree of how much we're wrong.

CHAIRMAN BIBLE: Let's talk about that. What sort of access do you have to additional financing? How could you—you no longer have pockets that appeared to be fairly deep. We could never determine. You are somewhat more restricted in your ability if you get the private placements of going back to the equity markets. What kind of cushions and what kind of reserves in the event things aren't according to projections? You start out on day one being the biggest book in the state of Nevada.

MR. AMERINE: Certainly most of our expenses outside of the mortgage are variable based on our volume. So we would have to make decisions with respect to if things did go very badly, which certainly we don't anticipate, but if they did, we have the ability I think to make adjustments very quickly with respect to the expenses, which are really for the most part payroll and your ongoing food and beverage expenses, and that is really it. There is not that much in the way of expenses for the company.[42]

Later, under questioning, Sam Schulman, chairman of Sport of Kings, assured the board that his wife "has millions of dollars of liquid assets" that could be used to bail out the business.

After the testimony, Bible said again that the Forsyths would make out very well with the 50-cent-per-share price, and in order to reduce the company's financial burden, the per-share price should be brought down to 30 cents.

Roche said that he was satisfied the Forsyths had been taken out of the project and that it could then move forward. He agreed with the 30-cent price for the Forsyths' stock and argued for limiting the Sport of Kings's license to two years so the board could take a look at the book again and keep tabs on its financial operations.

DuCharme commented that some of the Sport of Kings applicants had viewed the Forsyths as "white knight investors" who were "blind sided by the Nevada gaming regulators." But the Forsyths knew in 1989 they "were about to be objected to by the Gaming Board of Great Britain," he said. "It was tantamount to denial over there. . . . And still they tried to come over here and get involved in this operation. I think Sport of Kings, the company, embraced them and their money, their deep pockets. I think they should have known or they should have done some type of due diligence to find out the problems that they were going to run into."[43]

The Forsyths were "clearly unsuitable," said DuCharme, who did not believe the book's $4 million private placement or the profit and hold projections would pan out. "I think this just has too many cumulative problems for me to overcome. And even if we took out the Forsyths altogether, and brought this application on the table with the problems that it has outside of the Forsyths, I don't think I could go for it. So I'm not going to support it. That's that."

Roche replied that since the project was a unique one, not a casino, "while you can challenge the projections that are being offered here, we really don't know. And I guess you have both sides making judgment calls, and at least my theory on that is it's a free enterprise system where I think people have the right to fail."[44]

Hejmanowski said he would telephone the Forsyths in England to see if they would take the offer of 30 cents per share. He said they were waiting by a phone. Bible called for a recess. After 20 minutes Hejmanowski returned, saying he had spoken to Stephen Forsyth, who told him to accept it.

The final motion stated that the Forsyths could not enter Sport of Kings without giving 48-hour notice to the Gaming Control Board chairman or a designee but that they would be permitted to receive limited complimentaries from the book. The withdrawal requests from the Forsyths were referred back to staff and amended to applications for lender suitability, giving the board the right to continue to investigate them in the future.

The board vote was the same as in February, 2 to 1, with DuCharme dissenting. Bible said he had reservations about the low bankroll reserve and the $4 million private placement, but he added that without a license the project would be "at an almost impossible disadvantage" trying to sell the shares, without which the book could not operate.

Amerine and Schulman were recommended for licenses as officers and directors and to share in the gaming revenue. Sport of Kings was required to submit a surveillance system to the board for review and turn in monthly financial reports. It would purchase the stock from the Forsyths for 30 cents per share. Further, the book was required to hold at least $1 million in reserve to pay off bettors. Finally, no one would be able to acquire "beneficial ownership" in the book unless the Nevada Gaming Commission found them suitable.

The commission, in another special hearing for Sport of Kings on August 6, 1992, unanimously approved the application. Amerine and Schulman were licensed. But it took more than two months for the book's operators to fulfill the board's conditions.

Sport of Kings finally opened on October 12, 1992, with 110 employees, including waitresses, valet parkers, bet ticket runners, bartenders, and a chef. The private stock offering had been successful, netting the project the $4 million Amerine and Schulman said it needed.

Meanwhile, the Forsyths were effectively out of the project. But so were their deep pockets. And even more serious woes were yet to come for Sport of Kings.

Trevor Beaumont, the risk manager recruited to come over from England, declined to take the job, saying he was unconvinced he could operate the way he wanted to and with enough money behind him. Also, his son's leukemia made it hard for him to leave. It was clear from the time Sport of Kings opened that it would be unable to operate as planned.

Almost out of the box, the legal book was a failure as a business. One major factor was the decision by Amerine to offer sports wagering, a departure from the original idea to offer only horse-race betting. During its first 19 days of operation, Sport of Kings lost nearly $1 million, according to company records. Most of the loss came from sports wagering: $663,827, from a total of just under $11 million worth of bets. Race betting produced a loss of $308,000 on only $6.4 million in wagers.

The book was repeatedly defeated by the Las Vegas "wise guy" contingent. The smartest and luckiest of the bettors, Billy Walters, was said to have won $1 million betting on football games the first week the book opened. Jack Lysaght, director of the race and sports book and responsible for handicapping sports for Sport of Kings, was trying to make good on the promise to set up better odds than other books in Las Vegas.

"If a football game was at three points [for the favorite], he [Lysaght] would make it at four points," Peters said.[45]

But by that first week, Sport of Kings was already refusing bets to keep the losses down.

In November 1992, the operation continued to struggle. It actually turned a profit on race betting, winning $446,194 on $4.9 million worth of bets but losing $485,469 on a handle of $13.7 million on the sports side for a pre-expense profit of $99,302. From November 1992 to mid-1993, Sport of Kings posted winnings each month, ranging from a low of $356,000 in January 1993 to $831,000 in March 1993.

Despite the encouraging win figures, the book still suffered cash flow problems from staff payroll and other expenses. In late November 1992, the book laid off most of its valet parkers, ticket clerks, and waitresses. On November 25, Lysaght left his job with $50,000, or half his salary, in severance pay. Lysaght, formerly race and sports book director at the Riviera Hotel in Las Vegas, told the *Review-Journal* that he was "forced" to leave and that "I'll take responsibility for the [sports book] losses, but I was forced to adhere to a lot of policy changes I didn't agree with. I wanted to run it the right way, but they didn't want to win, they were playing not to lose. All they were doing was balancing the numbers. For cosmetic purposes, they made me the fall guy."[46]

In order to cut its losses from sports wagers, Sport of Kings drastically lowered its high betting limits on events. Limits on National Football League games were reduced from $50,000 to $10,000 per game. Limits went from $20,000 to $5,000 on college football games and from $3,000 to $1,000 for National Basketball Association games.[47]

The book also withdrew some of its biggest offers to bettors. Telephone wagering accounts were canceled. Fixed odds on races were all but eliminated in favor of straight pari-mutuel wagering with odds posted by the tracks.

"The horse racing sharpies immediately honed in on the Sport of Kings like sharks on a whale carcass," wrote Randy Moss, racing columnist for the *Dallas Morning News*. Moss quoted a race manager from a competing book as saying "I hope they make it. They're keeping the wise guys away from us."[48]

Still, Amerine said he would continue to set fixed odds and have high bet limits on some races. He told the *Review-Journal* the cost-cutting measures would help. "We're going to turn this thing around," he said.[49]

But what happened that November and December would eventually seal the fate of the Sport of Kings. In November, Amerine and William Vargas, the book's chief financial officer, approached wealthy local gambler Billy Walters about buying $950,000 worth of betting chips from Sport of Kings and holding onto the chips for several days. Walters agreed. The transaction, essentially a loan, was intended to enable the book to pay off the telephone betting accounts of winners and free up more of the book's reserves so it could take on more bets.

On November 21, 1992, Vargas withdrew $950,000 in chips from the cage at Sport of Kings and went with Walters to Binion's Horseshoe casino in downtown Las Vegas, where the chips were exchanged for Walters's cash. Vargas returned to Sport of Kings with the cash and deposited it into the cage.

Sport of Kings used the money to pay off and close its betting accounts. Four days later, on November 25, the book repurchased the chips from Walters. Vargas documented the money received on a currency transaction report, or CTR, which was required under state Regulation 6A for reporting cash transactions of more than $10,000 in casinos. The CTR on the money exchange was sent to the board.

The board later learned that Walters, in a separate transaction on November 22, 1992, reduced his account at the book by $823,000 and accepted chips in return.

On December 11, 1992, Sport of Kings issued a press release stating that the book had "obtained a 12-month loan in the principal amount of $2 million from Eric Nelson, a real estate investor in the Las Vegas area." What the release did not mention was that the loan was guaranteed with cash deposits at the American Bank of Commerce held by Walters and that Nelson was the go-between.

Both the chip transactions and the Walters-Nelson loan posed potentially lethal gaming control problems. Walters, a rich "wise guy" and investor, had been indicted in 1991 by a grand jury in Las Vegas, but not convicted, in connection with a highly publicized illegal betting operation known as the Computer Group. A loan from him would cause the Gaming Control Board great concern. Local news accounts about Walters's involvement in Sport of Kings alone appeared damaging to the state's desired image of strict control of gaming, not to mention to the integrity of Sport of Kings's officers. State gaming regulations required that the sources of loans to gaming businesses and the names of those involved be reported to the board. And, as with the Forsyths, the regulations required that moneylenders to gaming properties might themselves have to submit licensing applications for investigations into their backgrounds and suitability.

On December 17, 1992, Amerine resigned his $200,000-per-year position as president and chief operating officer, following reported disagreements, described as bitter, with Schulman and other Sport of Kings board members.[50] But the wheels were set in motion for the downfall of Sport of Kings after the board learned of the Walters loans.

The board held a hearing in Las Vegas on February 11, 1993, to consider whether to call Walters, his wife and business partner, Susan Walters, and Nelson forward to determine whether they were suitable to serve as lenders to a gaming operation and also require them to file gaming license applications.

To board members, it appeared as though Sport of Kings had sought to bypass reporting rules required under the gaming control process. To make matters worse, the transactions appeared to have had the blessing of former board member Amerine, who was asked to appear to answer questions.

John O'Reilly, a prominent gaming attorney who had a year earlier completed his term as chairman of the Gaming Commission, assisted Amerine at the meeting. Also at the hearing was Vargas, chief financial officer and acting president of Sport of Kings. Vargas was represented by Frank Schreck, another leading gaming lawyer and former member of the Gaming Commission. Representing Walters was Jeff Silver, another well-known gaming attorney who also once served as a member of the commission.

Board members questioned Vargas first about the chip transaction with Walters.[51] Vargas, 33, was a former certified public accountant for Arthur Andersen in Los Angeles and Las Vegas. He said the chip loan came about after Sport of Kings managers set out to put an end to the deposit accounts of the people who were beating the book on a regular basis, thus pressuring the house to raise its cash reserve. The plan was to use the money from Walters's chips to pay the other winning bettors what was in their accounts, and then Sport of Kings would refuse to take any further bets from them.

Problems with the book's reserve account began as early as the book opened in October 1992, when the wise guys were really beating the house. Their betting accounts at the book swelled as a result. Vargas said one reason Sport of Kings was losing was that betting limits were too high. He said he had feared that if he lowered the limits, bettors would run to withdraw from their accounts since they would need less money to place bets. At that point, the book would not be able to afford to pay the withdrawals because so much of its cash was tied up in its state-required minimum $1 million reserve account.

MR. VARGAS: The chip transaction resulted from a number of discussions that we had at the property.

CHAIRMAN BIBLE: Okay now, "we" being who?

MR. VARGAS: "We" being, management of the property, Dennis Amerine and myself, regarding the problems the company was having with respect to its reserve liability. And, when I say that, what I mean is that we had customers who we wanted to get rid of, and who were beating the property. But, we had no way to facilitate doing that.

CHAIRMAN BIBLE: Now explain, "getting rid of."

MR. VARGAS: We had certain customers, because of our location, the only types of customers we seem to get are "the wise guys." We have a very difficult customer base to try to manage. We felt that by eliminating those deposit accounts, those individuals would draw their money out and choose not to gamble with us anymore. Which would be exactly what we wanted.

CHAIRMAN BIBLE: And how would you eliminate those deposit accounts?

MR. VARGAS: By calling them and requesting them to come in and draw their money down and tell them we didn't want their business anymore.[52]

Vargas said that in mid-November 1992, he urged Amerine to go to the Gaming Control Board and ask for permission to take funds from the reserve to close the telephone accounts, but nothing came of it. However, from talking to Walters at Sport of Kings, "Mr. Walters indicated that he would be willing to purchase chips from us, to facilitate that," Vargas said.

"There were numerous conversations that were held with Mr. Walters," Vargas continued. "One thing that we did in trying to understand why we were losing so much money in the Sports Book, we went to the gentleman that was, basically, beating us, the worst [Walters]. And, what he had indicated to us was that he felt that our current, that the Race and Sports Book Manager at the time, was too opinionated with respect to his lines. And that when Mr. Walters made a wager, the line didn't move enough and Mr. Walters would then make another wager. And that created some very large liability for us.

"So, in the course of that conversation, as well as a conversation where I asked Mr. Walters if he would identify people that I had on phone accounts, as to what his knowledge of those people were. Whether they—since the names meant nothing, really, to me, other than they're customers.

"I requested him to look at that and to see if he recognized any of those names. Some of those names recognized were the accounts that we chose to eliminate."[53]

Vargas described how he facilitated the chip loan with Walters. He said he took 95 $10,000 chips from the book's cage and drove to Binion's with Walters, followed by a Sport of Kings security guard.

"At Binion's, we then went to the Binion's cage. I gave Mr. Walters the chips, Mr. Walters took the cash. And we came back and I—actually when I came back, I came back with the money, with the security guard and Mr. Walters went on his way.

"I went back to Sport of Kings, delivered the cash to the cage, at which time I had my cage manager fill out a CTR. I provided her with my driver's license as agent on the transaction and the CTR was appropriately filed."[54]

Vargas said that four days later, Amerine asked Bible to release funds tied up in Sport of Kings's reserve account since the telephone accounts had been paid and closed. On November 25, 1992, with the reserve funds released by a bank, Vargas said he reversed the transaction with Walters, going with him back to Binion's and Walters exchanging the Sport of Kings chips for his $950,000.

Under questioning, Vargas said Amerine was aware of the transaction at the time. Vargas said at first he himself did not perceive it as a loan but as a chip-and-cash transaction. He admitted he reported the loan seven days later and not "in a timely manner" as required by state Regulation 8.130. Vargas also admitted he was seven days late in reporting a $150,000 loan to the book from an Englishman named Charles Henry. Amerine was aware of the Henry transaction as well, he said.

"Because of Mr. Amerine's former association [with the board]," Vargas said, "I assumed that if there was a transaction that would be viewed negatively, by this body, he would make me aware of that."

Asked by board member Roche why he did not inform the board of the problems caused by money tied up in the reserve, Vargas again laid it on Amerine and on Bible, both of whom Vargas said were in communication at the time, leading him to believe nothing was amiss.

"I did not feel that it was my position to discuss the matters with you directly," Vargas said. "I spoke with Mr. Amerine about them. I was aware that he had often—that he often had conversations with Mr. Bible, though I don't—I'm not saying that any of these things occurred, I mean I don't know what these conversations were, but I presume that maybe, he would have requested that—that process of Chairman Bible—of the Chairman."[55]

Amerine himself was sworn in minutes later. He said his recollections differed from Vargas's regarding Walters. He said he wanted Walters to bet with chips rather than from a telephone account, which would require increasing the book's reserve requirement. He denied asking Walters to withdraw money from his account, convert it to chips, and leave it with Amerine for safekeeping, as Walters, in a sworn statement to board agents, had claimed Amerine had done.

Roche and DuCharme appeared skeptical of Amerine's answers and continued to question him about the $950,000 chip transaction. Amerine said he saw it as an opportunity, using "the chip float" to buy down the phone accounts at Sport of Kings, and that he thought Walters intended to gamble with the chips.

MR. ROCHE: But as far as, to summarize your testimony, Mr. Amerine, is you would assume to the extent that you were aware of a transaction where Mr. Walters would have acquired $950,000 worth of chips, that that was for no other purpose than for him to conduct gambling activities?

MR. AMERINE: That's right, that's right.[56]

Amerine admitted discussing with Walters guaranteeing the $2 million bank loan. But he said he did not know that Walters was the guarantor when the loan was actually made. He said he thought it was Nelson loaning the money to Sport of Kings. But Roche pointed out to him that Nelson told a gaming board agent that it was "the Gaming Control Board guy [Amerine] that was the point person on the loan negotiations." Then Bible began questioning his good friend about Walters.

CHAIRMAN BIBLE: At that point you had no knowledge of Mr. Walters's involvement?

MR. AMERINE: No. It was my understanding that he was not involved in that at all.

CHAIRMAN BIBLE: At the point you made the request of me in terms of lowering the—or changing the conversion ratio, you had no knowledge of Mr. Walters's involvement?

MR. AMERINE: Not at that time.

CHAIRMAN BIBLE: At what point did you first become aware that Mr. Walters had, in effect, guaranteed the loan?

MR. AMERINE: I had a conversation with someone. It was after I left [Sport of Kings in December], I had a conversation with someone outside the company and he said that it appears that Mr. Walters may have guaranteed that loan.[57]

Vargas attorney Schreck, taking the podium with Vargas, disputed Amerine's assertion that the $950,000 transaction was for gambling purposes. It was a loan, Schreck said. Walters still had more than $800,000, aside from the $950,000, deposited at the book to gamble with, he said.

"In light of the fact that there's $800,000 in Mr. Walters's account at the time he takes the $950,000 would belie the fact that he's asking for that money for chips, and it's something Mr. Amerine was well aware of. . . . For Mr. Amerine to disassociate himself from the use of those proceeds, is disingenuous."[58]

The board voted 3 to 0 to call Walters, his wife, and Nelson forward for lender suitability. Roche said the $2 million loan "from our perspective has some potential deceptive elements to it if one's not privy to it. I mean it, definitely after the fact, looks like it was done for a specific purpose to conceal his [Walters's] identity."[59]

Later that month the Gaming Commission voted unanimously to require Walters, his wife, and Nelson to file gaming license applications. Billy Walters, through his lawyer Jeff Silver, at first refused, saying the investigation would be too lengthy and expensive because of Walters's complex financial holdings.[60] However, with his money still tied up in the book, he was later persuaded to file an application.

But it was only a matter of time for the Sport of Kings to come to an end. In March 1993, the Gaming Control Board gave the book until that May to repay the $2 million loan guaranteed by Walters, threatening to take action if it did not, including forcing it to close.[61] But the book was unable to pay up.

At a board hearing in Las Vegas on May 5, 1992, members complained they were misled about the role Gregory Peters, the originator of the project, played at the book. Peters had earlier told the board he would just be a bettor there. Board members said they were not informed that Peters had helped operate the Sport of Kings and that he was paid more than $140,000 a year as a consultant. An employee of a casino making $75,000 or more would face licensing as a "key employee" under state regulations.

Board members told Peters he would be the subject of a suitability investigation if he continued to assist in managing the book. The board also denied Peters's request to withdraw his application for suitability as a shareholder in Sport of Kings, which under state regulations permitted the agency to keep the investigation on him active if needed.

Peters, who had sold off his stock in Sport of Kings prior to the hearing, denied he helped manage the book and insisted he had been open with the board's staff about his consulting work. He said he at first refused to consult for the book, fearing trouble from the board, but had been assured by Amerine that he would not face licensing. And anyway, his advice on how to operate it was not followed, he said.

"I have never been involved in the operation or management of Sport of Kings," Peters told the board. "If I was, it'd be a success today. That I can tell you. Because none of my concepts have been used. . . . The interest in seeing it being a success is only natural. It's like my baby. I created it. I'd love to see it be a success. But being involved in management, I'll give you a hundred instances of things I've said that haven't been done there. So you can't, there's no way I'm involved in management."[62]

Still bleeding from payroll and other overhead costs, Sport of Kings nonetheless continued to operate and beat most of its customers. The book dropped sports betting completely in March 1993 and had its best month. The book won $565,208 in May, $435,064 in June, and $464,076 in July.

But in June, when it became clear Sport of Kings could not attract further financing, the board drew up a complaint, issued by the state attorney general's office to the Gaming Commission, alleging the book failed to timely report the nearly $3 million in loans from Walters and did not keep enough money in its cash reserve. The book also should have had Peters file an application as a key employee and should not have allowed him to gamble there, the board said.[63]

If the commission sustained the complaint, the board would be empowered to impose a number of penalties, from a fine to license revocation and closure of the book.

Neither Amerine nor Walters was included in the complaint. Bible said that after "examination of all the evidence . . . we did not choose to take disciplinary action against either individual."[64]

With the board complaint looming and Vargas gone, the book's operation was entrusted to Blas Molto, Peters's business associate. The final blow took place in July 1993, when Sport of Kings learned it owed the Internal Revenue Service $365,000 in withholding taxes the book collected on the winnings of gamblers. With race book profits eaten up by expenses, the only alternative was to close.[65]

By July 1993, when it stopped taking bets, Sport of Kings's final tally, according to company records, showed it had taken in just over $75 million in bets, $37.8 million on race wagers, and $37.2 million on sports, with $4.1 million won from the races and $1.6 million lost on sports, for a total gaming win of $3.2 million over 10 months in operation.

Gaming regulators let the business shut down easily. The board permitted Molto to use money from the book's cash reserve account to pay its debts. He paid worker salaries, winning bettors, and vendors before shutting the doors of Sport of Kings down for good in December 1993, after 14 months in business.

The derelict bookmaking parlor became a boarded-up building like the Deville before it. Sport of Kings's stock, "ODDS," was delisted from NASDAQ in June 1993.[66]

According to Peters, not long after Sport of Kings closed, Stephen and James Forsyth suffered a financial setback in England and were forced to liquidate the Sport of Kings property. They gave Peters the job of selling the building and land to recoup some of their losses. All told, the brothers had lost about $7 million on the deal. The Sport of Kings debacle also cost the principals $1.5 million in the legal fees.[67]

The Forsyth brothers continued to talk to their Las Vegas lawyers about the possibility of resolving their problems and entering Nevada gaming, but they never did. In late 1996, James Forsyth collapsed while playing tennis in England and died at age 45. Dennis Amerine became a successful gaming consultant whose clients included casino gaming regulators in South Africa.

In the end, it was Billy Walters who struck the final blow on the Sport of Kings. As a partner in Berkeley Enterprises, which had the $2.5 million first deed of trust on the property, Walters forced the closed race and sports book into a foreclosure auction in early 1995.[68] With foreclosure, the property would revert to Walters if no one bought it. The March 30, 1995, auction, however, produced a winning bid of $3.5 million.

The new owners rebuilt the interior, removing the paintings of old English racetracks and other decorations. The building reopened in late 1995 as The Beach, a dance club frequented by young adults, with a small sports book leased by Tom's Sunset Casino, a locals-oriented casino based in Henderson. Instead of being the best use of the property, as the backers of Sport of Kings once said, the grandfathered betting operation served as a sideshow for the club's dancing, hard-drinking 20-something clientele. But the jinx on the gaming side of the property continued. On Christmas Day 1997, masked armed robbers broke into the nightclub and stole $15,200 from the sports book.[69] A couple of weeks later, on January 12, 1998, Tom's Sunset was forced to shut down its gaming operations, including those in Henderson and at The Beach, a day after its sports books lost big to bettors when the Green Bay Packers defeated the San Francisco 49ers in the NFC championship game.[70] In February 1998, in a housekeeping move, the board and the commission voted to formally deregister Sport of Kings as a public company.

And, these days, few Las Vegas race books, if any, offer fixed odds. Parimutuel pools rule the day.

Chapter Seven

A Cheater in Our Midst

Gaming Board Computer Whiz
Ron Harris Beats the System

On the afternoon of January 14, 1995, Las Vegas resident Ronald Dale Harris and Reid Errol McNeal were checked into a guest room at Bally's Park Place Hotel on the Boardwalk in Atlantic City. Harris and McNeal, longtime friends and former schoolmates in Las Vegas, often traveled together. They had gone scuba diving at the Cayman Islands in the Caribbean Sea and rafting down the Colorado River in Nevada. But this was an entirely different kind of trip. McNeal left to go downstairs to the casino while Harris stayed in the room. In the keno lounge, McNeal plunked down $100 to place $10 wagers on 10 keno games. McNeal watched the keno numbers, chosen by an electronic random-number generator, flash one by one on a message board. The computerized machine selected 20 numbers between 1 and 80 for each game. McNeal chose eight numbers for each game. Upstairs in their room, Harris sat in front of a big-screen television, tuned to a closed-circuit channel on which hotel guests could watch keno numbers as they were drawn.[1]

According to New Jersey State Police, Harris, with a small personal computer and monitor beside him, watched the numbers from each keno game and entered them into the computer in an attempt to predict numbers that might appear in the next game. Harris was telling McNeal the numbers to choose, but New Jersey police were never sure exactly how they communicated. McNeal was seen wearing some kind of earphone, and police later observed a pair of cellular phones in the men's hotel room.[2] Finally, on one keno game, the machine's random-number generator selected all eight of the numbers McNeal had marked on one of his cards, producing a $100,000 jackpot. It was the largest keno jackpot ever won in Atlantic City. The odds of winning it were more than 230,000 to 1.[3]

At first glance, the winning keno ticket and jackpot looked legitimate to Bally's employees. But when McNeal went to collect his winnings, his behavior aroused suspicion. He joked he had never played keno before despite having just spent $100 on 10 games with the potential of producing the maximum jackpot. He wanted to be paid the entire $100,000 in cash. When asked to provide a picture identification card, McNeal, a resident of the Cayman Islands, showed them a Nevada driver's license after he had produced a Cayman license while checking into the hotel. Casino officials knew that had McNeal shown the Cayman license, as a nonresident of the United States he would have had to immediately pay 33 percent of the jackpot to the Internal Revenue Service.[4]

As McNeal waited, Bally's employees discussed the matter with the casino vice president. The electronic keno game, manufactured by Imagineering Systems, Inc., of Reno, Nevada, had been installed for only a few months. The vice president telephoned Imagineering Systems in Reno, and Ron Mach, the company's head of engineering, took the call.[5] Other facts produced further suspicions. The vice president learned that in Canada the previous year, Imagineering's keno game was beaten for $200,000 in jackpots by one man who played the same numbers over three days. It turned out that each time the Canadian game was shut down for the night, the computer would reset the game's program. But when it was turned on the next morning, the numbers produced for the first game of the day were the same as the previous day's first game. The jackpot winner in Canada was found to have simply played the same list of numbers and had no knowledge of the glitch. Imagineering rewrote the game's program to avoid the problem before it was installed at Bally's and two other casinos in Atlantic City in the fall of 1994.[6]

After about an hour, McNeal grew restless and said he would wait in his hotel room. Bally's officials informed Mach that McNeal had checked in with a man named Ronald Harris. Mach said a man with the same name worked for the Nevada State Gaming Control Board and had examined the program of Imagineering's keno game.[7] The casino vice president then telephoned the New Jersey State Police's Division of Gaming Enforcement. Soon after McNeal rejoined Harris upstairs, two state police detectives were on their way to meet them.[8]

It was the beginning of the end of a scam orchestrated by Harris, at the time a 38-year-old divorced father of two. But the New Jersey swindle was nothing compared to the sinister plot Harris had hatched in Nevada, a statewide scheme Nevada gaming officials would not uncover until nearly eight months later. Explosive coverage of Harris on a network television program in 1997 would anger the Gaming Control Board and casino industry executives, who feared it would hurt the state's reputation for strict regulation of legalized gambling. Board chairman Bill Bible would later tell Nevada state criminal investigators that the Harris case was the most important cheating case in the history of slots.

An electronics engineer for the Gaming Control Board since 1983, Harris played a significant role in the evolution of Nevada's gaming control system. At the time he was in New Jersey in January 1995, he was responsible for checking the integrity of programs submitted by manufacturers of new and existing computerized gaming machines in Nevada, which then numbered more than 170,000 and accounted for more than 60 percent of gaming revenue in the state. In 1991, he developed and maintained the computer inspection program used by two three-person teams of board technicians—one in Carson City, the other in Las Vegas—to conduct surprise field tests of gaming machines in casinos, bars, and other locations throughout the state.[10] The tests were undertaken to make sure the devices by manufacturers such as International Game Technology (IGT) and Bally Gaming contained software programs approved by the board and the Nevada Gaming Commission. Harris also assisted the board in resolving player disputes over slot machine winnings and was the board's acknowledged expert at testing for slot programs that cheated gamblers. Coworkers noticed he was eager to learn how each new slot cheater did it in order to help the board prepare a complaint.[11] Back in 1988, Harris had helped the board and the commission understand the complexities of the Universal near-miss feature, which the commission later ordered prohibited. In 1989, he coordinated lab work that exposed the deception by partners of the American Coin Machine Company, which blocked thousands of jackpots in video poker machines in Las Vegas over a three-year period.

But Harris had his own deception to cover up. It lasted from 1992 to 1995, during which time Harris, McNeal, Harris's girlfriend, and his ex-wife won at least $47,000 in fraudulent jackpots. Prosecutors were able to prove they cheated seven machines in casinos in northern and southern Nevada but claimed Harris had rigged up to 44 machines for cheating purposes.[12] The resulting scandal produced changes in how the board keeps tabs on its employees. While Harris proved to be the only board representative involved in the cheating ring, his plot showed how one veteran board employee was able to control confidential information and corrupt the system without the knowledge of others for nearly three years. Nevada's vaunted gaming regulatory agency—regarded as state of the art by regulators in other states with casino gaming—showed it was vulnerable to the complexities of computerized gaming machines it regulated well into the 1990s. It was the worst known case of corruption in the history of the agency.

At about 4:45 P.M., January 14, 1995, New Jersey State Police detectives

Ronald Hungridge and William Ames responded to Bally's Park Place. Hungridge and Ames were met by hotel security guards who accompanied them to McNeal's room. After they knocked on the door, a tall, thin man with long, dark blond hair tied in a ponytail answered the door. It was Harris. Hungridge asked to speak to McNeal. Harris asked whether there was a problem. The 19-year veteran detective said he just wanted to talk to McNeal about the jackpot and that he would be free to go. McNeal appeared and agreed to go with Hungridge and Ames to the hotel's police office for questioning. Harris asked to go along, and Hungridge said he could. But after they went downstairs, Harris said he had to go back to the hotel room to wait for a phone call. The detectives returned to the guest room with him. Hungridge took down Harris's name and address from Harris's Nevada driver's license. While writing down the information, Hungridge looked around the room. He saw clothing on a ledge, duffel bags, suitcases, computer magazines, a police scanner, two cellular telephones, a calculator, and some notepads with handwritten information. He also spied a large number of keno game cards atop a large-screen television. Hungridge then got up to leave and told Harris it would not take long and that McNeal could go after being paid the jackpot.

Hungridge went downstairs to interview McNeal. While Hungridge took down McNeal's identification, the detective learned that Harris might have been employed by the Gaming Control Board. Imagineering had submitted an upgraded version of the computer software for its keno game to New Jersey gaming officials for approval in April 1994 and to Nevada in September 1994. In his position with the board, Harris would have had full access to the game's software. From the information on Harris's driver's license, detectives believed he was the same person. And from what they saw in the hotel room, the officers also believed there was enough evidence to sign criminal complaints against McNeal and Harris for alleged fraud involving the jackpot. The two detectives got McNeal's consent to search his room. Hungridge, Ames, and other state police detectives then went with McNeal to search the room, but by the time they got there—about 45 minutes after Hungridge last saw Harris—Harris was gone.[13]

Hungridge called security to scour the casino and hotel parking lot for Harris. While searching the hotel room, the detective noticed some clothing and suitcases were missing, as were the cellular phones, the police scanner, and a notepad with handwritten information on it. The officers confiscated the calculator, the keno cards, and a few notepads. They also seized two compact discs and a computer floppy disk that were sitting on one of the two double beds. One of the compact discs was in a case with "Michada backup 1-10-95" written on the label. When he was questioned again, McNeal decided to remain silent. The detectives proceeded to seek arrest warrants for McNeal and

Harris. They contacted the Gaming Control Board in Las Vegas to report that Harris was at large.

Meanwhile, Harris hastily drove out of the hotel's parking lot in a rented car to the airport in Newark, New Jersey. In the terminal, he placed the personal computer he used to predict the keno numbers into a storage locker and kept the key. He then boarded a USAir flight back to Las Vegas.

When a New Jersey State Police officer phoned the board sometime after 3 P.M. Pacific Standard Time, the call was routed to senior agent Robert Brown, a colleague of Harris's for more than 10 years.[14] The officer told Brown that a New Jersey judge had signed an arrest warrant for Harris in connection with "rigging a keno game to pay $100,000."[15] The warrant alleged Harris engaged in theft by deception, conspiracy to commit theft by deception, and computer theft, all felonies. New Jersey police transmitted a copy of the warrant to Brown and advised him that Harris was headed for Las Vegas on an airline out of Newark. Brown and two other gaming agents examined arrivals to McCarran International Airport and figured Harris would likely be aboard a specific USAir flight.[16] They went to the gate at McCarran and waited for Harris to emerge. Nevada authorities had already considered Harris a fugitive from charges in New Jersey.

While Harris was still on the plane to Las Vegas, Edward Allen, chief of the Gaming Control Board's Electronic Services Division, was informed of the warrant for Harris's arrest on alleged slot cheating charges. The Electronic Services Division oversaw the board's entire computer information system, which was used to keep track of gaming licenses, work permits, and tax records. The division's mainframe computer also stored detailed records of all approved gaming devices. Board agents used the mainframe to send results of field tests on the computer programs stored inside individual slot machines throughout Nevada. The division also coordinated the electronics lab, begun in the late 1970s, that tested and certified new gaming devices. Harris was assigned to the lab in 1983, and Allen had worked in the division alongside Harris since 1986. He considered Harris one of the best people the board had.[17]

Allen decided that in light of the New Jersey charges, Harris should be blocked immediately from using the division's mainframe computer to destroy potential evidence. Allen and his staff made sure Harris would be unable to log on to the board's mainframe from both within the board's offices and outside through phone lines. They also canceled Harris's ability to enter the building using his state-issued card that unlocked the board's computerized locking system. Allen enlisted Rex Carlson, manager of the computer lab, and the lab staff to help him begin searching the division's offices to see whether Harris had left behind any potential evidence. He also asked Carlson to start looking at what Harris had been working on in the lab.

Meanwhile, at McCarran airport, Brown and his fellow board agents watched the USAir plane land. As Harris entered the terminal, Brown approached and told him he was under arrest on the New Jersey warrant. Brown and the other agents escorted Harris to a Las Vegas police substation at the airport, where Harris was read his rights. He allowed the agents to search his baggage before they took him to the Clark County Detention Center in downtown Las Vegas. In a car on the way to the jail, Harris admitted he knew Reid McNeal but insisted the keno jackpot was legitimate.

"He said he hadn't done anything wrong, and at that point I asked him why did he leave the hotel or why did he leave the city," Brown told a grand jury in Las Vegas in 1996. Harris explained that he left because the jackpot had been won against "a gaming licensee [and] he became embarrassed [and] he figured he should leave," Brown testified.[18]

Following Harris's arrest, Allen asked Harris for an explanation of what happened in New Jersey. Not satisfied with the answers he got, Allen fired him.[19] The case immediately drew widespread publicity. Board investigators learned later that Harris had apparently found a weakness in how random numbers were generated in Imagineering's keno program after the software was submitted for his examination in 1994.[20] But instead of informing his superiors about the problem, Harris kept it to himself. He then developed a method of predicting keno numbers about to be chosen by analyzing the game's source code and algorithm—the mathematics used to write the game's random-number generator that selected the keno numbers. Imagineering engineers insisted that without the code and algorithm, there was no way anyone could predict the keno numbers.[21] Meanwhile, New Jersey police reported they received a description of a personal computer in Harris's hotel room while he was at Bally's, but the device was never recovered. They suspected a computer expert friend of Harris's might have custom-built the small device for him. But even gaming lab staffers in Nevada were unable to fully understand just how the computer whiz beat the Imagineering keno game.

In the weeks following the news about Harris in early 1995, Carlson and his gaming lab staff in Las Vegas looked into every one of the projects assigned to Harris for evidence of foul play.[22] One of Harris's assignments was to review the Winner's Choice multigame machine, for which manufacturer IGT had applied for approval in Nevada. The game, which offered video poker, video slot, and video keno games in the same machine, was well along in the approval process. It was on the required 60-day field trial in a casino, during which time the board's lab monitored the game's problems, the money it generated in and out, and its hold percentage on a weekly basis. On Harris's Michada-brand personal computer, Carlson reviewed the results of tests on Winner's Choice machines operating at Caesars Palace in Las Vegas. The records showed one of the machines had a negative hold percentage, meaning it was losing money. Carlson decided to take a look at the prototype of the machine that was still in the lab. He checked the machine's memory to look at the previous games played on it. There, he found the machine's keno game had awarded five or six rare hits, including eight spots out of eight. The board's lab technicians had done this kind of thing before, using a special device to trigger a maximum hit on a gaming machine to evaluate its reaction. But the special device had been broken for some time. Carlson thought about Harris. He suspected Harris had been practicing on the keno game in the Winner's Choice prototype. He decided to check out the machine's random-number generator for design deficiencies. The generator was supposed to produce game outcomes by constantly adding up different sets of numbers, then assigning the sums to specific positions on a reel, specific cards on video poker, or numbers on video keno. The rapidly changing additions and sums were derived from a table of digits so that they would be considered "truly random" within 95 percent certainty on a mathematical chi-squared test as required by state regulations. Experts deemed it virtually impossible for players to predict the outcomes of individual games.

After checking the software inside one of the machine's erasable programmable read-only-memory (EPROM) chips for about 10 minutes, Carlson determined the random-number generator was poorly designed and figured Harris had probably found out the same thing.[23] Harris, Carlson thought, had likely "defeated" the Winner's Choice machine in the field himself, and that was why the machine had a negative hold. Carlson and other board representatives later went to Caesars to review the W-2G forms that winners of jackpots of $1,200 or more are required to fill out for federal tax purposes. The tax records showed the field trial machine had awarded a keno jackpot of $10,000 on December 3, 1994, to a man named Reid McNeal. The state attorney general's office later theorized Harris and McNeal won the jackpot with a computer, as they had done in Atlantic City. But state officials decided they did not have enough evidence to bring a case, and no charges were ever filed.

Harris and McNeal were indicted by a grand jury in Atlantic City on March 29, 1995, on charges of computer theft, attempted theft by deception, and accessing a computer system.[24] Harris's trial and extradition to New Jersey, however, would not be scheduled until nearly three years later. The New Jersey Casino Control Commission voted on June 21, 1995, to place Harris onto the state's Exclusion List, barring him from entering hotel-casinos in Atlantic City.[25]

Aside from the pending trial, that was about it for the Harris case by the spring of 1995. Publicity about the caper had died down. But the Gaming Control Board in Nevada discovered a new twist that summer. On July 17, 1995,

Richard Kowach, an electronics engineer for the Electronics Services Division in Las Vegas, was performing a routine inspection of an EPROM computer chip containing the program of a spinning-reel slot machine made by Universal Distributing of Nevada.[26] A machine with the same program information was on the floor of the Horizon Casino at Lake Tahoe in northern Nevada. Kowach was trying to see whether the program on the machine's chip was the same one Universal had placed on the "master chip" for the game that was examined and approved by the gaming board and the commission before the machine was put into play in the state. The master chips and confidential source codes—the program or blueprint—of the Universal game and hundreds of other types of gaming machines were kept locked inside the division's file system.

But while comparing the machine chip with the master chip in a computer, Kowach found something strange. The program data on the two chips were identical, except the machine chip had a few pages of extra programming added to the end of it.[27] The added programming appeared normal, in the usual rows of ones, zeros, and letters. Kowach then ran a "check sum" test on both chips, where the computer adds up all the bits, each given a value of one or zero, on each chip. If the machine chip had been altered, the sum of the bits should have been different from the master. But the test showed the sums were the same for both chips.

Still confused, Kowach reported the problem to Carlson, who ordered Kowach and his colleague Joseph Giordino to "disassemble" the coding of the extra programming inside the Universal chip to find out what it was. That would enable them to read the original source code of the added programming. When the two engineers examined the source code, they were alarmed to read that the additions were references to reel stop positions and credits in the memory of the machine. The extra programming would automatically fill the reel stops with jackpot symbols. It appeared as though someone put the coding there to manipulate the reel stops and credits to produce a guaranteed jackpot—in other words, a cheating device, or gaff.[28]

After further analysis, Kowach and Giordino learned the added coding was programmed to permit a player to receive extra credits after wagering an exact sequence of coins, such as one coin in the first game, then two coins in the second, then one, and then two again.[29] One program had a sequence that lasted for 16 games and another for 21 games. The sequencing would be read by the machine and modify a location in the memory of the computer chip that held the number of credits the player had. The program would add a "2" to the hundreds place of the credits the player had; if the player had 10 credits, it would be changed to 210. As the player continued to play, credits would be added automatically along the way without any winning combinations lined up on the reels. In the 21-coin sequence game, once the 200-credit level was reached, the betting sequence would change to only one coin wagered per game for 239 games.[30] On the 239th game, the inserted program would jump into the machine's added code to automatically assign a line of jackpot symbols to the game, then jump back into the normal code. The 16-coin sequence program required maximum bets after reaching 200 credits to activate a jackpot.[31] Either way, the cheater would have to follow the sequences exactly in order to win; a counter had been inserted into the program to record the coins put in, and if the player varied from the preset sequence, the counter would reset to zero.[32]

The board engineers also found that the program in the gaffed Universal chip would block about 50 percent of the legitimate jackpots that would have been won by players who did not bet the set sequence. The person who programmed the cheating device had done this deliberately. Casino operators normally check the payouts of machines daily and probably would have removed and examined a machine that paid out an unusually high amount. But since half the jackpots normally won by the public had been blocked, the auditors would not notice the machine had awarded much more than usual if the cheater had won a large jackpot.[33]

Carlson contacted the board's three-agent slot examination teams in Las Vegas and Carson City and directed them to go to as many of the Universal machines in the field as possible to see whether any others contained the gaff. He soon learned that board agents had found the same anomaly inside a machine at the Imperial Palace casino in Las Vegas in 1992, three years earlier. Harris, who was then handling reports from the field tests, knew of the discrepancy but did not report it. The gaff placed inside the machine at the Imperial Palace would not have worked with the kinds of strips affixed to the machine's reels. But Carlson believed Harris had done it to begin developing the capability to cheat a machine.

Carlson proceeded to examine reports from field inspections stored in the lab's database. He was shocked to find three other gaffed chips in the field, in three different casinos. How could someone gaff machines at three different locations? When he looked into the records of where the Universal game was in the state, the reports showed each of the gaffed machines had been previously inspected at random by the board in the field. In addition, the gaffed programs were written to defy what is called Cobatron signature checking, a method hotels use to make sure the computer chips in a machine are not set up by employees to hit jackpots. The programming allowed the gaffed chips to pass the Cobatron test. Harris, Carlson thought, might have rigged it so the field inspectors would unwittingly insert the cheating device into the machines they tested.

"I had a tremendous fear at that point that Harris was involved," Carlson said in testimony to the grand jury in 1996. "Harris had developed a way to beat the Cobatron test."[34]

Carlson dispatched two field agents to the Frontier Hotel in Las Vegas, where inspectors had checked the same types of Universal machines in 1993. Carlson had the serial number of the machine he figured was gaffed. When the agents called the lab to report one of the machines had been gaffed, the serial number matched. Carlson was concerned the inspection program might still be programming the Universal machines in Nevada to cheat. After examining the field inspection program itself, known as DEPROM, he determined it could not be producing the cheating programs. A decision was made to contact New Jersey and make a copy of one of the compact discs seized from Harris's hotel room in Atlantic City six months before, the one labeled "Michada 1-10-95." Edward Allen called the New Jersey State Police in Atlantic City and requested that an officer travel to Las Vegas with the disc.

On August 2, 1995, a New Jersey state detective arrived in Las Vegas with the disc labeled "Michada 1-10-95." Allen recognized the handwriting on the label as Harris's. He had the disc duplicated on a recording device in the electronic services division. The original disc was handed back to the detective, who returned to Atlantic City to replace it in the state police evidence vault. Allen had Mark Robinson, a senior programmer and analyst in developing software for the Gaming Control Board, examine the copy of the disc. Allen and other staffers figured that "Michada" referred to the lab's old Michada computer, used only by Harris.

Carlson scanned the board's copy of the Michada disc and found it contained the DEPROM program used by agents to inspect gaming machines in the field. Harris himself had conceived of and written DEPROM. Carlson theorized that Harris programmed DEPROM to recognize the Universal slot machine when it was being inspected and then insert the gaff at the end of the machine's program. The special gaff program would not be applied to other brands of machines because it obviously would not work. DEPROM would recognize the Universal chip through a string of 32 numbers and letters, called an "electronic fingerprint," unique to the Universal machine.[35] Only then would it insert the cheating program. The program would ignore the 32-character fingerprints of other brand machines. When Carlson examined the compact disc, he found the same unique string of characters in several files for Universal machines in Nevada casinos. Carlson then used a laptop to perform an inspection of a chip to see whether the gaff would be installed. He loaded the compact disc into the laptop and made copies of the uncorrupted Universal software. After testing the software with DEPROM, he found that the cheating device had been inserted.[36]

Robinson oversaw an eight-member staff of electronics technicians in the lab. He had known Harris since joining the board in 1987. He was there when Harris created and wrote the D E P R O M program to read the fingerprints of gaming machines during the random inspections. Robinson also admired Harris's skills in uncovering cheating programs.

"When we would get a cheating incident in from the field, Ron was always very anxious to work on that problem and try to determine how the player cheated and determine what was involved and try to bring the case together so we can bring it to some kind of legal action," Robinson told the grand jury in 1996.[37]

Allen and Carlson discussed the situation with Robinson. They wanted him to find out more about how the Michada disc installed the cheating programs. All three figured Harris was behind the cheating "because he was the only one who ever did any maintenance on D E P R O M," Robinson testified.[38]

Robinson was assigned to examine the D E P R O M program and other information found on the disc. Board agents had used standard I B M laptop computers with the D E P R O M program loaded inside to read the E P R O M chips in the gaming machines under test. The database in each laptop would then be used to determine whether the program inside the chips was the same one approved by the board and the commission. The D E P R O M program then would automatically write a record of each inspection into the laptop's memory.

Carlson handed Robinson a computer floppy disk with the information copied from the compact disc. One part of it was an "object module," some numbered coding that was a piece of a larger "executable" type of software program, such as WordPerfect or Lotus 1-2-3. When Robinson decoded the object module into assembly language he could read, he found the program was much larger than expected. It contained gaffed programs and the fingerprints of approved programs. Part of the module was legitimate, but another part placed the gaffs inside certain gaming machines during the field tests.

Robinson speculated that Harris had entered seven items into the module. One item was a program with the ability to decode encrypted information. The program had decoded the name of a file used by field agents when they sent reports on inspected machines to the board's mainframe computer. Robinson then made an astonishing discovery after further decrypting the coding. Harris's program, he found, had encrypted data that were automatically decoded to "0703" in the field agent's files. Robinson figured the 0703 stood for the month and day of Harris's birthday, July 3.[39] Thereafter, a small piece of the cheating program would find the end of the file, then back up slightly and write "0703." After a machine was field tested, Harris's program code would then look through a table including the electronic fingerprints inside 13 particular E P R O M S. If the tested machine had one of the 13 fingerprints, Harris's program would jump to the valid part of the good program and insert the jackpot-producing language.[40]

It went further. Harris's program installed gaffs into four different types of EPROM chips, three for Universal machines and another type the board could not identify. However, his program would not install the gaff every time a machine with the chip was tested. It would wait until the laptop had inspected one of the four targeted chips eight times. It would then gaff the chip only on the ninth test, then no other until the laptop was turned off or the program was restarted. Harris programmed the device to place the 0703 on the eighth machine tested, which he could then view on the mainframe computer and know that the next machine tested had been gaffed. Robinson produced a list of gaffed machines by conducting a search for 0703 and printing out the records of the next machines that were tested.

Harris had also fixed it so the gaffing was activated only on the Gaming Control Board's laptops, manufactured by Dell Corporation. He made sure the cheating program would not work on the board's office computers, which he knew would be easier to test to see whether they were capable of gaffing chips.

With the inspection reports, Harris was able to locate exactly where the gaffed machines were. Robinson found machines with the inserted cheating program at the Imperial Palace, Westward Ho, and Frontier casinos in Las Vegas; the Ramada Express casino in Laughlin; and the Horizon at Lake Tahoe. Harris gaffed his first machine on November 3, 1992, at the Imperial Palace; the next on November 25, 1992, at the Frontier; the next on April 5, 1993, at the Ramada; and then on May 5, 1994, at the Horizon. Gaffed machines were also found later at the Crystal Bay Club Casino at Lake Tahoe and Fitzgerald's in Reno. Since Harris's program could not differentiate coin denominations, the gaffs were inserted into nickel, quarter, and dollar machines, which offered varying sizes of jackpots.

Allen, Carlson, and Robinson were convinced it was an inside job. The Michada disc, created in 1993, included directories identical in structure to ones in Harris's Michada computer and contained a file directory named "Ron."

The Gaming Control Board then turned to investigating slot machine jackpots at the casinos. When agents examined federal tax forms for gaming winnings, they found that Harris's former wife, Victoria Elaine Berliner, had won a $9,000 jackpot on a machine at Fitzgerald's casino in Reno on October 13, 1993. McNeal won $9,000 on the same machine at Fitzgerald's on December 15, 1993. Berliner also won a jackpot of $5,000 on a machine at the Crystal Bay Club on February 11, 1994. Investigators further suspected Harris of tampering with a machine at the Comstock Hotel in Reno in 1994. Harris and Berliner had been divorced since 1988.[41]

Board officials took stock in what Harris had done. They figured that his motive to cheat might have come from the Leo Weeks computer cheating case he helped crack in 1993. Harris had uncovered the method Weeks used to cheat video poker machines made by IGT. Weeks used a small palmtop computer to help anticipate jackpots. He was convicted of felony cheating for using the device to win $12,000 at the Horizon casino in Lake Tahoe, sentenced to probation and community service, and ordered to pay the $12,000 back. Board investigators and lab personnel claimed that Harris openly resented the light sentence Weeks got after the work Harris did to stop him. "When Weeks got probation, Ron didn't like that," one board source said.

Evidence, however, shows that Harris began to gaff machines using the field inspection program back in 1992, a year before Weeks was sentenced. Old-fashioned greed and the desire to share the wealth with his friends must have been the motive. However, Harris learned how Weeks had cheated machines with the small computer. Weeks's computer, later dubbed the "Weeks Box," located the pattern of how cards were selected by the random-number generator within a video poker machine. With the pattern, the computer figured out what cards were about the come up. Harris, after gaffing machines to cheat with his DEPROM program, would later use a computer to predict the outcomes of video keno games in Nevada. This "predictive" method would be his next move.[42]

Harris was indicted by a grand jury in Reno on June 12, 1996, on 15 counts in connection with alleged felony cheating at gaming on four occasions in northern Nevada. The counts pertained to the three jackpots at Fitzgerald's involving McNeal and Harris's girlfriend, [Lynda] Lee Doane, and the jackpot at the Crystal Bay Club involving Berliner.[43]

Meanwhile, the state was pursuing another probe of Harris in Las Vegas on alleged cheating in casinos in southern Nevada. Criminal investigators for the Nevada attorney general's office obtained a search warrant in April 1996 to enter Harris's Las Vegas home. Inside the residence, the investigators found a legal-size notepad with notes that witnesses would say later was Harris's handwriting. Authorities claimed the pad contained instructions for part of the coin betting pattern that would cause a jackpot in one of the gaffed machines in southern Nevada.[44]

On July 18, 1996, the closed-door grand jury proceedings in Las Vegas against Harris began. The state sought indictments on four felony counts of "unlawful acts regarding computers." Prosecutors alleged that Harris knowingly modified, without authorization, data or a program in order to devise a scheme to defraud or illegally obtain property. The counts came from alleged cheating to trigger jackpots in gaming machines at the Ramada Express in Laughlin and the Frontier, Westward Ho, and Imperial Palace in Las Vegas between November 3, 1992, and May 5, 1994.

In his summation to the grand jury, Deputy Attorney General Victor H. Schulze II said that aside from the electronic records, the gaffing program allegedly written by Harris on the notebook seized at his home was "the most damning evidence" against him.

"[T]his is a new kind of crime that we as a society are going to start seeing and hearing more of because the age of high-tech white-collar crimes has hit, and in my view it's not a matter of if it was going to hit. It's a matter of when it was going to hit, and they're starting to hit," Schulze told the jurors. "We know we're talking about programs because gaming is computerized now. That's why this is a computer crime, and we know he did it with the intent to defraud because from what we know now of the changed or altered program, the very purpose of the program was to cheat the casinos out of the money. . . . If a knowing player sat down at a machine and played the triggering sequence of coins, the expert testimony was here today [that] not only does it increase your odds of winning, the testimony was you must win. It does not reduce the elements of chance. It destroys it. There is no chance. That is not gaming. Gaming is only gaming when the odds are the same for everybody, and in this case there was no element of chance to Harris. I would submit to you this is an open and closed case, and would ask for return of an indictment."[45]

The jury left the courtroom at 5:10 P.M. and returned only three minutes later to announce it had voted to charge Harris on all counts. The indictment was filed a day later, July 19, 1996, charging Harris with four felony counts of "unlawful acts regarding computer" in connection with gaffing the machines in Laughlin and Las Vegas.[46]

With the indictment in Clark County, Harris also faced the cheating charges in Reno. Initially, he pleaded not guilty to the charges in Reno. But as part of a bargain with prosecutors there, Harris agreed to plead guilty to four felony cheating-at-gaming charges during a hearing on August 9, 1996, before state District Judge Peter I. Breen. In exchange, Deputy Attorney General David L. Thompson agreed to drop the remaining 11 alternative charges in the indictment. In addition, Harris's attorney, Scott Freeman, made a surprise announcement: that as part of the negotiation with prosecutors, Harris would stipulate that he had no objection to being named to the Gaming Control Board's List of Excluded Persons, people banned for life from entering any casino in Nevada, under penalty of a gross misdemeanor. Harris agreed to stay out of casinos immediately. Each of the cheating-at-gaming charges carried a sentence of 1 to 10 years in state prison and a $10,000 fine. Under questioning in open court by Judge Breen, Harris admitted that what he did was illegal and wrong and that he was guilty.[47]

But later, Thompson realized that under the law, Harris would have to be charged and tried in each Nevada county where he was alleged to have cheated at gaming: Douglas, Lyon, Washoe, and Clark. To prevent further trials and to see Harris "whipped around the fleet," Thompson decided to allow Harris to drop his plea to the cheating charges in exchange for entering a guilty plea to a single count of racketeering, which carried a maximum penalty of 20 years in prison.[48]

According to Thompson, Harris gaffed a total of 44 machines in Nevada, including some at casinos unmentioned in the indictments. Harris, he said, cheated in two ways. He started in 1992 with "intrusive gaffing" by using the DEPROM program inserted by board agents. The method was used to obtain a jackpot starting in 1993. In 1994, Harris started with "predictive gaffing" with the specially constructed personal computer he later used on the keno machine in Atlantic City and on keno devices in Nevada.[49]

With the computer, Harris would determine at what point the random-number generator of a gaming machine was within a "curve," or set, of numbers. At some point in the curve, a sequence of numbers would repeat itself. Harris was able to identify where on the curve the generator was and then predict the repeating pattern of numbers after only 10 games. To cheat, Harris used McNeal to read the numbers to him as they were drawn so he could type them into the special computer. By the 10th game, Harris would figure out the curve where the repeating sequence was, then tell his accomplice the keno numbers or video poker cards to play to win. McNeal used cellular phones to relay the numbers to Harris. McNeal also used an "ear bud," a tiny earphone placed in the ear that looked like a hearing aid, to communicate with Harris.[50]

It would take Harris four-and-a-half minutes to get the computer in sync with the targeted machine, Thompson said. By examining Harris's phone records, authorities found "loads of calls in excess of four and a half minutes," Thompson said. "He had 11 cell phones in his home."

According to Thompson, Harris said that the locker where he had left the computer in Atlantic City was cleaned out later by McNeal, who took the device with him to the Caymans.

After his arrest in Atlantic City, Harris continued to cheat machines in Nevada with a different accomplice that Harris refused to identify, according to Thompson. But in the months after the arrest in January 1995 and before Kowach's discovery of the gaffed Universal chip that summer, investigators found little, aside from McNeal's $10,000 jackpot at Caesars, which was seen at the time as an unprovable case.

A search warrant executed by the Gaming Control Board at Harris's home at 4155 Big Dipper in Las Vegas following his January 1995 arrest yielded nothing. Thompson said that at one point, Nevada state investigators placed Harris under surveillance. But when two investigators were sent to watch Harris's home from a car, they were surprised to see Harris walk out of his house and come over to talk to them. He knew who they were, and the investigators could not understand why. The state did not find out how until the next search warrant was executed, on April 26, 1996, at Harris's home and the Las Vegas–area abodes of Harris's girlfriend, Sunshine Hall; Harris's father and mother; his uncle; and his brother's girlfriend. In all, some 15 investigators performed the searches. Since they knew Harris had permits for two automatic weapons, nearly all the investigators were armed during the searches.

This time, Thompson knew more about what to look for. He had filed a 62-page affidavit in state court in which he asked the judge for a warrant permitting a broad search, one that included Harris's weapons, electronic equipment, and collection of recorded music on compact discs. Harris watched as investigators confiscated a bunch of pistols and rifles, address books, computer programs written by him in notebooks, and printouts of state gaming machine inspection sheets.

They then opened and played in a stereo each of Harris's audio compact discs to see whether any of the boxes contained a disc with gaming machine source codes. After they found one with the codes, Harris admitted that he had hidden another disc in the box of a country-and-western recording. In all, Harris had two other compact discs with source codes in addition to the two found in Atlantic City 15 months before. One of the discs found at Harris's home contained the random-number generator source codes of hundreds of gaming machines, including all the source codes turned in to the Gaming Control Board by gaming machine manufacturers in 1994. One of the discs also contained a list of 900 locations of a game called Player's Edge made by IGT. Harris had placed the disc inside his customized personal computer and referred to the source codes to predict jackpots.

Also from Harris's home, Nevada investigators recovered loads of elaborate electronic scanning equipment capable of picking up radio broadcasts on specified bandwidths. Thompson said that Harris had apparently gone to Nellis Air Force Base in Las Vegas and purchased surplus sophisticated government radio detecting devices. With that equipment, he was able to listen to communications by law enforcement officers surveying his home. However, because the Nevada attorney general's investigators did not have radios in their state-issued cars—the state legislature declined to provide funding to buy them—Harris was caught unawares during the April 26, 1996, raid.[51]

State authorities also carted away some miniature television surveillance equipment they found on Harris's property. Thompson suspected Harris and another unknown person rigged a tiny black-and-white surveillance camera that could be worn and then pointed at gaming machines. The camera would send television signals of the games to Harris in a hotel room or somewhere nearby. Harris could then use his computer to record the keno numbers or poker cards to try to predict a jackpot.

"I said to him, 'I think you're still cheating,'" said Thompson, after the television equipment was found. "And he said, 'We tried it, but it didn't work. There were too many lines on the screen.' He wouldn't say who he did it with."[52]

"He was more of a computer nerd than a cheat, at first," Thompson added. "Then as he went along, he learned by doing. What he did was extraordinary and sophisticated, because of his depth of understanding of the workings of the devices, the care and planning of the offense, and because he was a law enforcement officer and a criminal."

Thompson later learned that Harris even had a method of choosing with whom he would split the jackpots once he had located a gaffed machine. Harris recruited people whom Thompson called "collectors." Harris would test a person by taking them to a machine without telling them it was set up to cheat, play it for a while, and then have the other person play, urging him or her to bet the maximum each time. Then he would leave. Harris would later see whether the person offered to give him half the jackpot. He told one of his accomplices, ex-wife Vicki Berliner, that he knew of a "design flaw" in the machines that triggered jackpots.

Harris asked for about half the value of the jackpots won. He admitted to collecting $15,000 to $17,000 of the $47,000 his attorney said was won by the ring. But evidence of those jackpots came only from the federal w-2G forms they filed. State investigators believe they won thousands more from a slew of small jackpots in the range of $300 to $600 that did not require w-2G forms.[53]

The other known members of the cheating ring entered guilty pleas in Reno in exchange for suspended sentences, probation, and agreeing to pay back the jackpots to the northern Nevada casinos. McNeal pleaded to conspiracy to commit fraudulent gaming acts, a felony, and was fined $2,000 and compelled to repay his $9,000 jackpot to Fitzgerald's. Berliner pled to a gross-misdemeanor charge of aiding and abetting a nuisance and trespassing and was ordered to repay the $7,000 she got in jackpots she shared with Harris at the Crystal Bay Club and Fitzgerald's. Lynda Lee Doane, one of Harris's girlfriends, was convicted of misdemeanor trespassing and required to repay her $9,000 jackpot to Fitzgerald's. They were not charged in the other counties where the cheating ring operated.[54]

In November 1996, the Gaming Control Board took Harris up on his offer to sign a stipulation not to contest his nomination to the state's List of Excluded Persons. Under Nevada Revised Statutes 463.151, the board could call for Harris's exclusion by declaring him "a person of unsavory or notorious reputation whose presence in a licensed gaming establishment would adversely affect the public confidence and trust that gaming is free from criminal or corruptive elements."[55]

At a hearing that month in Las Vegas, the board recommended that Harris be added to the list, given his guilty pleas to the four cheating charges in Reno, his arrest in New Jersey, his placement on New Jersey's Exclusion List, and the publicity his case had drawn. Board chairman Bible said that "this individual not only cheated at gaming, but he violated the public trust that he had as an employee of the board. He used his knowledge and skills he gained here to further his cheating practices. And if anything, the industry not only in this state but in all states needs to be advised of this individual's tendencies, plus his skill levels."[56]

Board member Steve DuCharme said that "the public policy of this state clearly declares that the continued growth and success of gaming is dependent upon public confidence and trust that licensed gaming is conducted honestly and competitively. It further states that public confidence and trust can only be maintained by strict regulation of gaming. . . . As the chairman pointed out, this is a very dark portion of regulation in gaming in Nevada's history."[57]

Joe Ward, a deputy state attorney general, testified that "as you know, your background checks on Gaming Control Board employees [are] extremely thorough. But even the most intense background investigation may not detect a character flaw or an integrity flaw."

"We're like any other organization," Bible replied. "You'll find throughout society that organizations have individuals that work for them that have problems. I think today demonstrates that this system works."[58] The board voted unanimously to nominate Harris to the list, and the commission formally placed him on it in February 1997.

But Harris drew attention of a different sort in February 1997, this time on national television. The ABC-TV news show *PrimeTime Live* broadcast a segment featuring interviews, on grainy videotape, that Harris had given to the Nevada attorney general's office in 1995. Harris agreed to the interviews in order to show he was cooperating with investigators. The tapes were supposed to be secret but were leaked to the network. In them, Harris alleged that the Gaming Control Board gave special treatment to some of Nevada's larger slot manufacturers. He claimed board officials, including Chairman Bible, had quietly intervened on behalf of machine maker Bally Gaming to stop an investigation into a video poker machine that made it hard for players to win two jacks or better. Slot manufacturing giant IGT, Harris alleged, was able to trigger jackpots on its Megabucks statewide progressive system from a central computer center in Reno. And, he claimed, some gaming machine companies deceived players and induced them to bet more by creating near-miss results in slot machines, making players think they nearly won a jackpot.

During the *PrimeTime Live* show, Bible appeared nervous when a reporter blindsided him with questions about Harris's charges, which the chairman denied. An IGT executive, also interviewed for the show, awkwardly attempted to dismiss the allegations. Both men came off as defensive, and the program left the impression that Nevada's gaming industry was not well regulated, especially regarding slot machines. After the broadcast, Thompson, who had conducted the 1995 confidential interviews with Harris, said he investigated but found no evidence to back any of Harris's allegations, and he denied leaking the tapes.

The *PrimeTime Live* segment, however, set off a storm of criticism from members of the Nevada state legislature, casino industry, and news media. Some feared it would hurt the reputation of legalized gambling in the minds of tourists. All heaped vitriol on Harris, most labeling him an "admitted slot cheat" who lacked credibility. One state lawmaker demanded an investigation into who leaked the tapes to ABC. Some blamed the leaks on State Attorney General Frankie Sue Del Papa, who answered that her office was not responsible and that copies of the tapes had been sent to other authorities, including gaming regulators in New Jersey. However, no one in Nevada called for a new investigation into Harris's explosive allegations about the board and the gaming industry. The FBI interviewed Harris about the allegations, but no charges emerged from it.

Harris attorney Scott Freeman complained that his client's allegations had been "dismissed as the ranting of a convicted felon. As far as Ron is concerned, from his observations they [the board and gaming industry] work very closely together. You see a lot of ex–gaming board people working in the industry. Ron Harris was dismissed out of hand by both the regulators and by the industry."[59]

Harris was convicted on the single racketeering charge in 1997 but was allowed to stay free on his own recognizance pending sentencing. During that time, he helped a friend open a small computer business in Las Vegas. At Harris's sentencing hearing in Reno, on January 9, 1998, Freeman argued for probation, saying Harris had no previous criminal record and had cooperated with the attorney general's office by explaining how he had cheated the machines. Thompson, however, argued for prison time, saying Harris had acted deliberately and without remorse for years on his cheating scheme. Judge Breen sentenced Harris to seven years.[60] Board chairman Bible was in the audience watching as Harris—whose ponytail had been shorn at the urging of his attorney—was handcuffed and led to the Nevada State Prison in Carson City. Thompson said later that it was the only time he could recall that someone in Nevada got jail time for a first offense related to cheating at gaming.[61]

In an interview with the *Las Vegas Review-Journal* in early 1998, Harris said that he knew what he did was "wrong, but the attention I've gotten, it was way out of proportion."[62] As to why he put the cheating scheme together, he told the paper that "there's no explanation. I'll tell anyone it was stupid. I think just working [at the Gaming Control Board] I lost the feeling that it was wrong to do. Just from working there you end up not rooting for the casinos. In some ways, I was the little guy against the casinos."

Despite the black eye the state received from the Harris case, Nevada gaming officials remained convinced of the state's ability to police the casino gambling industry. It certainly did not discourage gamblers, either in Nevada or outside it.

During his testimony to the grand jury hearing the Harris case in Las Vegas in 1996, Ed Allen, chief of the Gaming Control Board's Electronic Services Division, said, "We've progressed to the point where we are now where regulations regarding electronic machines have been revised, and we feel we have the best regulatory system in the United States."

Chapter Eight

Profiles of Nevada State Gaming Control Board and Nevada Gaming Commission Members

Steve DuCharme

When the casino gaming industry in Nevada was intent on expanding to other states in the early 1990s, Nevada State Gaming Control Board member Steve DuCharme was concerned. DuCharme and board chairman Bill Bible did what they could to block the Nevada industry's efforts to break into what was then called "foreign gaming."

DuCharme and Bible pointed out that other states did not have established regulatory agencies to oversee casino gaming. They feared that lobbying efforts by the Nevada casinos and the lack of a regulatory framework might produce a scandal that could hurt the industry's reputation.

"I felt that it was not beneficial to the state of Nevada and the gaming industry in Nevada to have our licensees out promoting gaming legislation and gaming opportunities in these other jurisdictions," DuCharme said.

Ultimately, the industry convinced the Nevada Gaming Commission and the state legislature that expanding gaming to other states would benefit Nevada companies.

In retrospect, DuCharme said that "realistically, [with] the kind of capitalist system that the United States operates under, it's probably impractical to try to restrict or restrain business opportunities. But we wanted to at least slow it down to the extent that we could ensure that our licensees would conduct themselves properly in jurisdictions that had proper regulation. . . . The majority of the efforts have been successful, and Southern Nevada has experienced an unprecedented boom over the past eight or nine years."

DuCharme arrived in Las Vegas with his family in 1960 at age 12, one of seven kids. To make ends meet, his father sold insurance and wholesale foods and at times worked nights in the slot department at the Stardust hotel-casino.

DuCharme graduated from Las Vegas High School and entered Nevada Southern University, now the University of Nevada, Las Vegas (UNLV), as a business major. In 1970, before finishing his degree, he decided to join the Clark County Sheriff's Department at the urging of a family friend, the department's undersheriff, Lloyd Bell.

"I kind of looked up to him," DuCharme said. "So I became a reserve deputy, which meant you worked a couple of days a month without pay, and right from the start I couldn't believe that they would pay people money to have that much excitement. So I kind of got hooked and went on as a regular deputy."

DuCharme then spent nine years as a narcotics officer and two years with the street vice squad. He obtained a bachelor's degree in criminal justice at UNLV after attending night classes. In 1977, he shot and killed a suspected drug dealer at a Las Vegas convenience store. The suspect had earlier told an undercover officer and an informant that he was going to leave town and that he was armed. DuCharme and the other officers quickly set up an undercover buy-bust, but after the transaction, the dealer fled to the store. When DuCharme and his partner told the man to come out, the suspect reached into a shoulder holster purse to destroy the marked bills the officers used for the buy, but it looked like he was reaching for a gun. DuCharme's partner hollered, and DuCharme fired the fatal shot. A coroner's jury reviewed the case, found no wrongdoing, and ruled the shooting was justified.

For much of his life in Las Vegas, DuCharme had kept in contact with Bob Miller, whom he had known in both high school and college. Miller, two years older than DuCharme, would prove to be an invaluable contact. Miller, who had earned a law degree, worked as a deputy for the sheriff's department in Las Vegas and later became a justice of the peace, Clark County's district attorney, and in 1989 governor of Nevada. Miller appointed DuCharme to the Gaming Control Board in 1990 to replace the retiring Gerald Cunningham as the member representing law enforcement. At the time, DuCharme was public information officer for Sheriff John Moran, a close friend of Miller.

"Obviously, the governor's going to appoint someone to that position that he either knows personally or somebody that has the reputation and the requisite credentials," DuCharme said. "It's kind of being at the right place at the right time with the right background."

When Bible retired after nine years on the board in September 1998, the chairmanship was passed to DuCharme, who took over heading an agency with 430 employees.

Before becoming chairman, DuCharme oversaw the board's Enforcement Division, whose board agents perform background checks on applicants for licenses and work cards. When he became chairman, DuCharme, in addition to overseeing the enforcement department, was responsible for personnel, budgeting, and other administrative duties for the entire agency. While based in the Grant Sawyer State Building in Las Vegas, DuCharme will typically travel to the board's offices in Carson City two or three times a month, two or three days each time, except longer when Nevada's biennial legislature is in session.

DuCharme said that when he first came on the board, "I was shocked at the amount of reading that is required of the board members."

The week before each board meeting (the first Wednesday and Thursday of each month), the board's staff arranges the stacks of investigative reports into eight-inch-thick notebook binders and labels the exhibits. Each board member will read the materials from Friday through Monday, which "is like cramming for finals once a month," DuCharme said.

Some individual items in board hearings, he added, become marathon affairs.

"Two or three times a year, you're going to have a very contentious licensing hearing, where there will be a huge investment, both in time and money, that brings to light some areas of concern regarding one or more of the applicants," he said. "Since there is so much money involved and hanging in the balance, waiting for a favorable licensing recommendation, these hearings take a lot of time and effort on everybody's part. The [board] investigators spend thousands of hours investigating it, the applicants' attorneys spend thousand of hours preparing their case, and we sometimes argue it back and forth in public hearings. Like in the Sport of Kings [race book hearings in the early 1990s], we probably had 30 to 40 hours, back and forth."

Generally, the licensing investigation of an average applicant "requires the same amount of preparation," he said. "It's just that there are no areas of concern that arise and so you don't have as much discussion on the record. But the amount of research, investigation and review by the board members, by the applicants' attorneys, is the same."

In the future, one of the issues that will receive a lot of attention by the board and the industry it regulates will be problem, or compulsive, gambling, DuCharme said.

"Before, Nevada had enjoyed the thought that people would come to Nevada from someplace else, that they would come out and stay up too late, probably drink too much and eat too much and maybe gamble too much, and then they'd go home and say, 'Boy, I had a great time but I can't do that again for a couple months.' And we really didn't have the problem locally. But with the advent of video poker and neighborhood or convenience store gaming, we've seen a lot of our local citizens having problems with gambling . . . and we just haven't addressed it previously. At least now we are addressing it.

I think we'll probably have to look at it closer and try to develop some programs to help people."

Whether that ought to involve curbing new businesses offering gambling in Las Vegas, "that's a tough issue," DuCharme said. "The Nevada Gaming Commission and the Legislature have looked at it and have been unable to successfully figure out how we're going to curb it in the future and not inhibit everybody's right to be successful. If we just say from now on, no grocery store can have slots, how can a new grocery store compete with the grocery store across the street that has a considerable source of income from the slots? All of these issues have been discussed, they haven't been able to resolve them, and there will be discussions in the future."

Robert N. Peccole

While a member of the Gaming Commission in the 1980s, Robert N. Peccole was best known for his outspokenness, frequently taking positions at odds with the opinions of gaming board members and his fellow commissioners. Peccole, for instance, strongly questioned the state's legal case for placing reputed mob associate Frank Rosenthal on the List of Excluded Persons in 1988, before voting—"reluctantly," he said—in favor of it with his colleagues. He also raised concerns about the legal reasons for fining Imperial Palace owner Ralph Engelstad $1.5 million in 1989 for embarrassing the state by holding Hitler birthday parties at the Strip hotel. And he declared his opposition to imposing regulations meant for large casinos in Las Vegas and Reno—such as requiring new casinos to build at least 200 hotel rooms—on small Nevada cities and counties.

But Peccole most often served as the thorn in the side of the commission during the panel's normally routine consideration of work card denials. He remembers himself as the lone vote in favor of many gaming work card applicants who were recommended for denial by the Gaming Control Board solely because of previous felony convictions. Peccole felt that as long as the employer knew about it and accepted it, ex-felons should be eligible to make a fresh start. That was something his father, Robert J. Peccole, a longtime casino worker and owner in Las Vegas, had taught him.

"I had a real problem with the fact that just because a person had been convicted of a felony, they shouldn't have a work card," Peccole said. "I learned this from my dad in watching him in the [gaming] industry. He would hire people who couldn't get jobs anywhere else, but he let them know up front that he knew their background, and that he would give them a chance. If they turn him around, they are gone; this is their last shot. And he turned a lot of guys around that stayed in the business and became top notch employees. . . . That's one of the areas that a lot of [former] commissioners now, when I see them, kid me about it."

Peccole also took on the state's use of the exclusion list, or "Black Book." It was hard for him to understand how the industry benefited from the list. Since a casino faced licensing problems and fines if a Black Book member entered the property, the book therefore "jeopardizes a licensee," Peccole said. He objected to how the process was used to add James Tamer to the list in 1988, nearly 10 years after Tamer was convicted in federal court for helping Detroit mobsters hold a hidden financial interest in the Aladdin hotel in Las Vegas. Rosenthal was also put on the list in 1988, a decade after the Gaming Commission denied him a key employee license. "There should be a statute of limitations," Peccole said.

From his law office, a converted former home on Sixth Street in downtown Las Vegas, Peccole now practices gaming, personal injury, and business law for Peccole & Peccole, the firm he operates with his son Robert N., Jr., who also helps him oversee the development of 17 acres they own in southwestern Las Vegas. William Peccole, Robert N., Sr.'s, uncle, once owned the land where the expansive Peccole Ranch housing and golf course development was built in the same section of Las Vegas.

Former commissioner Peccole, 60, said he grew up in what he calls a "gaming family" in Las Vegas, headed by his father. "So, I've got a lot of juice," he said. His father worked in downtown Las Vegas casinos as early as the 1930s, dealt blackjack for Bugsy Siegel at the Flamingo hotel in the late 1940s, and was once a partner in the Westerner Club casino with Binion's Horseshoe casino founder, Lester "Benny" Binion. Peccole's father told him stories about what it was like when the state did little to control the goings-on in Las Vegas casinos in the 1930s and 1940s.

"He started in gaming a year before he was twenty-one, before they had [age] restrictions," Peccole said. "He said it was really funny, because all [the Nevada Tax Commission] did was collect taxes. There was no enforcement."

Peccole's dad took over the Cal-Neva Lodge in Lake Tahoe for several years, soon after its former owner, singer Frank Sinatra, lost his gaming license for hosting Chicago mobster Sam Giancana in 1963. That year, Robert N. Peccole, a graduate of the University of Southern California, was admitted to the Nevada Bar Association along with his friend Richard Bryan. Peccole's friendship with Bryan, with whom he attended Las Vegas High School and the Hastings College of Law in San Francisco, would shape his career. Peccole practiced criminal law until 1965, when Bryan, who was appointed to serve as public defender in Las Vegas, chose him to be his chief deputy. Peccole left four years later to form a private practice and represented gaming license applicants before the board and the commission. After 10 years as a private lawyer, his buddy Dick Bryan, who was elected attorney general of Nevada, asked him to take the chief deputy attorney general job in Las Vegas. Bryan appointed him to the Gaming Commission in February 1985, where Peccole stayed until 1989.

Less than a year after leaving the commission, Peccole made the controversial decision to work for Ralph Engelstad as legal counsel at the Imperial Palace. He took the position before the state legislature enacted a law barring former board and commissioner members from accepting jobs in the casino industry for one year after they left office. Peccole said that he learned of the job opening in a classified ad for an in-house counsel at a casino, the name of which was not mentioned in the ad. He applied at his wife's urging and said he was "surprised" to hear it was from the Imperial Palace. He took the position following an interview with Engelstad. Peccole said he had no problem accepting it, pointing out that most of his fellow commissioners had agreed with him that the 1989 fine levied on Engelstad was excessive. He said he was hired because "Ralph Engelstad really demands loyalty, and I think that he probably in those [commission] meetings saw that there was the possibility that I could be very loyal to him."

One of the things that struck him most about his commission job was the amount of work required, scanning verbatim transcripts of Gaming Control Board hearings and other material shipped to his office in boxes. Each review took at least three days, eight hours a day, before each monthly commission meeting.

"It's a very demanding job," he said. "The commission was only part-time, and it wasn't a very high paying job. It was only about $12,000 [a year], something in that range. You don't realize how demanding it is until you have to start preparing. . . . We had to read all the summaries, know all the backgrounds of who these [applicants] are, and then you would have to read the transcripts to see what kind of questioning the board had done. That's preparation. I mean, many times we were starting [commission meetings] at nine in the morning and stayed until midnight. I always found it fascinating because there were so many different kinds of issues coming up."

Thomas Roche

At his fifth-floor office inside the palm tree–lined Howard Hughes Center complex a few blocks east of the Las Vegas Strip, Thomas Roche is constantly busy and driven. He regularly logs 12-hour days as a partner for the international accounting firm Arthur Andersen LLP. Including the work he brings home, his normal workweek covers 70 to 80 hours. Casino corporation clients such as Mirage Resorts, Hilton Hotels, Harrah's Entertainment, Station Casinos, and M G M Grand seek his expertise and guidance to avoid the kinds of accounting errors or money-handling mistakes that might incur the wrath of the Gaming Control Board or the U.S. Treasury Department.

Arthur Andersen's casino customers use the firm to make sure they follow the Gaming Control Board's strict cash reporting and documentation rules— a kind of insurance policy against possible fines or licensing penalties. And Roche knows what the board requires. A certified public accountant, Roche was a member of the board from December 1989 to October 1993, serving as its accounting and auditing expert. He received a B.S. degree in accounting at the University of Southern California and joined Arthur Andersen in 1979, when he was immediately assigned to help audit the Marina and Circus Circus casinos in Las Vegas and the Cal-Neva Lodge in Lake Tahoe. Roche is one of 2,400 partners in the Arthur Andersen company, which is one of the "Big Five" accounting firms and the largest of those firms involved in the gaming industry.

To Roche, the most significant change in gaming policy while he served on the board was enforcing compliance with the board's cash-handling and anti-money-laundering statute, Regulation 6A. The board sent out agents in undercover roles to put money on deposit, make wagers, and other "participatory transactions" at casinos to see whether employees followed Regulation 6A cash management procedures. The board as a result began issuing complaints and assessing fines for noncompliance. Roche said the penalties were healthy for the industry because they showed the Treasury Department that Nevada licensees were being tested for following rules written to deter money laundering. Nevada casinos, Roche said, would rather face tough regulation by the state than regulation by federal officials.

"I think that the industry really hunkered down and made that a high, high priority for themselves, once they saw the direction the board was taking," Roche said.

When Arthur Andersen audits a casino client, "we look pretty much at the internal controls—the general environment that they establish to control and safeguard the assets, and recognize revenues," he said. Most of the time, Roche and his auditors engage in "compliance testing," where an "engagement team" of staffers is sent to perform surprise inspections of a casino licensee's internal money-handling and accounting procedures. The team might go to the casino in midmorning and enter the count rooms, watch a new shift take over at a slot change booth, and count the markers (loans to gamblers) being held in the casino cage. An audit of a large casino can take 1,500 to 2,000 hours over a year's time. What emerges is the Audited Financial Statement, which each casino is required to submit to the Gaming Control Board annually under state Regulation 6.080, and, for public companies, Form 10K to the Securities and Exchange Commission. But most important, Roche said, the auditors seek to reach the conclusion that the casino's cash control environment is such that the financial information is reliable and not misstated.

The independent auditors further submit to the Gaming Control Board a state Regulation 6.090 report, showing whether the licensee adhered to its minimum internal control plan for money handling, and a report attesting to the casino's compliance with Regulation 6A. Meanwhile, the board's Audit Division performs its own independent audit of each casino.

"The gaming industry is unique in the sense that they do require the CPA firms to perform certain prescribed tests and submit the results of that testing directly to the board," Roche said. "Nevada has set the standard that others throughout the world have adopted as the optimal configuration."

The most common internal control breakdowns inside casinos, according to Roche, include "lack of accountability over the assets in terms of chips and currency held in the [casino] cages reconciling to paperwork; and/or there being weaknesses in controls in hard count [coins and tokens] and soft count [currency] rooms. More hard count than soft count, but those are typically the areas we focus in on, because they segue into, again, this issue of safeguarding of assets, and, more importantly, the recognition of revenues. So, we also are sensitive to issues such as skimming, management fraud, those types of issues. I think, overall, the level of control quality here amongst the Nevada licensees who are our clients is pretty outstanding. At least that's what we have concluded, especially with all the different checks and balances the state has imposed on those clients."

With the state's strict auditing controls in place, discrepancies are the exception to the rule in the casinos the company audits, Roche said. Those that he and other auditors do find are usually due to individual human error. "The way a cage works is that you have a cage accountability, where the paperwork will roll forward the activity that goes on in a cage during a shift. So, at the end of that shift, you'll know what should be in the cage, because the paperwork will tell you that, and you physically count down the assets and compare the two. So, the end checks and balances that occur, like in a cage, are essentially: 'Here's what the paperwork shows should be there, and here's what you counted, and here's the difference.' And that's what traditionally generates the overs and shorts you find on cage accountability worksheets. The physical count of assets is different from the paperwork and what it shows should be there. And that's pretty much the same concept that you apply throughout the casino, whether it's tabletop inventories, hard count, soft count, whatever it may be."

A typical day for Roche is fielding questions from casino executives, floor personnel, out-of-state casino licensees, and others about internal control, licensing, accounting, debt, and equity issues. They will also call him at home, where he spends what little off-time he has with his young son, William, and his wife, Lisa Miller-Roche, a former state deputy attorney general who works as an attorney in the Hughes Center a couple of blocks from his office.

"I've been pretty much preoccupied with throwing most of my time into work," Roche said. "I don't spend a lot of free time, as I'm sure Lisa can tell you."

Michael Rumbolz

A native Las Vegan, Michael Rumbolz took full advantage of the opportunities offered by the many casino businesses around him while he grew up. He worked as a busboy at the Stardust casino when he was 16, dealt poker at the Golden Nugget while a student at UNLV, and then dealt blackjack at Circus Circus before entering law school at the University of Southern California.

After graduating from law school in 1980, Rumbolz moved right back to Las Vegas with an interest in entering casino-related business law. His rise was rapid. He joined the firm of Jones, Jones, Bell, Close & Brown (later renamed Jones Vargas), which had quite a few gaming clients. Over the next few years, Rumbolz worked for about a dozen gaming license applicants, poring over the details of Summa Corporation's sale of the Sands Hotel and the purchase of the Aladdin Hotel by Ed Torres and Wayne Newton.

Then, in 1983, Brian McKay, the state's attorney general, convinced Rumbolz to take over the position of chief deputy attorney general in Las Vegas. In June 1984, McKay appointed him chief attorney general for the office's gaming division, "which really in terms of the offices, was a demotion," Rumbolz said. "But it clearly provided me with the day-to-day work that I was most interested in." Only several months later, what Rumbolz described as "a series of coincidences" occurred. Patty Becker, a member of the Gaming Control Board, announced she would step down. Board member Bart Jacka became chairman. As a result, Rumbolz, barely in his 30s, was appointed by Governor Richard Bryan to the board as its legal and law enforcement member in January 1985. Two and a half years later, Rumbolz replaced Jacka as board chairman, where Rumbolz remained until Bill Bible took over as chairman in January 1989.

"I've had sort of a unique position," Rumbolz said. "I'd been able to look at gaming control from the board member position, and from the outside as private counsel representing applicants. I also had the ability to look at it from the inside as attorney for the gaming regulators. . . . [What] I found exhilarating was actually being involved as a decision maker in the process, and being able to help shape the policies and decisions of the board and the commission, and being able to do it in a public forum where a vote could be taken and where we could exchange ideas with the public, but also amongst ourselves."

Casino gaming was centered in Nevada and New Jersey during Rumbolz's years on the board, a time when the U.S. government once again indicated that a tax might be levied on the industry. For Rumbolz, that possibility "brought into focus a lot of the states' rights and federalist concerns that are truly involved in a much larger picture of the gaming industry and how it fits into our society." In the 1980s, the federal government "determined that casinos were banks, for all intents and purposes, which was a major shift, both in theory as to how this industry operates under statutes they may apply to it, but also in content, as to what and when casinos would be required to provide reports to anybody, let alone the federal government," Rumbolz said. "We were able, I think, to find a common ground with the federal government to access information they were interested in, without taking away from the state the right to control the industry and to be the real regulators over how the industry conducted its business."

By adopting stringent cash-reporting rules for casinos to follow under state Regulation 6A, Nevada used its own regulatory system to share the information with the federal government. New Jersey, meanwhile, took another view and permitted the federal government to regulate its casinos as banks.

"Eight or nine years later, it has certainly been confirmed to me by several executives who worked in both Atlantic City and Nevada that the industry was put into a much better position by being able to report to the Nevada regulators under the Nevada format than the Atlantic City casinos were left in the federal [government's] hands," Rumbolz said.

Nevada also fostered the spread and acceptability of legalized gambling in other states in the 1990s, he said, by instituting a "thorough housecleaning" in the late 1970s and early to mid-1980s. State gaming officials, he said, successfully rid the industry of corruption in public and private corporations, such as mob-involved Teamster Union pension fund investments and hidden mobster ownership at the Stardust, Fremont, Tropicana, and other Las Vegas hotels.

The rise of public equity investments and debt offerings involving Las Vegas casino businesses in the 1980s "helped to give a much more legitimate grounding to the financial side of our industry, and people with backgrounds in other businesses before they came to gaming," Rumbolz said. "So, part of the clean up both of individuals and financial dealings in our casinos helped other jurisdictions look at the industry in a different light and actually feel that there was a way of controlling it and allowing it in your state without a lot of corrupting influences coming with it. That was also enhanced by New Jersey's extremely rigorous attitude regarding associations and potential corrupting influences."

Rumbolz also credits meetings among gaming regulators—starting with international conferences sponsored in the 1980s by the International Association of Gaming Attorneys and the formation of the International Association of Gaming Regulators in 1988—for fostering discussions on gaming industry issues (the backgrounds of executives, slot cheating rings, and fraud) and streamlining gaming regulations in other states and countries. Gone are the days, in the 1980s, when Nevada had to review the entire regulatory structures of other states and foreign countries, including Great Britain and Australia, before allowing a Nevada gaming licensee to operate there, he added.

After his exit from the board at the end of 1988, Rumbolz had to contemplate a variety of lucrative job offers. He accepted one with New Jersey casino owner Donald Trump and became president of Trump's Nevada company. When Trump decided against a Las Vegas casino project, Rumbolz moved to Atlantic City, where he helped open Trump's Taj Mahal casino and served for two years as executive vice president of Trump Castle. Rumbolz then came back to Las Vegas and worked as director of corporate development for Circus Circus Enterprises. Since 1995, he has held the position of president and chief operating officer of Anchor Gaming, Inc., a slot manufacturer and route operator based in Las Vegas. His boss is slot machine and table game pioneer Stan Fulton.

Rumbolz describes himself as a "bad golfer" and, "if you ask my wife, a workaholic." His off-work interests include reading and amateur geology. "I like to get in the desert and explore different mine sites, collect various samples," he said. "Nevada is sort of a geologist's heaven, or nirvana, just because of the physical structure of our valley."

Sue Wagner

Labor Day, 1990, changed Sue Wagner's life. It was the day before the September primary election, in which Wagner, a Reno-based veteran state legislator, was running for her Republican Party's nomination for lieutenant governor. Wagner had just finished campaigning in Fallon, Nevada, when she and four others entered a small private airplane, piloted by Bob Seale, Nevada's state treasurer. But once the plane was airborne, it plummeted to the ground. Seale's wife was killed, and the other passengers were injured. Wagner suffered serious injuries; her neck and back were broken. She was placed into a body cast. Her candidacy, however, was successful. She won the nomination and the general election. She was paralyzed when she was sworn in.

While in office, Wagner went through a long convalescence, during which some of the vertebrae in her neck and back were fused. She also contracted a disease associated with paralysis. She left office after her term expired in 1994, and though still suffering constant back pain, she accepted her appointment by Governor Bob Miller to the Gaming Commission in April 1997.

"I'm always in pain, and I can never do a full-time job," Wagner said. "Some of the commission's meetings last 12 to 14 hours, so they've provided me with a special chair. But I still need to take breaks to lie down on a chaise lounge."

Wagner brought with her a lot of experience on gaming issues from the legislative side. After six years as a member of the state assembly, she was elected to the state senate and served 10 years, including two legislative sessions chairing the Judiciary Committee, through which all gaming-related bills must pass. But only after she joined the Gaming Commission did she realize, she said, "how little I did know" about the industry and its regulation.

"What I like about it is making policy decisions," Wagner said. "I think I'm more tough, very hard-nosed, by virtue of being a legislator. I question motives. I have a cynical outlook. I'm not a housewife from Reno. I've got a questioning mind and I would rather be tougher than not. I think there is a difference between being a legislator and a regulator. A legislator seeks compromise, whereas a regulator sees it one way or another. I don't see [being a regulator] as consensus-building. Although, by placing a condition on a license or limit on a license, you could compromise by doing that."

Wagner's tough-mindedness on the commission was often shared by another female member, Debbie Griffin, who served for eight years before leaving in 1998. Wagner said she and Griffin often agreed in taking hard stands on gaming applicants, and there were many 3-to-2 votes with the two of them voting against the applicants. "I don't know if it is [because we're both women]," Wagner said. "I think that people who might think that would think we would probably be more likely to give everybody a second shot."

One gaming issue that interested her while on the commission concerned whether Nevada ought to restrict the proliferation of new slot machines in small businesses. "I don't think there is a problem," she said. "We might have them in grocery stores and Laundromats, but that is part of our history, and I think it's unfair to go back and say, 'no more.'"

Wagner also disagrees with the argument put forth by some in Nevada that kids are hurt by the presence of gaming machines inside stores and other public places. She asked her son, an attorney in Pacific Grove, California, and her daughter, who holds a doctorate in education from the University of Arizona, whether they felt affected by slots as children in Reno, "and they thought that was crazy," she said.

Another important topic for her is compulsive gambling. Wagner's interest got her appointed in 1998 by Gaming Control Board chairman Bill Bible to a statewide committee charged with studying the problem. Approaches to solving compulsive gambling in states that are relatively new to gaming might not work in Nevada, she said. In Missouri, for instance, policymakers suggested simply ejecting people who are identified as problem gamblers from the state's riverboat casinos. Wagner said that expelling problem gamblers would not be practical in Nevada's larger casinos.

Originally from Maine, Wagner moved in 1950 to Arizona, where she met her future husband. They moved to Nevada 18 years later. "I was horrified by the neon lights and the casinos," she said. "It was a shock to see slots in stores, in airports, at first." Wagner, however, won a seat in the state assembly only five years after they settled in Reno.

Memories of the 1990 plane crash remain with her, and Wagner, who flies from Reno to Las Vegas about once a month, will fly only in a commercial airliner. Ironically, her husband, Dr. Peter Wagner, an atmospheric physicist, was killed when his small plane crashed while he was performing tests over the Sierra Nevada in northern Nevada in 1980.

"Some people I sit next to in the plane are like white knuckle [about flying]," she said. "But I don't even think about it. In a large plane, I feel safe."

John F. O'Reilly

After working his way through a B.S. degree in accounting and finishing law school in St. Louis in 1969, John F. O'Reilly set out with his wife for Las Vegas to serve out a stint as a captain in the U.S. Air Force. They fully intended to return to their hometown of St. Louis, but after only a couple of years "the choice became obvious to stay," he said. The opportunities were there. O'Reilly served as a military judge, prosecutor, and military contracts head at Nellis Air Force Base, where he also took courses that led to a master's degree in business administration from UNLV.

In 1974, his military obligation at an end, O'Reilly, having received a license to practice law in Nevada in 1972, put his sights on a private law career. Then he got to know Milt Keefer, the first chairman of the Gaming Commission, and handled gaming-related cases for him. O'Reilly obtained a real estate license and worked in the audit and tax departments for the accounting and consulting firms Arthur Andersen and Ernst and Ernst. Over the years, he has served in numerous positions, professional and volunteer, including chairman of the Las Vegas Chamber of Commerce's board of directors, regent for Loyola Marymount University in Los Angeles, and an alternate municipal judge in Las Vegas. O'Reilly even received a gaming license as an "investor" in the Casablanca hotel-casino in Mesquite, Nevada, in June 1998.

O'Reilly is best known for his service as the chairman of the Gaming Commission from 1987 to 1991. During his years on the commission, O'Reilly was known as a take-charge guy, the dominant one who did most of the talking at hearings.

Nevada in the late 1980s was entering a new era of huge public stock offerings to finance casinos when O'Reilly took over as chairman. The commission reviewed and approved recapitalizations by the Holiday Inn and Caesars Palace hotel-casinos that represented the first two billion–dollar stock issues in state history. O'Reilly also held court during the debate over revising more than 50 state gaming regulations that led to the 1992 "Status of Gaming" report. The commission under O'Reilly further moved to, as he termed it, "clean up some of the issues left over from previous decades" by entering mob associates from the 1970s, such as Frank Rosenthal, into the Black Book. And O'Reilly aided the state's successful case for autonomy in regulating casino cash transactions by personally assuring the deputy director of the FBI that Nevada would cooperate with federal law enforcement.

Now a gaming licensee himself, O'Reilly said that the casino industry is "like any business; it's exciting, it's satisfying, and it's got its challenges. I've always looked at gaming as an entertainment business. It's good if you like seeing the smiles on people's faces, and providing them with a good time."

A good time for O'Reilly is being in the outdoors, tooling around in his 28-foot boat, which he has owned since 1974. He takes it out for waterskiing and sometimes fishing on Lake Mead outside Las Vegas. He will also drive it on the Pacific Ocean from San Diego to some islands off the coast of Mexico. "It's a power boat," he said. "I don't have the patience to sail."

William Urga

When William Urga, born and raised in Las Vegas, graduated from law school at the University of California, San Francisco, in 1970, he considered entering commercial litigation, not gaming law, as a career. In fact, he did not even want to practice in Las Vegas. But he did apply to a Las Vegas law firm that included former Nevada governor Grant Sawyer, considered by many the father of modern gaming control. After being interviewed by Sawyer himself, Urga was impressed enough to accept a job.

With Sawyer's influential and politically connected firm, Lionel, Sawyer & Collins, Urga began practicing his specialty, Nevada corporate law, including work on the merger of the International Leisure Company with Hilton Hotels Corporation. He later became part of Jolley, Urga, Wirth, and Woodbury, another powerful Las Vegas law firm. But Urga's lack of gaming experience did not necessarily disqualify him from serving on the Gaming Commission. When Governor Bob Miller requested he join, he accepted.

"Well, the governor asked me to do it," said Urga, 53, with a slight sigh. "And the fact that I was a native, I felt that I had a responsibility to do it. I decided it would be something that I would enjoy. I don't think [lacking a background in gaming] was as much a problem because a lot of the things you're working on have nothing to do with the hands-on, day-to-day operation of gaming. The process, the system you have to learn a bit, but that comes fairly quickly. I spent a lot of time preparing and reviewing for the monthly meeting."

As other part-time commission members can attest, the work was heavy before the meetings, usually 50 to 80 hours per month, although some months were easier than others, Urga said. The pay was about $40,000 per year while he was a member, he said. Gaming Control Board agents would truck in boxes containing transcripts of board meetings to his law firm, and Urga said he would spend all of Saturday and Sunday and parts of Monday, Tuesday, and Wednesday studying them before the Thursday commission meetings. Hearings on the possible revocation of casino employee work cards seemed to take up a lot of the commission's time, more so than the time it took to consider nonrestricted casino license applications.

"In some respects, [work cards] got a disproportionate amount of attention," Urga said. "You spent a lot of time on work cards because the person's livelihood may be on the line, and even though the rules said that there weren't supposed to be any new facts or argument. . . . Chairman [Bill] Curran would give the employees some latitude, and they would come up and make a pitch and you'd have to review all that material."

In his six years on the commission, Urga said he never once felt any political pressure to vote one way or another. "Absolutely none, at least on me," he said, "and I don't believe there was on anyone else. The governor never stepped in, the legislators never stepped in, lobbyists never stepped in. It just didn't happen, which is probably a rarity in a government agency. But I really, truly felt it was hands-off. We voted the way we felt. We turned down people who were licensed in other jurisdictions and licensed around the world."

One of the things he recalls that commissioners found unacceptable enough to turn down gaming license applicants from foreign countries was bribery, Urga said. "They would use the excuse that it was an acceptable business practice to take regulators out to dinner, or to give them gifts. Some of them were just bad people."

Many applicants for licenses to participate in the major casino projects in Las Vegas in the 1990s were big players who tended to be involved in many deals that had to be examined by the board and the commission, he said.

"What I think takes time now is just investigating all of the business transactions that these people engage in because they are so active in business," Urga said. "But most of the big business people keep good records."

Overall, Urga said he enjoyed the process while on the commission, if not all the reading—often thousands of pages per month—to prepare for meetings. "I read it because I didn't want the [applicants'] lawyers telling me something different than what was in the record."

Urga, married with four grown children, liked growing up in Las Vegas. He played football and basketball while at Las Vegas High School and was never a gambler.

"It was fun because the gamers knew everybody, in the sense that they were your neighbors, so as a kid before you even had swimming pools, if your dad knew somebody, you could go swim in the hotel pools," he said. "I guess I enjoyed Las Vegas because I guess I didn't know any better."

Appendix One

Organizational Structure of the Nevada State Gaming Control Board and the Nevada Gaming Commission

The Nevada State Gaming Control Board and the Nevada Gaming Commission make up the two-tiered system charged with regulating the Nevada gaming industry. The conduct and regulation of gaming in Nevada are governed by Chapters 462, 463, 463B, 464, 465, and 466 of the Nevada Revised Statutes and are further clarified by the regulations of the Nevada Gaming Commission and the Nevada State Gaming Control Board. The commission and board administer the state laws and regulations governing gaming for the protection of the public and in the public interest in accordance with the policy of the state.

Nevada Gaming Commission

The Nevada Gaming Commission is a five-member lay body appointed by the governor that serves in a part-time capacity. Its primary responsibilities include acting on the recommendations of the Gaming Control Board in licensing matters and ruling in work permit appeal cases. The commission is the final authority on licensing matters, having the ability to approve, restrict, limit, condition, deny, revoke, or suspend any gaming license. Additionally, the commission is charged with the responsibility of promulgating regulations to implement and enforce the state laws governing gaming.

State Gaming Control Board

The State Gaming Control Board is a three-member body appointed by the governor that serves in a full-time capacity. The board is responsible for regu-

Source: Gaming Control Board Web site

lating Nevada's gaming industry 24 hours per day on a daily basis. Its purpose is to protect the stability of the gaming industry through investigations, licensing, and enforcement of laws and regulations; to ensure the collection of gaming taxes and fees, which are an essential source of state revenue; and to maintain public confidence in gaming. The board implements and enforces the state laws and regulations governing gaming through seven divisions. The board has offices in Carson City, Las Vegas, Reno, Elko, and Laughlin.

DIVISIONS OF THE GAMING CONTROL BOARD

The Administration Division provides administrative, technical, and support services to the board, the commission, and the other six operating divisions in such areas as legal services, budgeting, personnel, payroll, accounting, management analysis, central files, special investigations, training, purchasing, gaming research, and hearings, thus providing them the resources to efficiently and effectively regulate the industry.

The Audit Division audits the records of nonrestricted licensees (whose annual gross gaming revenues are $1 million or more) to determine whether taxable gaming revenues have been properly reported. The division performs special investigations involving financial records, advises the board concerning licensees' equity and debt positions and bankroll adequacy, and provides expertise in matters concerning financial statements and accounting standards. The division also evaluates each nonrestricted licensee's systems of internal control and conducts interim observations to ensure continuing compliance with regulations. The Audit Division is responsible for the enforcement of Nevada Gaming Commission Regulation 6A, which implements federally mandated cash transaction controls.

The Corporate Securities Division monitors, investigates, and analyzes activities of registered, publicly traded corporations and their subsidiaries involved in the Nevada gaming industry. Actions that might affect the industry, such as changes in control, public offerings, involvement in foreign gaming, and recapitalization plans, are scrutinized by the division and reported to the board.

The Electronics Services Division examines, tests, and recommends gaming devices for approval or denial by the board and commission. The division inspects gaming devices in its laboratory and in the field to ensure continued integrity and assists in resolving gaming patron disputes through analysis of device electronics. The division also develops and manages computer applications for the board's internal information management system.

The Enforcement Division inspects licensed games, devices, casino surveillance systems, and gaming premises. It investigates reported violations of gaming law, organized crime allegations, and potential candidates for the List of Excluded Persons. The division develops intelligence information, compiles information on criminal activities, and produces criminal cases resulting in arrest and prosecution of criminal offenders. The division also reviews the issuance of work permits for all gaming employees; processes applications for new games, charitable bingo, and charitable lotteries; and regulates the conduct of horse racing.

The Investigations Division investigates all gaming license and key employee applicants to determine their viability, business integrity, and suitability for licensure or approval. Division investigators produce detailed reports that are used by the board and commission as the basis for licensing recommendations/decisions.

The Tax and License Division issues all state gaming licenses approved by the commission. The division collects, controls, and accounts for all state gaming fees, taxes, fines, and penalties. It provides a complete accounting of gaming revenues collected and deposited to the state general, distributive, and dedicated funds. The division also monitors the activities of nonrestricted licensees (whose annual gross gaming revenues are less than $1 million) and restricted licensees through a field compliance program.

Gaming Policy Committee

The Gaming Policy Committee is an 11-member committee that meets at the call of the governor to discuss matters of gaming policy. The committee is advisory in nature—its recommendations are not binding on the commission or the board. The Gaming Policy Committee is composed of the following:

- The governor (who chairs the committee)
- One member of the state senate
- One member of the state assembly
- One member of the Nevada Gaming Commission
- One member of the Nevada State Gaming Control Board
- One member of a Nevada Indian tribe
- Five members appointed by the governor: two representatives of the general public, two representatives of nonrestricted gaming licensees, and one representative of restricted gaming licensees.

The state's public policy concerning gaming, in part, is as follows:

The legislature hereby finds, and declares to be the public policy of this state, that:

- The gaming industry is vitally important to the economy of the state and the general welfare of the inhabitants.

- The continued growth and success of gaming is dependent upon public confidence and trust that gaming is conducted honestly and competitively, that the rights of the creditors of licensees are protected and that gaming is free from criminal and corruptive elements.
- Public confidence and trust can only be maintained by strict regulation of all persons, locations, practices, associations and activities related to the operation of licensed gaming establishments and the manufacture or distribution of gambling devices and equipment.
- All establishments where gaming is conducted and where gambling devices are operated, and manufacturers, sellers and distributors of certain gambling devices and equipment must therefore be licensed, controlled and assisted to protect the public health, safety, morals, good order and general welfare of the inhabitants of the state, to foster the stability and success of gaming and to preserve the competitive economy and policies of free competition of the State of Nevada.
- To ensure that gaming is conducted honestly, competitively and free of criminal and corruptive elements, all gaming establishments in this state must remain open to the general public and the access of the general public to gaming activities must not be restricted in any manner except as provided by the legislature.

Appendix Two

Budget for the Nevada Gaming Commission and the Nevada State Gaming Control Board, Fiscal Years 1997–1999

Fiscal year 1998:	$24,491,240
Fiscal year 1999:	$25,036,690

Personnel (listed by department, both classified and unclassified employees, as well as full- and half-time positions, for fiscal year 1998):

Administration:	48.5
Audit:	114
Corporate Securities:	17
Electronic Services:	27
Enforcement:	115
Investigations:	77
Tax and License:	23
TOTAL POSITIONS:	421.5

Gaming Licenses Issued and Active during the Quarter Ended June 30, 1997:

Restricted:	1,978
Nonrestricted (Groups 1 and 2):	2,047
Nonrestricted (Group 3):	182
Slot route operators:	64
Manufacturer/distributor:	185
Wire service and simulcasts:	7
TOTAL:	4,463

Licensed Devices during the Quarter
Ended June 30, 1997 (by game):

TABLE GAMES

21:	3,536
Baccarat:	86
Mini-baccarat:	92
Craps:	463
Roulette:	408
Keno:	174
Caribbean stud:	138
Let It Ride:	205
Race books:	104
Sports pools:	131
Poker:	500
Pan/other related games:	26
Balance (other games):	379
TOTAL:	6,242

SLOT MACHINES (BY WAGER)

Restricted Locations (15 slots or less, no table games)

$.05:	1,404
$.25:	13,741
$1.00:	2,019
Other:	109
TOTAL:	17,273

Nonrestricted Locations

$.05:	38,405
$.25:	97,211
$1.00:	35,951
Other:	8,304
TOTAL:	179,871
TOTAL SLOT MACHINES:	197,144
TOTAL TABLES AND SLOTS:	203,386

Total Gaming Win and Collections for Fiscal Year 1997
(by county, with percentage of statewide total in parentheses)

Clark:	$5,930,331,040	(78.3%)
Washoe:	$980,778,417	(13%)
South Lake Tahoe:	$305,551,279	(4%)
Elko:	$199,698,952	(2.6%)
Carson Valley:	$72,387,149	(1%)
Other counties:	$83,751,368	(1.1%)
STATEWIDE:	$7,572,498,205	(100%)

Slot Win and Game and Table Win for Fiscal Year 1997

Slot win:	$4,767,779,214
Game and table win:	$2,804,718,991
TOTAL:	$7,572,498,205

Ranking of Slots and Table Games Win to Total Win

SLOTS

$.05:	7.6%
$.25:	30.4%
$1.00:	19%

TABLE GAMES

21:	13.4%
Baccarat:	60.5%
Craps:	5.1%

Tax/Fees Collections (state gaming taxes and license fees, by county, with percentage of statewide total in parentheses)

Clark:	$445,883,326	(78.2%)
Washoe:	$74,476,792	(13.1%)
South Lake Tahoe:	$21,945,895	(3.9%)
Elko:	$14,640,250	(2.6%)
Carson Valley:	$5,806,456	(1%)
Other counties:	$7,209,426	(1.3%)
STATEWIDE TOTAL:	$569,962,145	(100%)

General Fund and Dedicated Fund Collections from Gaming

General fund: $516,506,205

Dedicated funds (schools, counties): $53,455,940

Tax/Fees Collections by Category (with percentage of statewide)

Percentage fees:	$444,975,675	(78.1%)
Entertainment tax:	$36,316,362	(6.4%)
Quarterly nonrestricted slot tax:	$14,227,841	(2.5%)
Quarterly games tax:	$7,106,885	(1.2%)
Quarterly restricted slot tax:	$5,716,463	(1%)
Annual slot tax:	$50,835,574	(8.9%)
Annual games tax:	$2,725,858	(0.5%)
Other collections:	$8,054,487	(1.4%)
TOTAL:	$569,959,145	(100%)

Paperwork Filings a Typical Nevada Casino Would Be Required to Send to the Gaming Control Board, 1998 (with due dates)

Quarterly 5.050: Lending Agencies (April 1, July 1, October 1)

Annual Standard Financial Statements (September 15)

Changes to Internal Control System (April 30, October 31)

Annual Drop Time (July 15)

Entertainment Tax Form NGC-11 (the 24th day of each month)

Games and Slots in Operation Form NGC-15 (March 31, June 30, September 30)

Gross Win Tax Form NGC-1 (the 24th day of each month)

Race Track Handle Report (filed with NGC-1 form, 24th day of each month)

Race and Sports Unpaid and Futures Report (the 10th day of each month)

Key Employee Listing: Hard/Soft Count (January 10, April 10, July 10, October 10)

Number of Games in Operation Form NGC-2 (December 31)

Number of Slots in Operation Form NGC-4 (June 20)

Selected Annual Salaries of Gaming Control Board and Commission Members and Employees as of 1998

Nevada Gaming Commission, chairman:	$55,000
Nevada Gaming Commission, member:	$40,000
Gaming Control Board, chairman:	$100,786
Gaming Control Board, member:	$93,715
Chief, investigations:	$67,647
Chief, enforcement:	$67,647
Chief, audit:	$67,647
Chief, corporate securities:	$67,647
Chief, tax and license:	$67,647
Chief, administration:	$67,647
Chief deputy, administration:	$61,441
Executive secretary, gaming commission:	$61,441
Manager, electronics lab:	$67,647
Chief, electronics:	$72,669
Electronics engineer:	$65,141
Electronics lab engineer:	$65,141
Senior agent, corporate securities:	$49,277
Senior agent, investigations:	$49,277
Senior agent, audit:	$49,277
Senior agent, tax and license:	$49,277
Senior agent, enforcement:	$49,277
Intelligence analyst:	$49,277
Agent, corporate securities:	$43,939
Agent, audit:	$43,939
Agent, investigations:	$43,939
Agent, research:	$43,939
Agent, tax and license:	$43,939
Electronics technician:	$42,202
Legal researcher, gaming:	$32,254
Senior research analyst:	$51,014
Research specialist:	$58,959
Programmer analyst:	$49,613
Special agent:	$53,040
Agent:	$43,939

Notes

INTRODUCTION: AN OVERVIEW
OF GAMBLING IN NEVADA, 1861 TO 1999

1. Adam R. Collings, *Nevada: The Silver State* (Anaheim, Calif.: Adam Randolf Collings, 1989), 14.

2. Ibid.

3. Gilman M. Ostrander, *Nevada: The Great Rotten Borough, 1859–1964* (New York: Alfred E. Knopf, 1966), 198.

4. Nancy Christian Miluck, *Nevada—This Is Our Land: A Survey from Prehistory to Present* (Genoa, Nev.: Dragon Enterprises, 1978), 60–61.

5. Ibid., 71.

6. Ibid., 72.

7. Jerome Skolnick, *House of Cards: The Legalization and Control of Casino Gambling* (Boston: Little, Brown, 1978), 104.

8. Ibid.

9. Miluck, 79.

10. Ostrander, 12.

11. Skolnick, 105.

12. Ibid.

13. Ibid.

14. Ibid., 106.

15. Ostrander, 207.

16. Ibid.

17. John R. Goodwin, *Gaming Control Law: The Nevada Model—Principles, Statutes and Cases* (Columbus, Ohio: Publishing Horizons), 15.

18. Russell R. Elliott, *History of Nevada* (Lincoln: University of Nebraska Press, 1973), 252.

19. Ibid., 263.

20. Ibid., 273.

21. Ibid., 274.

22. Ibid., 289.

23. Ibid., 291.

24. Ibid., 278.

25. Ibid.

26. Skolnick, 108.

27. Elliott, 282.

28. Minutes, Las Vegas Board of Commissioners, Las Vegas City Clerk's office, January 4, 1924.

29. Ibid.

30. Ibid.

31. Ibid., January 6, 1928.

32. Ibid., January 3, 1931.

33. Ibid., March 20, 1931.

34. Ibid., April 7, 1931.

35. Ibid.

36. Ibid., April 9, 1931.

37. Ibid., April 13, 1931.

38. Ibid., April 17, 1931.

39. Ibid., April 22, 1931.

40. Ibid., May 8, 1931.

41. Ibid., May 29, 1931.

42. Ibid., May 19, 1931.

43. Ibid., May 20, 1931.

44. Ibid., July 6, 1931.

45. Clark County Commission minutes, Clark County Clerk's Office, Las Vegas, March 5, 1929.

46. Ibid.

47. Ibid., March 7, 1929.

48. Ibid., March 21, 1931.

49. Ibid., April 29, 1931.

50. Robert D. McCracken, *Las Vegas: The Great American Playground* (Reno: University of Nevada Press, 1997), 39.

51. Clark County Commission minutes, January 5, 1933.

52. Ibid., November 21, 1933.

53. Ibid., November 5, 1935.

54. McCracken, 53.

55. Ibid.

56. Ibid., 54.

57. Skolnick, 110.

58. Ibid.

59. Clark County Commission minutes, January 7, 1944.

60. Robert Laxalt, *Nevada: A Bicentennial History* (New York: W. W. Norton, 1977), 106.

61. Mary Ellen Glass, *Nevada's Turbulent '50s: Decade of Political and Economic Change* (Reno: University of Nevada Press, 1981), 26.

62. Clark County Commission minutes, August 5, 1946.

63. Ronald A. Farrell and Carole Case, *The Black Book and the Mob* (Madison: University of Wisconsin Press, 1995), 22.

64. Laxalt, 105.

65. Glass, 27.

66. Laxalt, 105.

67. Skolnick, 117.

68. Ibid.

69. Jerome J. Vallen, ed., *Nevada Gaming License Guide* (Las Vegas: Lionel, Sawyer & Collins, 1988), 10.

70. U.S. Congress, *Senate Special Committee to Investigate Organized Crime in Interstate Commerce,* Third Interim Report (Washington, D.C.: U.S. Government Printing Office, 1951), 4.

71. Ibid.

72. Ibid., 3.

73. Ibid., 32.

74. Ibid., 18.

75. Ibid., 8.

76. Ibid.

77. Ibid., 24.

78. Ibid.

79. Ibid., 32–33.

80. Vallen, 13.

81. Laxalt, 108.

82. Vallen, 97.

83. Ostrander, 212.

84. Ibid., 212–13.

85. Ibid., 213.

86. William R. Eadington, "The Evolution of Gambling in Nevada," *Nevada Review of Business and Economics,* 1982, 57.

87. Ed Reid and Ovid Demaris, *The Green Felt Jungle* (New York: Trident Press, 1963), 155–56.

88. Ibid., 155.

89. Ibid., 177.

90. Ibid., 146.

91. Ibid., 79.

92. Ibid., 88, 38.

93. Ovid Demaris, *The Boardwalk Jungle* (New York: Bantam Books, 1986), 100.

94. Ibid., 101.

95. James W. Hulse, *The Nevada Adventure: A History* (Reno: University of Nevada Press, 1969), 255.

96. Reid and Demaris, 69.

97. Eadington, 57.

98. Ibid., 91.

99. Glass, 34.

100. Vallen, 13.

101. Goodwin, 6.

102. Ibid., 17.

103. Grant Sawyer, *Hang Tough! Grant Sawyer: An Activist in the Governor's Mansion* (Reno: Oral History Program, University of Nevada, 1993), 85.

104. Farrell and Case, 8.

105. Ibid., 51.

106. Ibid., 8.

107. Sawyer, 91.

108. Reid and Demaris, 192.

109. Eadington, 57.

110. Laxalt, 111.

111. Eadington, 57.

112. Albert Woods Moe, *Nevada's Golden Age of Gambling* (Reno: Nevada Collectibles, 1996), 98.

113. Omar Garrison, *Howard Hughes in Las Vegas* (New York: Lyle Stuart, 1970), 75.

114. Ibid., 77.

115. Moe, 100.

116. Ibid., 254.

117. Skolnick, 140.

118. Ovid Demaris, *The Last Mafioso* (New York: Bantam Books, 1981), 247.

119. Skolnick, 139.

120. Ibid., 208.

121. Eadington, 57.

122. Ibid., 217.

123. Farrell and Case, 78.

124. Skolnick, 220.

125. Nicholas Pileggi, *Casino: Love and Honor in Las Vegas* (New York: Simon & Schuster, 1995), 186.

126. Demaris, *The Blackboard Jungle,* 313.

127. Ibid., 312.

128. Farrell and Case, 91.

CHAPTER ONE. CHEATING AND MURDER: THE AMERICAN COIN CAPER

1. *State of Nevada vs. John Sipes a.k.a. Vito Bruno,* Clark County District Court, Case No. 92-C148458.

2. Jeff Burbank, "Employee 'Ordered' to Make Cheat Devices," *Las Vegas Sun,* August 1, 1989, B1.

3. Interview, Lisa Miller-Roche, former Nevada deputy attorney general, gaming, 1997.

4. Jeff Burbank, "Inspectors Will Check Devices for Integrity," *Las Vegas Review-Journal,* November 5, 1991, A1.

5. Interview, Eric Jorgenson, 1997.

6. Nevada State Gaming Control Board, hearing transcripts, May 9, 1979, 93.

7. Ibid.

8. Ibid., 94.

9. Ibid., 95.

10. Nevada Gaming Commission, hearing transcripts, May 17, 1979, 19.

11. Nevada State Gaming Control Board, November 10, 1981, 19.

12. Nevada Gaming Commission, November 19, 1981, 31–32.

13. Nevada State Gaming Control Board, October 12, 1983, 71.

14. Nevada Gaming Commission, October 20, 1983, 167.

15. Complaint, *NGCB vs. American Coin Machine Company et al.*, Case No. 89-11, August 1, 1989, 2.

16. Interview, Gerald Cunningham, 1996.

17. *NGCB vs. American Coin Machine Company et al.*, Case No. 89-11, August 1, 1989, 33–34.

18. Ibid., 28–32.

19. Interview, Cunningham.

20. Ibid.

21. *NGCB vs. American Coin Machine Company et al.*, Case No. 89-11, August 1, 1989, 8.

22. Interview, Dennis Amerine, 1996.

23. Interview, Ellen Whittemore, 1997.

24. Ibid.

25. Howard Stutz, "American Coin Files for Bankruptcy," *Las Vegas Review-Journal*, August 5, 1989, B1.

26. *NGCB vs. American Coin Machine Company et al.*, Case No. 89-11, August 22, 1989, 1–19.

27. *NGCB vs. American Coin Machine Company et al.*, Case No. 89-11, February 22, 1990, 2.

28. *State of Nevada vs. David E. Lemons*, Clark County District Court, Case No. 92-C108725.

29. Warren Bates, "Police Arrest Vegas Man in Slaying," *Las Vegas Review-Journal*, September 10, 1992, B1.

30. *State of Nevada vs. David E. Lemons*, Clark County District Court, Case No. 92-C108725.

31. Ibid.

32. Carri Geer, "Slaying Case Goes to Jury," *Las Vegas Review-Journal*, April 2, 1993, B1.

33. *State of Nevada vs. David E. Lemons*, Clark County District Court, Case No. 92-C108725.

34. Carri Geer, "LV Jury Acquits Murder Suspect," *Las Vegas Review-Journal*, April 8, 1993, B1.

35. Carri Geer, "Man Acquitted in LV Slaying Arrested in Apartment Melee," *Las Vegas Review-Journal*, May 7, 1993, B10.

36. Dave Berns, "Man Acquitted in 1990 Murder Case Purportedly Confesses in Letter," *Las Vegas Review-Journal*, September 23, 1997, B4.

37. *State of Nevada vs. John Sipes a.k.a. Vito Bruno*, Clark County District Court, Case No. 92-C148458, opposition to defendant's motion to set bail, February 17, 1998, 4.

38. Ibid., 1–7.

39. Ibid., 5.

40. Ibid., 6.

41. Interview, David Roger, 1998.

42. Ibid.

43. *State of Nevada vs. Soni Beckman*, motion to continue district court arraignment, February 13, 1998.

44. Warren Bates, "Ex-Slot Company Owner Wins Judgment against Partners," *Las Vegas Review-Journal*, May 18, 1995, B4.

45. Interview, Roger.

46. Bates, "Ex-Slot Company Owner Wins Judgment against Partners."

47. Dave Palermo, "Slot Machine Scheme Defendant Seeks Release from Deal," *Las Vegas Review-Journal*, May 24, 1996, B2.

48. Dave Palermo, "Slot Cheating Case Ruling to Stand," *Las Vegas Review-Journal*, July 26, 1996, B3.

49. Burbank, "Inspectors Will Check Devices for Integrity."

CHAPTER TWO. TO RALPHIE FROM ADOLPH:
RALPH ENGELSTAD AND THE WAR ROOM AT THE IMPERIAL PALACE

1. Based on an interview with Joseph I. Cronin, 1998, and decision by Nevada Supreme Court in *Joseph I. Cronin vs. Eighth Judicial District Court of Nevada et al.*, Case No. 19890, November 2, 1989, 636–43.

2. Howard Stutz, "Engelstad Made His Fortune in Construction," *Las Vegas Review-Journal*, February 19, 1989, A14–A15.

3. Nevada State Gaming Control Board, complaint, Case No. 88-11, December 8, 1988.

4. Ibid.

5. Interview, Scott Scherer, 1997.

6. Interview, Gerald Cunningham, 1996.

7. Interview, George Dickerson, 1998.

8. Interview, Owen Nitz, 1998.

9. *Joseph I. Cronin vs. Eighth Judicial District Court of Nevada et al.*, Case No. 19890, November 2, 1989, 636–43.

10. Ibid.; interview, Cronin.

11. *Joseph I. Cronin vs. Eighth Judicial District Court of Nevada et al.*, Case No. 19890, November 2, 1989, 636–43.

12. Ibid.; interview, Cronin.

13. Nevada State Gaming Control Board, complaint, Case No. 88-11.

14. Interview, Nitz.

15. Imperial Palace, Publicity Department news release, September 30, 1988.

16. "Chronology of Events," *Las Vegas Review-Journal,* February 19, 1989, A14.

17. Nevada State Gaming Control Board, complaint, Case No. 88-11.

18. "Chronology of Events."

19. "Learning of a Casino Owner's Birthday Parties for Hitler, Even Jaded Vegas Is Outraged," *People Weekly,* October 24, 1989, 52.

.20. "Chronology of Events."

21. Howard Stutz and Alan Tobin, "North Dakota Group Tours Nazi Room," *Las Vegas Review-Journal,* October 10, 1988, A1.

22. Timothy Heider, "ADL Probe Begins," *Las Vegas Sun,* October 11, 1988, B1.

23. Michael L. Campbell, "Hecht: Bryan 'Dragging His Feet' in Probe," *Las Vegas Sun,* October 11, 1998, B1.

24. "Chronology of Events."

25. Jeff Burbank and Jeff German, "County May Probe Engelstad," *Las Vegas Sun,* October 11, 1988, A1.

26. Jeff Burbank and Jeff German, "Museum May Not Accept Nazi Memorabilia," *Las Vegas Sun,* October 13, 1988, B1.

27. Bob Shemeligian, "Two Factions Protest in Front of Imperial Palace," *Las Vegas Sun,* October 14, 1988, B1.

28. Jeff Burbank and Jeff German, "Gamers Probe Imperial Palace Party 'Prostitutes,'" *Las Vegas Sun,* October 19, 1988, B1.

29. Steve Schmidt, "Jewish Groups: Engelstad Owes More Than Apology," *Grand Forks (North Dakota) Herald,* October 20, 1988, 1.

30. Howard Stutz, "Engelstad: A Private Life Exposed," *Las Vegas Review-Journal,* February 19, 1989, A4.

31. "Chronology of Events."

32. Ibid.

33. Ibid.

34. Ibid.

35. *Scanlon vs. Engelstad,* December 5, 1988.

36. Letter from the Office of the Attorney General to George Dickerson, Esq., re: *GCB vs. Imperial Palace, Inc., et al.,* January 6, 1989.

37. *Imperial Palace vs. State Gaming Control Board et al.,* Case No. A271707, February 6, 1989.

38. Nevada Gaming Commission, *State Gaming Control Board vs. Imperial Palace,* Case No. 88-11, February 24, 1989, 3.

39. Ibid., 6–7.

40. Ibid., 8–9.

41. Ibid., 13.

42. Ibid., 18–19.

43. Ibid., 21.

44. Ibid., 24.

45. Ibid., 32.

46. Ibid., 39.

47. Ibid., 41.

48. Ibid., 46.

49. Ibid., 48.

50. Ibid., 55.

51. Ibid., 60.

52. "Fine to Fund," *Las Vegas Review-Journal,* February 25, 1989, A15.

53. Howard Stutz, "Debate Continues over Fine Levied on Engelstad," *Las Vegas Review-Journal,* February 25, 1989, A1.

54. Ibid.

55. "Ex-Imperial Palace Executives Settle Lawsuit against Resort," *Las Vegas Review-Journal,* December 2, 1989, B3.

56. Interview, Nitz.

57. Interview, Bob Peccole, 1998.

58. Interview, Cunningham.

CHAPTER THREE. WHO'S MINDING THE CASINO CAGE?
JOE SLYMAN AND REGULATION 6A

1. Ed Reid and Ovid Demaris, *The Green Felt Jungle* (New York: Trident Press, 1963), 6.

2. *U.S. vs. Charles W. Broun et al.,* United States District Court, Middle District of Florida (Tampa), Case No. 83-043MW, Criminal indictment filed December 2, 1983.

3. Clyde Weiss, "Stardust License Suspension Ordered," *Las Vegas Review-Journal,* December 5, 1983, A1.

4. Dave Palermo, "New Rules Worry Many at Casinos," *Las Vegas Review-Journal,* August 16, 1993, B1.

5. "Nevada Beats Fincen to Punch with Casino SAR Rules," *Money Laundering Alert,* vol. 8, no. 6 (March 1, 1997), 1.

6. Ibid.

7. "Casino Cash Rules to Change," Associated Press, March 12, 1997.

8. Jake Mattox, "Casinos' Cash Rules Could Change," *Las Vegas Business Press,* August 14, 1996, 1.

9. *U.S. vs. Broun et al.,* statement of David H. Burris, special agent, Criminal Investigation Division, IRS, on behalf of the three unnamed federal undercover agents for the DEA, the IRS, and the FBI, who used the assumed names "Mike Hansen," "Robert Mangione," and "Jon Bartel," respectively, while working the case, March 9, 1983, 1–13.

10. Ibid.

11. Ibid.

12. Ibid.

13. Ibid.

14. Ibid.

15. Ibid.

16. *U.S. vs. Broun et al.*, Grand Jury indictment, count 2, 5.

17. Alan Tobin, "Royal Casino Execs Cleared," *Las Vegas Sun*, September 28, 1984, A1.

18. Jane Morrison and Richard Cornett, "Casino Owner Found Innocent in Federal Court," *Las Vegas Review-Journal*, September 28, 1984, B1.

19. Ibid.

20. Ibid.

21. Nevada State Gaming Control Board, Item No. N88-0465, August 3, 1988, 3.

22. Nevada State Gaming Control Board, September 7, 1988, 93.

23. Ibid., 119–20.

24. Ibid., 136.

25. Ibid., 145.

26. Ibid., 147.

27. Ibid., 154–56.

28. Nevada State Gaming Control Board, Item No. N88-0465, September 28, 1988, 9.

29. Ibid., 67.

30. Ibid., 68.

31. Ibid.

32. Ibid., 257–58.

33. Jeff Burbank, "Recommendation Expected on Slyman License Request," *Las Vegas Sun*, September 28, 1988, B3.

34. Nevada State Gaming Control Board, October 11, 1988, 1.

35. Ibid., 45.

36. Ibid., 190.

37. Ibid., 193.

38. Ibid., 201.

39. Ibid., 204.

40. Ibid., 231.

41. Ibid., 237–39.

42. Ibid., 253–56.

43. Ibid., 261.

44. Ibid., 264–65.

45. Ibid., 289.

46. Nevada Gaming Commission, Item No. 14-10-88, October 19, 1988, 23.

47. Ibid., 33.

48. Ibid., 39, 42.

49. Ibid., 46.

50. Carri Geer, "Friendship Lost: Dottore Turns on Bongiovanni," *Las Vegas Review-Journal*, December 11, 1997, A1.

51. Ibid.

52. Carri Geer, "Prosecution Witness Says He Betrayed Ex-Judge's Friendship," *Las Vegas Review-Journal*, December 12, 1997, B12.

53. Nevada Gaming Commission, Hearing on Regulation 6A amendments, January 23, 1997, 65.

54. Ibid., 72.

55. Ibid., 73.

56. Ibid., 95.

CHAPTER FOUR. NEAR MISS: THE RISE AND FALL OF SLOT
MACHINE INNOVATOR UNIVERSAL DISTRIBUTING OF NEVADA

1. Interview, Gary Harris, 1997.

2. Marshall Fey, *Slot Machines* (Reno: Liberty Belle Books, 1994), 43. Author Fey is the grandson of three-reel-slot inventor Charles A. Fey (1862–1944).

3. Interview, Harris.

4. Ibid.

5. Ibid.

6. Nevada State Gaming Control Board, Tax and License Division.

7. Interview, Harris.

8. Interview, Frank Schreck, 1998.

9. Interview, Harris.

10. Interview, Schreck.

11. Nevada State Gaming Control Board, memorandum to the Nevada Gaming Commission, Regulation 14 Amendments, July 13, 1989, 1–2.

12. Nevada Gaming Commission, Commission Events Index, June 29, 1995, File No. 00331, Case No. 88-04, Text ID No. 235, 1.

13. Interview, Harris.

14. Universal Company, Ltd., "Universal: Always Creative," company prospectus, 1987, 27.

15. Ibid., 9.

16. Ibid.

17. Ibid., 17–25.

18. Fey, 43.

19. Nevada State Gaming Control Board.

20. Marshall Fey, *Slot Machines: Learn to Play to Win* (Sparks, Nev.: Reno-Tahoe Specialty, 1989), 8.

21. Nevada State Gaming Control Board memorandum, Regulation 14 Amendments, July 13, 1989, 1.

22. Nevada Gaming Commission, Commission Events Index, June 29, 1995, File No. 00331, Case No. 88-04, Text ID No. 235, 3–4.

23. Nevada Gaming Commission, December 1, 1988, Case No. 88-4, 6.

24. Ibid.

25. Ibid., 9.

26. Ibid., 10.

27. Ibid., 15.

28. Ibid., 19–21.

29. Ibid., 20.

30. Ibid., 22.

31. Ibid., 31.

32. Ibid., 42–43.

33. Ibid., 44, 46.

34. Ibid., 89–90.

35. Ibid., 93.

36. Ibid., 98.

37. Ibid., 118.

38. Ibid., 111–12.

39. Ibid., 121.

40. Ibid., 132.

41. Ibid., 139.

42. Ibid., 141.

43. Ibid., 163.

44. Ibid., 167.

45. Ibid., 172–73.

46. Ibid., 174.

47. Ibid., 183.

48. Nevada Gaming Commission, January 26, 1989, 273.

49. Ibid., 274.

50. Ibid., 275.

51. Ibid., 276.

52. Ibid., 262.

53. Ibid., 264.

54. Ibid., 273.

55. Ibid., 278.

56. Ibid., 272.

57. Ibid., 279.

58. Ibid., 292.

59. Interview, Schreck.

60. Interview, Harris.

61. "Firm Reportedly Made Concessions to Sell Slot Machines," Associated Press, reported in *Dallas Morning News*, February 21, 1995, B13.

CHAPTER FIVE. CASINO POLITICS: THE GAMING BOARD VS. SHELDON ADELSON AND THE LAS VEGAS SANDS

1. Jeff Burbank, "Adelson's Plans Less Ambitious," *Las Vegas Review-Journal*, November 11, 1992, F1.

2. Ibid.

3. Gregory A. Patterson, "Taking a Gamble on Las Vegas . . . ," *Boston Globe*, May 8, 1988, A1.

4. Nevada State Gaming Control Board, Case No. 88-0889, February 8, 1989, 2.

5. Ibid., 3–4.

6. Ibid., 8.

7. Ibid., 12.

8. Ibid., 28–29.

9. Ibid., 36.

10. Ibid., 39.

11. Howard Stutz, "Drexel Paved Path of Gaming in 1980s," *Las Vegas Review-Journal*, February 12, 1989, B1.

12. Nevada State Gaming Control Board, Case No. 88-0889, February 8, 1989, 46.

13. Ibid., 51.

14. Ibid., 70–71.

15. Ibid., 77–78.

16. Ibid., 97.

17. Ibid., 102.

18. Ibid., 139.

19. Ibid., 142–43.

20. Ibid., 478.

21. Ibid., 502.

22. Ibid., 518.

23. Ibid., 524.

24. Ibid., 525–29.

25. Ibid., 585.

26. Jon Ralston, "Control Board Strikes a Blow against Juice in Lewin Case," *Las Vegas Review-Journal*, February 22, 1989, B9.

27. Nevada Gaming Commission, February 23, 1989, 82.

28. Ibid., 131–41.

29. Ibid., 149–50.

30. Ibid., 179.

31. Ibid., 200–201.

32. Ibid., 209–10.

33. Interview, Gerald Cunningham, 1996.

34. Howard Stutz, "Henry Lewin Sues Sands, Owner," *Las Vegas Review-Journal*, April 4, 1991, D1.

35. Alan Tobin, "Testimony Blasts Adelson," *Las Vegas Review-Journal*, December 2, 1992, B1.

36. Alan Tobin, "N.Y. Architect Wins Judgment against Hotel," *Las Vegas Review-Journal*, January 31, 1993, B5.

37. Gary Thompson and John Thompson Wilen, "Venetian Builds toward Monumental Gamble," *Las Vegas Sun*, January 3, 1999, E1.

38. Christina Binkley, "Huge Casino Project Does the Unthinkable: It Rattles Las Vegas," *Wall Street Journal*, December 4, 1997, A1.

39. Thompson and Wilen.

40. Robert Macy, "A Touch of Venice," Associated Press, published in *Las Vegas Review-Journal,* July 10, 1998, D1.

41. Ed Vogel, "Venetian wins Preliminary License," *Las Vegas Review-Journal,* February 11, 1999, D1.

CHAPTER SIX. FIXED ODDS AND WISE GUYS: THE SPORT OF KINGS

1. Interview, Gregory Peters, 1997.

2. Memo by Dennis Amerine, president of the Nevada Pari-Mutuel Association, 1990, 19.

3. Ibid., 20.

4. Ibid., 19.

5. Ibid., 21.

6. Sport of Kings, Inc., Form 10-Q for third quarter ending August 31, 1991, SEC report 91-23-5649, filed October 15, 1991, 3.

7. Ibid., 8.

8. Interview, Peters.

9. SEC Form 10-Q, 9.

10. Ibid., 8.

11. Jeff Burbank, "Sport of Kings Stock Continues to Surge," *Las Vegas Review-Journal,* March 13, 1992, D7.

12. Ray Poirier, "Sport of Kings Probe Reads Like Mystery Novel," *Sports Form Casino Gaming Weekly,* July 4, 1992, 1.

13. Nevada State Gaming Control Board, Case Nos. 92-0067 and 92-0068, February 13, 1992, 714–16.

14. Ibid., 823.

15. Ibid., 808.

16. Ibid., 804.

17. Ibid., 763.

18. Ibid., 828.

19. Nevada State Gaming Control Board, February, 19, 1992, 853.

20. Ibid., 855.

21. Ibid., 982–83.

22. Ibid., 884.

23. Nevada Gaming Commission, February 20, 1992, 243.

24. Ibid., 241.

25. Ibid., 245–47.

26. Ibid., 254.

27. Jeff Burbank and Alan Tobin, "Sport of Kings Lender Linked to IRA," *Las Vegas Review-Journal,* March 9, 1992, D1.

28. Ibid.

29. Jeff Burbank and Alan Tobin, "Forsyths Past Association Scrutinized," *Las Vegas Review-Journal,* February 28, 1992, D8.

30. Burbank and Tobin, March 9, 1992.

31. Interview, Peters.

32. Ibid.

33. Jack Welsh, "Callaghan Jumps from Investigator to Director," *Sports Form,* June 13, 1992, 2.

34. Interview, Peters.

35. Press release, Sport of Kings, Inc., July 16, 1992.

36. Nevada State Gaming Control Board, Item No. 01-07-92, July 23, 1992, 6.

37. Ibid., 12.

38. Ibid., 29.

39. Ibid., 27–28.

40. Ibid., 46.

41. Ibid., 65.

42. Ibid., 94–95.

43. Ibid., 145–46.

44. Ibid., 147.

45. Interview, Peters.

46. Jay Richards, "Lysaght Latest in Line of Cuts to Sport of Kings," *Las Vegas Review-Journal,* November 27, 1992, E9.

47. Ibid.

48. "Horse Betting Elite Win Big on Failed Las Vegas Gamble," *Dallas Morning News,* November 27, 1992, B14.

49. Richards, "Lysaght Latest in Line of Cuts to Sport of Kings."

50. Jay Richards, "Amerine Resigns Post as President of Sport of Kings," *Las Vegas Review-Journal,* December 18, 1992, E13.

51. Nevada State Gaming Control Board, Item No. N93-0581, February 11, 1993, 26.

52. Ibid., 26–27.

53. Ibid., 29.

54. Ibid., 33–34.

55. Ibid., 43.

56. Ibid., 61.

57. Ibid., 72–73.

58. Ibid., 79–80.

59. Ibid., 103.

60. Dave Palermo, "Sport of Kings Gets 60 Days," *Las Vegas Review-Journal,* March 10, 1993, E7.

61. Ibid.

62. Nevada State Gaming Control Board, Item No. N92-0836, May 5, 1993, 265, 269.

63. Dave Palermo, "State Files Sport of Kings Complaint," *Las Vegas Review-Journal,* June 3, 1993, D8.

64. Ibid.

65. Dave Palermo, "Race Book to Close for Two Months," *Las Vegas Review-Journal,* July 17, 1993, A1.

66. Sport of Kings company report, Investext, Market Guide, Inc., October 23, 1995.

67. Interview, Peters.

68. Thomas Moore, "Sport of Kings to Be Auctioned," *Las Vegas Business Press*, March 6, 1995, 1.

69. Dave Berns, "Sun Sets in Henderson on Casino," *Las Vegas Review-Journal*, January 16, 1998, A1.

70. Ibid.

CHAPTER SEVEN. A CHEATER IN OUR MIDST: GAMING BOARD
COMPUTER WHIZ RON HARRIS BEATS THE SYSTEM

1. Based on grand jury transcripts, *Nevada vs. Ronald Dale Harris*, Case No. 96GJAG3A, July 18, 1996, including testimony of Detective Ronald Hungridge and Detective William Ames, both of the New Jersey State Police, Division of Gaming Enforcement, 11–26; interview, Ronald Hungridge, 1998.

2. Interview, Hungridge.

3. Interview, Carl Conti, spokesman, Imagineering Systems, Reno, 1998.

4. Interview, Hungridge.

5. Interview, Conti.

6. Interview, Hungridge.

7. Interview, Conti.

8. Interview, Hungridge.

9. Grand jury, *Nevada vs. Ronald Dale Harris*, Case No. 96GJAG3A, July 18, 1996, 115.

10. Ibid., 117.

11. Interview, David Thompson, deputy attorney general, Criminal Justice Division, state of Nevada, 1998.

12. Interview, Hungridge; grand jury testimony, *Nevada vs. Ronald Dale Harris*, Case No. 96GJAG3A, July 18, 1996, by Hungridge and Ames, 11–26.

13. *Nevada vs. Ronald Dale Harris*, Case No. 96GJAG3A, July 18, 1996, 31.

14. Atlantic City Municipal Court criminal complaint against Ronald Dale Harris, January 15, 1995, Case Nos. C-38295 and C-38395.

15. Grand jury, *Nevada vs. Ronald Dale Harris*, Case No. 96GJAG3A, 32.

16. Ibid., 61.

17. Ibid., 33.

18. Ibid., 63.

19. Interview, Robinson.

20. Interview, Conti.

21. Grand jury, *Nevada vs. Ronald Dale Harris*, Case No. 96GJAG3A, 92.

22. Ibid., 95.

23. Superior Court of New Jersey indictment, Case No. 95-03-0735-C-CP, 1–2.

24. New Jersey Department of Law and Public Safety, *Division of Gaming Enforcement vs. Ronald D. Harris*, preliminary order of exclusion, Docket No. 95-0239-EL, June 21, 1995.

25. Grand jury, *Nevada vs. Ronald Dale Harris,* Case No. 96GJAG3A, 73–74.

26. Ibid., 74–75.

27. Ibid., 79.

28. Ibid., 97.

29. Ibid., 152, 159.

30. Ibid., 152.

31. Ibid., 81.

32. Ibid., 82.

33. Ibid., 100.

34. Ibid., 104.

35. Ibid., 107.

36. Ibid., 117.

37. Ibid., 122–23.

38. Ibid., 129–30.

39. Ibid., 131.

40. Interview, Thompson.

41. Ibid.

42. Washoe County District Court, Reno, Nevada, *Nevada vs. Harris et al.,* Case No. CR 96-1349, June 12, 1996.

43. Interview, Thompson.

44. Grand jury, *Nevada vs. Ronald Dale Harris,* Case No. 96GJAG3A, 177–78.

45. Clark County District Court, Las Vegas, *Nevada vs. Harris,* Case No. C137187, July 19, 1996.

46. Washoe County District Court, Reno, Nevada, *Nevada vs. Harris et al.,* Case No. CR96-1349, August 9, 1996, 2–9.

47. Interview, Thompson.

48. Ibid.

49. Ibid.

50. Ibid.

51. Ibid.

52. Ibid.

53. Ibid.

54. Nevada State Gaming Control Board, Case No. 96-36, November 8, 1996, 332.

55. Ibid., 335.

56. Ibid., 335–36.

57. Ibid., 336.

58. Interview, Scott Freeman, 1997.

59. Sean Whaley, "Former Gaming Official Sent to Jail for Slot Scam," *Las Vegas Review-Journal,* January 10, 1998, A3.

60. Interview, Thompson.

61. Dave Berns, "Fall from Grace: Confessions of a Slot Cheat," *Las Vegas Review-Journal,* January 11, 1998, A1.

Selected Bibliography

Collings, Adam R. *Nevada: The Silver State.* Anaheim, Calif.: Adam Randolf Collings, 1989.

Demaris, Ovid. *The Boardwalk Jungle.* New York: Bantam Books, 1986.

———. *The Last Mafioso.* New York: Bantam Books, 1981.

Elliott, Russell R. *History of Nevada.* London & Lincoln: University of Nebraska Press, 1973.

Farrell, Ronald A., and Carole Case. *The Black Book and the Mob: The Untold Story of the Control of Nevada's Casinos.* Madison: University of Wisconsin Press, 1995.

Fey, Marshall. *Slot Machines.* Reno: Liberty Belle Books, 1994.

———. *Slot Machines: Learn to Play to Win.* Sparks, Nev.: Reno-Tahoe Specialty, 1989.

Garrison, Omar V. *Howard Hughes in Las Vegas.* New York: Lyle Stewart, 1970.

Glass, Mary Ellen. *Nevada's Turbulent '50s: Decade of Political and Economic Change.* Reno: University of Nevada Press, 1981.

Goodwin, John R. *Gaming Control Law: The Nevada Model—Principles, Statutes and Cases.* Columbus, Ohio: Publishing Horizons, 1985.

Hulse, James W. *The Nevada Adventure: A History.* Reno: University of Nevada Press, 1969.

Laxalt, Robert. *Nevada: A Bicentennial History.* New York: W. W. Norton, 1977.

McCracken, Robert D. *Las Vegas: The Great American Playground.* Reno: University of Nevada Press, 1997.

Miluck, Nancy Christian. *Nevada—This Is Our Land: A Survey from Prehistory to Present.* Genoa, Nev.: Dragon Enterprises, 1978.

Moe, Albert Woods. *Nevada's Golden Age of Gambling.* Reno: Nevada Collectibles, 1996.

Moehring, Eugene P. *Resort City in the Sunbelt: Las Vegas, 1930–1970.* Reno: University of Nevada Press, 1989.

Ostrander, Gilman M. *Nevada: The Great Rotten Borough, 1859–1964.* New York: Alfred A. Knopf, 1966.

Pileggi, Nicholas. *Casino: Love and Honor in Las Vegas.* New York: Simon & Schuster, 1995.

Reid, Ed, and Ovid Demaris. *The Green Felt Jungle.* New York: Trident Press, 1963.

Sawyer, Grant. *Hang Tough! Grant Sawyer: An Activist in the Governor's Mansion.* Reno: Oral History Program, University of Nevada, 1993.

Skolnick, Jerome H. *House of Cards: The Legalization and Control of Casino Gambling.* Boston: Little, Brown, 1978.

U.S. Congress. *Senate Special Committee to Investigate Organized Crime in Interstate Commerce*, Third Interim Report. Washington, D.C.: U.S. Government Printing Office, 1951.

Vallen, Jerome J., ed. *Nevada Gaming License Guide*. Las Vegas: Lionel, Sawyer & Collins, 1988.

Index